TRACING THE HISTORY OF YOUR HOUSE

This Indenture made the ... day ...

... in the County of Essex aforesaid yeoman of the other part **Witnesse** ...

... of the said Jacob Kingsbury his Executors administrators and assigns ...

... the said Jacob Kingsbury his premises administrators and assigns ... **All that** ...

... and therein belonging to the same more or less with the appurtenance ...

... belonging situate lying and being in Essex aforesaid the same now or late ...

... or part thereof ... of lands & ... and being in Essex aforesaid now or ...

... and appurtenances the said messuage tenement and farm premises belonging or there with ...

... under wood ... Timber ... the deed and ... now standing growing or being or there ...

... be required ... assigned servants & labourers, workmen in & thorough ... upon the said premises ...

... deed & ... at & during & set the ... & condition of the premises and to repair & amend the same ...

... or their ... or ... or ... to be as convenient may be **To have and to hold** ...

... under ... their ... of their appurtenances (except before excepted) unto the said Jacob Kingsbury his ...

... for term during and unto the full end & term of ... & twenty years from the next ... & ...

... thereunto for as the same may be ... without ... for ... and & of other ... **yeilding** ...

... yearly Rent or sum of thirty pounds of good and lawful money of great Britain ...

... at & be required or assigned the yearly Rent or sum of thirty pounds of the lawful money of great ...

... at ... at all ... & ... & the first payment thereof to begin & be made on the ...

... thereof to be ... or in part or in all of the space of one & twenty years next over or ...

... & assigned unto the said messuage premises or any part thereof in the name of the whole ...

... thereof in any wise notwithstanding **And** the said Jacob Kingsbury for himself his ...

... & in form following (that is to say) that if the said Jacob Kingsbury his Executors administrators ...

... thirty pounds & thirty pounds of good & lawful money of great Britain on the days of payment ...

... have & distrained all the ... rents or ... rents due or payable to the ... or ... & ...

... his heirs and assigns and the said premises & every part thereof ... being seized or ...

... timber during the said term at the ... own proper costs & charges well & substantially ...

... & ... & in all other materials for ... & ... that the wall and ... thereof ...

... well & substantially in & as & in like manner make or cause to be made fifty ... & new ditching ...

... well & substantially repair amend maintain & keep all & every of the ...

... maintain and keep all the ... in & ... rails & ... belonging to the said premises in the ...

... expiration or other sooner determination of this present ... said shall & will quietly and peaceably ...

... & fences as aforesaid **And Moreover** that neither the ...

... [interlined] by ... or otherwise in and upon the said demised premises ... shall at his own ... or ...

... upon the said premises for the better Improvement thereof **And** shall during the said term ...

... remainder ... either to pash or to ... & thereof & sufficient ... shall & will ...

... his Executors administrators that neither he nor they shall or will at any time or times ...

... persons whatsoever for the whole or any part of the term hereby granted without leave first had ...

... thereof **And** the said John Starpe for himself his heirs and assigns and for every of them ...

... following (that is to say) that he the said John Starpe his heirs or assigns shall and will forthwith ...

... sufficient repaired **And** shall and will at his own ... own proper costs and charges ...

... **And** also shall allow & ... unto the said Jacob Kingsbury his Executors administrators or assigns ...

... and payable within ... for and in lieu of Plough boot and cart boot **And** shall and will ...

... or assigned within ... & ... days after such desire or request assigned to ... or ... sufficient ...

... said parties to these presents that if the said John Starpe his heirs or assigns shall neglect or ...

... request of the said Jacob Kingsbury his Executors administrators or assigns or within twenty ...

... Executors administrators or assigns to fall out of the said ... before ... & pitch ... & ...

... administrators and assigns from time to time and at all seasonable times in the year to ... &

... demised every year during the said term as much ... in & all the said Jacob Kingsbury ...

... but not the whole **And** also that it shall and may be lawful to and for the said John ...

... that shall arise or be taken out of one ... field belonging to the said premises within ...

Tracing the history of your house

2ND EDITION

Nick Barratt

the national archives

The National Archives
Kew, Richmond
Surrey, TW9 4DU, UK
www.nationalarchives.gov.uk

The National Archives (TNA) was formed
when the Public Record Office (PRO)
and Historical Manuscripts Commission
(HMC) combined in April 2003

ISBN   1 903365 90 2
        978 1 903365 90 8

A catalogue card for this book is available
from the British Library

Frontispiece: Part of a sale indenture from 1753, one of the most common forms of title deed
that the house historian will encounter. (C 103/12/1)

Front cover: Photograph of Gold Hill, Shaftesbury, Dorset by Derry Brabbs
Back cover: Photograph of Nick Barratt in Walcot Square, London by Mike Pearcy
www.words-pictures.co.uk

Designed & typeset by Ken Wilson | point 918
Cover designed by Briony Chappell
Printed by TJ International Ltd, Padstow, Cornwall

Contents

4 LAND LAW AND CONVEYANCING *76*

Preface

So much has happened in the world of personal history since I first wrote *Tracing the History of Your House* – not least the fact that the Public Record Office now forms part of the National Archives. Perhaps the most important change in the world of personal history and archives relates to the availability of documents to researchers. Since 2001 there has been an explosion in the amount of material available online, which has transformed the way we now examine the past; everyone can access material that sheds light on not just who their ancestors were, but also the way they lived, and the communities in which their lives unfolded.

The enormous interest in family history has been boosted of late by the BBC series *Who Do You Think You Are?*, in which celebrities trace their roots and discover key relatives who changed the course of their family's history. An important component of the series was the emotional and geographical journey each celebrity took, which often involved revisiting old childhood homes, or discovering the site of an important ancestral property for the first time. For example, one of the more dramatic sequences from the first series came when the satirist and broadcaster Ian Hislop discovered that his great grandfather Murdo Matheson was a soldier in the late eighteenth century; Ian then retraced Murdo's footsteps around the globe, only to end up back at Murdo's birthplace in Uig, Scotland, amid the stone ruins of an eighteenth-century crofter's cottage. The beauty of the two series made to date lay in the fact that, in essence, it was not about family history; the people that our celebrities encountered acted as the gateway to a wider social history of the times through which they lived. It has been traditional to keep the fields of local, family, social and house history separate, although experienced family historians have operated in the fields of local and social history for a long time.

In the wake of *Who Do You Think You Are?* there has been a growing realization that it is increasingly counter-productive to pigeonhole these various types of research; you cannot 'do' family history without looking at the social conditions under which your relatives laboured, or fully understand them unless you consider the history of the area in which they lived. This applies equally to house history. As you will see from the chapters in this book, you cannot fully understand the history of a property until you have investigated the people who made it their home, or considered the impact of events within the local community over a long period of time. Many of the questions you may have about your current house, or an ancestral home, cannot be answered specifically through documents relating to the particular property. However, you can start to construct a sense of what life was like by widening the scope of your research, and investigating the community at the time.

I still stand by the words of introduction below, four and a half years after I put pen to paper for the first edition – or, in these days of technology, fingers to keyboard – and, if anything, the experiences of the thousands of people who have been inspired to research their personal past in the light of *Who Do You Think You Are?* are an endorsement of the fact that history is alive, history is important, history is popular and, somewhat controversially, history is something that we all have a duty to record. After all, what would our ancestors have given for the chance to express their thoughts the way we can through the miracle of the information highway that is at our disposal?

This is not a book about family history, though the history of your family may well have led you to trace the history of your ancestral home. However, tracing the history of a house – whether it is your own home, a childhood residence, a property once dwelt in by a relative decades ago, or even a building in your local area that intrigues you – is perhaps the most gratifying line of research, and one that takes you to the heart of family life that took place decades, even centuries, ago. After all, countless families once considered the bricks and mortar that you now call home as their place of domestic security, and through records in the public domain, coupled with a closer study of the fabric of your house, you can get that bit closer to understanding the past that surrounds you.

*   *   *

Before you begin using this guide, I would like to offer a few words of encouragement. There is no great mystery to house history. It is something that anyone can do. I should know, as I basically taught myself from scratch. I have been lucky enough to investigate the histories of the properties featured in the last three series of the BBC's *House Detectives*, and each one has given me an insight into different sources and alternative approaches to the subject.

I wandered into house history by accident. However, I did have some experience from a school project, over fifteen years ago, when I was chosen to take part in an 'experimental' O-level course. It focused on local history, and the key element was a field trip to research the history of a street in the community. Luckily for me, the chosen site was a road adjoining my own, and consequently I was able to amaze fellow students with the casual way in which I assigned dates to houses that I had seen constructed as a child.

But it is rarely as easy as that. Each property will require you to follow a unique research trail – one that might be obscure or full of unexpected twists and turns, with dead ends lurking around every corner. This is all part of the fun, as you never know what secrets you will uncover; yet it makes trying to write a comprehensive guide to the subject all the more difficult. I have concentrated on the main sources that I tend to use when I begin investigating the history of a house, and ones that will yield the most fruitful results in the majority of cases. However, don't be afraid to experiment with other sources, and let the history of the local community guide your approach.

I would like to express my gratitude to several people who have contributed to this volume in various ways. First and foremost, to Stella Colwell, Paul Carter and Amanda Bevan for reading through the entire text for accuracy – I am eternally grateful to them for doing so and any errors that remain are mine alone; to the specialists at the National Archives for their help and support (they know who they are); to Nicky Pattison, Tim Dunn and Basil Comely for giving me my initial opportunity at the BBC; to Dan Cruickshank, who has been a font of knowledge about domestic architecture; and to Martin Cross, who first introduced me to local history many years ago. Above all, I would like to dedicate this book to my wife, Sarah, a fellow house detective, for her constant support that allows me to pursue a career that is also a lifelong interest.

So take heart, and with a deep breath set foot on your own unique detective trail. Good luck!

Nick Barratt

2001 and 2006

AN INTRODUCTION TO HOUSE HISTORY

1

House history

The communities that we live in today are products of one of humanity's most basic needs: shelter. Throughout the ages people have constructed dwellings to protect themselves from the elements, from the smallest peasant's hovel to the grandest royal palace. The United Kingdom is blessed with a rich architectural heritage, and historians have tended to focus their attention on the grander buildings of the past – castles, cathedrals and palaces. Yet there are thousands of equally fascinating buildings waiting to be discovered, with stories to tell about who used to live there, and what roles they played in their local community. In short, you can use your own house, an ancestral or childhood home – or indeed any property you consider to be of interest – as the starting point for a voyage of discovery through the ages.

The questions you want to ask about your house will ultimately determine how you approach the research. In general, most house historians start by attempting to find out when their chosen house was built. This can be a difficult task, as records that are specific to the construction of an individual property are few and far between. A house detective therefore faces the task of reconstructing a chronology of a property from a variety of sources in which dwellings have perhaps left a trace, and it is best to be realistic about the outcome – you may simply discover a rough range of dates between which construction *might* have occurred.

Rather than focusing on when the bricks and mortar were put in place, one of the best – and most interesting – ways of finding out about a house is by researching its owners or occupiers, the people that made it *their* home before you. Thus, the house detective needs to combine many techniques when looking at a property, such as elements of genealogy (or family history). Furthermore, you should try to investigate the way in which your house has evolved over the ages, not only in terms of its architecture, but also in terms of the way it would have been furnished on the inside – after all, the people you have uncovered through the records would have gone to great lengths to make it comfortable and homely, just as we do today. If you have a plot of land with your house, you might uncover broken pots or household rubbish; it is highly likely that these were left behind by previous occupants, and they can sometimes offer clues for dating purposes.

Whether you focus on construction dates or occupants, the processes you follow will start to reveal a chronology of your house, incorporating construction or alteration dates, and the names of the people who owned the house or resided there. The next step is to put your house into a wider context. Try to find out about the *way* people used to live, and what the local community was like at key moments in your house's past. Ask yourself what made it a good time to build your house, or why there was a sudden need to add another storey or wing. How did local events impact upon the lives of past occupants? Was there an important local industry that might give an indication as to why your householders moved to the property, or whether the house was built specifically as worker accommodation for a nearby factory perhaps? All of these are areas of research that will bring the past vividly back to life, and give you a greater understanding of the past. However, it is important to begin your research with realistic expectations – not everyone is going to be in the situation where they can trace a house back to the thirteenth century, or, as outlined earlier, be able to pinpoint a precise date of construction. You will almost certainly encounter problems along the way, and you may well feel that you have come to the end of the road. Don't give up – it is always worth trying a slightly different approach, or a new set of documents.

1.2 About this guide

House construction over time has varied from region to region, and from age to age. This variance in style can often provide valuable clues about when your house was built. Indeed your house might even be the last manifestation of many previous constructions that have stood on the same site, so always treat documentary evidence with care and remember to use other clues, such as architecture, to help date the property. Brief guidance on architectural style and building technique has been included in CHAPTER 2 of this book for reference purposes, but details of relevant literature to help you date your house through regional building styles and specific architectural features are given in 'Useful publications' at the end of the book. The initial purpose of this guide is to provide a basic introduction to the many and varied techniques required to trace the history of your house, and thereafter to explain and illustrate some of the main documentary sources that can be used to construct a house chronology.

The present chapter, and the next, introduce house history as a discipline, illustrate architectural styles (as mentioned above), and suggest useful ways of beginning your research. Relevant skills and tools of the trade are explained, and guidance is given about how and where to look for particular types of document. A word on archives in general is also provided, as they can be daunting places for the uninitiated. Chapters 3–13 then examine the most relevant documentary sources, with additional search tips, as well as explanations of how to use the material and where it can be located. Finally, a research plan has been suggested (CHAPTER 14) and a detailed case study given (CHAPTER 15) of Plymouth House (whose history has also inspired a number of the figures reproduced in the book). Additionally, four 'property profiles' summarize the life stories of four selected houses, and suggest how a variety of sources, from official documents to newspapers, can combine to create a vivid picture: these profiles appear between some of the chapters. The principal coverage throughout is of England and Wales, but you will also find in the book some reference to Scottish and Irish house history. The sources described are primarily to be found at the National Archives in Kew, although sources that exist in local archives are covered in some detail where relevant.

Some houses will be easier to trace than others, and there are no sets of rules to follow – each house will dictate where you will look for clues. House history is an imprecise art, and houses from disparate regions, constructed in various chronological periods, will require you to examine many different sources. Consequently, this guide is not intended to be a comprehensive survey of all sources that you may encounter. Instead, it reflects the main areas of research that will provide the best results most of the time, and the sources suggested should provide you with sufficient material to allow you to investigate with confidence. However, each house will have its own unique story to tell, with a unique documentary path to follow – that is one of the joys of house history, as you embark on a real voyage of discovery; so be prepared to experiment with a range of sources according to the circumstances. You can be amazed by the facts you uncover, and should find the detective work enjoyable and ultimately rewarding.

GETTING STARTED

2

2.1 Introduction

One of the most important tasks in any piece of research is deciding how and where to start. This chapter provides some advice on your first steps along the detective trail, and suggests some ideas about where you can look for initial clues before you even set foot in an archive. This will involve talking to neighbours, previous owners or estate agents who were involved in past sales, and the important task of familiarizing yourself with the local area. Once you have completed these background searches, and armed with any preliminary information you might have uncovered, you can consider moving on to researching primary source material. The next task will therefore be to locate the most relevant county record office (hereafter CRO) or national institution, as it is here that you will find documentary evidence that will contain information pertinent to the history of your house. Archives can be difficult places to work in, particularly if you have never been to one before, so a few hints are offered which should make the experience seem less intimidating and ultimately more rewarding. Tips about reading original source material are also provided, as you will soon discover that the vast majority of sources require some degree of interpretation, or indeed translation, before you can extract useful information.

Given that the aim of this book is to introduce documents that are primarily held at the National Archives, the chapter concludes with a more detailed introduction to the electronic catalogues, paper guides and indexes that you will need to use to obtain the National Archives document references. Advice on document ordering and Internet searches is also given.

2.2 First steps

BEGINNING LOCAL RESEARCH: TALKING TO PEOPLE

House history can be a very sociable pastime, as one of the best ways of finding out a bit more about your house and the road and area that it stands in is to talk to neighbours or previous owners. They may well know some snippet of information or interesting story that can lead you a little further back in time, or give you an avenue of research to pursue. They may even have done some research of their own. But remember to exercise diplomacy – not everyone will share your enthusiasm, so please phone or, better still, write before marching in demanding to know about the time they spent in the house. However, the opposite is sometimes also true, and you may not always like the tales that you are told about your present home. Remember that oral information is not always going to be accurate, and that it is your job as a house detective to corroborate these stories with hard facts, especially if you are looking for clues to the date of construction.

You may also find that people are willing to show you old photographs of the house. These might contain images of previous owners or occupants that you can later identify; there may also be evidence of different structures or building styles. You can check your attic or basement (if you have one), as people have a habit of squirrelling away old photos, along with papers and files, that get forgotten or left behind in a move – one person's junk is another's treasure trove. It may seem surprising, but it is also worth checking roof fillings in earlier houses, as all sorts of material were used as insulation – including clothes and personal papers that were no longer required, all of which can be used to help with dating the property; it has been known for old title deeds to appear in the eaves of old buildings, especially those that were written on parchment!

Don't just restrict your search to the interior of the house; the garden may also contain clues about the lives of former occupiers. For example, you may have uncovered items such as clay pipes, broken pots or other domestic goods, as in the days before organized waste disposal people often used their gardens as personal rubbish dumps. Although dating objects can be difficult, and there is no guaranteed link to your property, they can at least tell you something about the use of the site, and local historians or museums may be able to provide further guidance. Furthermore, you may come across evidence of old foundations as you dig, which again can provide telling clues about outbuildings such as stables, stores or indeed an entire earlier dwelling. These are all avenues that can be explored in more detail when you progress to archives, and at the very least can shed light on the way people used to live.

Away from the house itself, you can always talk to estate agents or solicitors who handled previous sales of the property. If your house stands in a fairly small community, try the local estate agents first; otherwise, go back to the firm that handled the sale of the property when you first moved in. If the property you are researching is not your own, you might be able to find this information from the present occupiers, or indeed locate the date of the last

2.2

sale via the Land Registry (*see* CHAPTER 5) and work from there. It is worth running these searches, as you may be pleasantly surprised as to the amount of information estate agents and solicitors can provide about the house, from sale catalogues to commissioned reports and surveys, even down to old title deeds that have never been collected by previous occupants – documents that often fail to make it into archives. Again, caution is urged when making your approach, as these people are busy professionals who might not have that much time to spare for enthusiastic house detectives.

RESEARCHING THE HISTORY OF YOUR LOCAL COMMUNITY
Another important step to take before commencing archival research is to pinpoint precisely where your house is situated in the local community. Not only will you need to know which street it is in, and feel confident enough to locate it on older maps that might not contain modern landmarks, but also you will need to find out about the administrative districts in which it fell, as many documents are grouped or arranged by these districts. The easiest to identify is the name of the parish, although modern parish boundaries might not equate to older ones, and you will need to be aware of the dates of these changes; similarly, ecclesiastical and civil parish boundaries may not be the same, and many small parishes were incorporated into larger ones, or new parishes were created in response to the massive population expansion in urban areas throughout the nineteenth century. Nevertheless, parish boundaries should be marked on modern Ordnance Survey (OS) maps. Similarly, you should find out if your house once formed part of a larger estate, and more importantly the name of the manor that it fell in; for further advice about the manorial system, turn to CHAPTER 6. Other administrative units that you will need to at least make a note of include the modern and historic parliamentary constituency; Poor Law union; urban, rural or district council; and the county division (for example, the name of the hundred, rape, riding, etc.).

To find out this information you will need to do some preliminary reading. Luckily there are some detailed publications to help you. Relevant volumes in the *Victoria County History* series (*VCH*) give a county by county guide to places, divisions and events of note, although not all areas are covered. Similarly, English Place Name Society volumes can give you some useful information about the origins of place names, and where they appear in documentary sources, as do topographical gazetteers, antiquarian studies and local history society publications. Local trade or street directories are another good source of information that can provide details about the administrative district of which your house was once a part. All of these publications should be available at your local studies library or CRO, which should be your first port of call, and a list of sources is provided under

'Useful publications'. At this stage it is advisable to make a working copy of a map that shows your area and mark these boundaries on it for future reference.

It is well worth taking some time to research a bit about the history of your community before focusing on your house, as you will often uncover social or economic developments that may have provided the reason for its construction in the first place. Major changes to the community will have influenced the way people lived their lives and therefore built their houses. Some of these issues are covered in more detail in CHAPTER 11, where the impact of national events on the locality is considered. However, the following questions are ones that you can usefully ask yourself as part of the process of putting your house in a wider chronological context:

- What was the local industry, and was your house associated with it (for example, docks, canals, factories)?
- What impact (if any) did the railways have?
- Do street or house names reflect the name of a local major landowner or estate?
- Does the house name reflect a previous use of the property (for example, Miller's Cottage)?
- Do you live in a suburb of a town or city that enjoyed a period of rapid expansion at some stage in the past?
- Was there any bomb damage caused in the Second World War?

All of these questions reflect aspects of the social history of your area, and will help you to understand why your house was constructed at a particular time, or may even determine where you will need to look for a particular type of document. For example, the construction of the railways in the mid-nineteenth century was coupled with the creation of dwellings for railway workers, and many other industries followed a similar pattern. Factory owners often erected rows of workers' cottages near their main establishment to reduce the time it took their employees to walk to work, with the result that many industrial towns experienced rapid suburban growth throughout the nineteenth century as the new communities of workers were connected to the historic heart of the town.

Architectural clues 2.3

Of course, one of the most obvious places to start dating your house is with the house itself. The way in which it was built – its architectural fingerprint – will often tell you a vast amount about the period in which it was constructed, although it will be difficult to pinpoint a precise date. Instead, you should use the building style of your property to provide a wider date period within which it was probably constructed. However, reading architectural clues can be tricky if you are not sure what you are looking out for. Although it is not within the remit of this guide to outline all of the tell-tale signs that you should be looking for – that would require a book in its own right – some of the main aspects of external domestic architecture are listed below, and will certainly give you enough ammunition to assign a rough construction date to your property.

REGIONAL BUILDING STYLES – VERNACULAR ARCHITECTURE

Perhaps the first thing you should do is step back, and look at your house in its entirety, before moving on to examine more specific sections of its architecture. The size, shape, floor plan and even location of your house can tell you a lot about when or why it was built. By reading these clues, you can start to assign a rough construction date to your house, or at least various parts of it, bearing in mind that older properties have probably been re-built, re-styled, added to or altered over the centuries.

The term used by house historians to describe the way in which builders in the various regions across the UK adopted different styles of house construction is *vernacular architecture*, and it covers all domestic and agricultural buildings. Regional construction styles tended to be phased out in favour of more style-conscious or nationally uniform types of house construction from the fifteenth century to the late nineteenth, with the dates varying greatly in different parts of the country. This means that you can broadly identify when your house was constructed by looking for evidence of any remnants of vernacular architecture in the structure of your property. Bearing in mind that every region had its own unique way of building houses, which makes comprehensive cataloguing beyond the remit of this book, a few of the most common regional styles you should look out for in England and Wales are described below.

Building styles were most affected by the materials that were commonly to hand. Only the richest people could afford to import expensive materials from a distance, such as quarried stone, so the house styles described below reflect housing for the lower to middle levels of society in a particular area.

Northern England

From the Norman Conquest to the dawn of the Industrial Revolution in the late eighteenth century, the north of England has traditionally been one of the least populated parts of the country. Stone buildings tend to dominate northern vernacular architecture, with the geology of each area defining the type of building material used. Consequently, sandstone is the main choice in the North West, moving from millstone grit in the Pennines to limestone in the North East and into Yorkshire, while slate was commonly used in the

Lake District into Wales. Timber houses were constructed, but tended to be higher-status properties and were most heavily concentrated towards the south of the region, particularly in Cheshire, where access to wood was more widely available. Types of buildings varied, but were most commonly long-houses built on farmsteads (PLATE 10). The long low construction shape offered greatest protection against the elements in exposed areas. Given the somewhat turbulent relations between England and Scotland during the Middle Ages, many houses closer to the border incorporated elements of military fortification into their design, with towers and strengthened walls more reminiscent of castles that domestic dwelling. These are often referred to as Tower houses or Pele Towers (PLATE 1).

Central and Midlands region

Within this area are a great variety of vernacular building styles, ranging from the stone-built houses that give Cotswold villages (PLATE 7) their own special character, to grandly constructed timber frame buildings in the western side of the region that survive in great numbers throughout Shropshire, Worcestershire and Herefordshire. Where stone was used to construct houses, it was predominantly limestone, varying in colour according to where it was quarried. In areas such as Staffordshire, where the local soil is clay-based, bricks were produced in large numbers at a far earlier date than elsewhere, giving rise to many very early brick-built properties in the region compared to other parts of the country. The use of bricks was fuelled by the rise of industrial towns in the area, which led to the growth of numerous brickworks to mass-produce enough materials to construct sufficient cheap housing to shelter the growing urban population throughout the late eighteenth and early nineteenth century. Because bricks have been used over such a long period in the Midlands, great care should be taken when attempting to date your house if you are basing it on the appearance of brickwork alone.

East of England

Traditionally, East Anglia and the east of England were among the most prosperous parts of the country, based on the wool trade that saw vast fortunes flow into the area from the Continent. One legacy of this prosperity is the large number of stone churches that dominate the East Anglian skyline, even though many of the villages that surround them have subsequently declined and are now only hamlets. The main building material in Suffolk and Essex was timber, giving rise to some of the country's best surviving timber framed houses. Most of them are easy to spot, as the external timbers have been left exposed, with wattle and daub panelling covered in plaster used to fill in the wall spaces (PLATE 6). Another common feature was the use of thatch as a roofing material. Brick was also used from an early date in property construction – another continental influence – so once again take care when dating your house. Some of the largest concentrations of brickworks can be found the closer you get to the Midlands. To the north of the region, particularly in Norfolk, other building materials were used. Flint, cobbles and pebbles were frequently used to construct houses, but stone was less popular.

South East region

As with the east of England, the South East was historically a prosperous part of the country and therefore could afford grander properties. There is no one single type of house construction style in the area, as there was an abundant supply of timber from forests, good clay-based soil to provide raw materials for brick-making, and plenty of sources of sandstone in Sussex and Kent. Therefore, large timber framed houses jostle with some of the earliest brick-built properties, set alongside grand stone dwellings. If one house type could be said to typify vernacular architecture in the South East, it would have to be the Weald house, which was a double-ended hall house – a central hall on two storeys with chambers attached to both ends. These houses were constructed of timber, contained under a single roof, with rooms on the upper storey extended out on jetties. In Kent and Sussex weatherboarding was much used. In terms of roofing, many properties were thatched, but stone or tile was sometimes employed to keep the occupants safe from the weather.

South West region

The further west you go, the more the influence of local stone starts to prevail. In Wales, for example, flint becomes the predominant construction material, as is the case in Cornwall. However, the main stone of choice in the county was granite, though the durability of the stone made it difficult to work, resulting in many dry-stone walled properties. Also in the west, particularly throughout Devon, cob-built houses were the norm. 'Cob' was the term given to the mixture of mud, grit and straw combined to create mud-walled houses. The walls were thickly built, with deeply set windows and doors, rounded corners, protected against the elements by limewash, and then topped with thatch (though in parts of Cornwall, where slate was more readily available, this was used instead). Cob-built houses also stretched into Somerset, Dorset, Wiltshire and Hampshire, though other local materials, such as chalk, were used to make the mixture, giving the houses a different colour and texture. Longhouses were also popular in parts of Cornwall and Devon, particularly on higher ground, and a particular feature of the region was the employment of long, tapering chimneys. Stone was more readily available in the West Country, with Dorset particularly rich in resources, so stone-built properties were more common. Indeed, many building materials were exported to other parts of the country and were prized for their quality, such as Purbeck, Portland and Chilmark stone.

Further information about identifying the materials used to build your house, and then using them to assign an architectural style and period, is provided in 2.3: Using architectural features to date your house.

NATIONAL BUILDING STYLES – POLITE ARCHITECTURE

The previous section has identified how locally available materials influenced the way in which houses were constructed in each region. However, from the fifteenth to the eighteenth centuries, regional styles of vernacular architecture were gradually replaced by national styles during a period often referred to as the great rebuilding when many of the traditional forms of housing were replaced by new properties. This was a period in which builders made a conscious decision to replicate fashions in architecture from not just within England and Wales but also around the world. The umbrella term used to describe these styles of building is *polite architecture*, and many are defined by a distinct chronological period; for example, we refer to Georgian architecture (PLATE 11), or a house being of 'Queen Anne' vintage. Of course, vernacular architecture continued alongside polite architecture, particularly as many of the styles of building were so costly that they were often restricted to the upper echelons of society. Below is a brief guide to the development of different styles of polite architecture, traced chronologically. If you wish to study the intricacies of such a vast subject, further reading is suggested at the end of the book, but an overview will at least allow you to focus on some of the main architectural features of each style and period.

Before the impact of the Renaissance took hold in the sixteenth century, ecclesiastical architecture was the main influencing factor in the construction of many of the more important or prominent secular buildings. Most houses of the lower ranks of society were relatively poorly built in vernacular style, while the manor houses of the middle classes – the knights and 'squirearchy' who formed the main pool of people from whom local administrators were drawn – altered little from the standard 'hall house' (PLATES 3 and 4), so-called because it incorporated one large open space – the hall – within which the family lived. Although these 'hall houses' gradually developed over time, with the addition of private partitioned chambers and new uses of traditional space, it was the higher echelons of society that first absorbed cultural influence from outside the local area. As the aristocracy moved away from fortified castles towards grander domestic properties, they incorporated elements of ecclesiastical architecture, particularly the

Architectural clues | 25

pointed arches used in churches. Consequently, properties that survive from the late fifteenth century onwards are often referred to as 'gothic', after this style of building that first appeared in the late eleventh and early twelfth centuries. However the impact of the Renaissance in the sixteenth century brought new cultural influences from the Continent into domestic space, with more flamboyant carving, increased use of brickwork (including a conscious use of patterns as visual art), artistic flourishes, and grander and more exotic designs for external features, such as ornate chimney stacks which were embraced rather than hidden away (PLATE 8). Thus gothic architecture made way for baroque, a trend that continued into the eighteenth century.

As the seventeenth century drew to a close, a new desire for symmetry took over, which was fully embraced throughout the eighteenth century. For example, Queen Anne architecture was far more regular in shape, with windows placed at standard intervals, facades becoming more symmetrical, and an increased use of brickwork or stone provided an imposing front to a house. Yet this 'rococo' style was transformed in the later Georgian period when the influence of classical architecture – columns, arches and pediments – fused with a greater spending power throughout the lower ranks of society (PLATE 12). Thus the merchants, who were making their fortune through trade and the emerging money markets, were able to adopt the style of the landed aristocracy, who were busy constructing fabulous country houses with landscaped gardens that incorporated further classical features such as temples, lakes and terraces. Town houses were dressed in stone, with regular frontages aggrandized by the addition of a parapet that hid the roof, thus making the property look larger than it was. Floor plans were usually based on a rectangular pattern, with staircases becoming an important internal feature and being used to break up the living space into rooms, rather than having a central hall; a typical Georgian 'double pile' house, for example, would have space at the back for domestic activity – cooking, cleaning, storage – while the living space would be at the front. Yet the latter half of the eighteenth century also witnessed the Gothic Revival, when builders rather playfully looked back to the medieval period to influence features on houses. Therefore high arched windows, Tudor chimneys, turrets and battlements started to appear in domestic dwellings, often inspired by literary works that had a medieval setting. Consequently there was little attempt made at historical accuracy during construction, and a return to medieval floor plans was avoided.

Towards the end of the Georgian period, into what is known as Regency (covering the first quarter of the nineteenth century), more exotic influences from abroad started to mix with the more formal classical lines. In the larger country houses, strange ornamental buildings – grottoes, ruins and follies – were constructed in the gardens. Designs from around the world reflect

Britain's growing global influence during this period, yet many architectural influences from China, India, Africa and the Middle East were imported back and appeared in domestic houses; one of the most spectacular is at Sezincote, near Moreton-in-Marsh, which was built in 1810 to an Indian design. Yet alongside these exotic displays came a more sober phase of construction, with long rows of terraced houses appearing in the expanding towns, and there was a widespread use of ironwork for the first time, particularly in the form of railings, which came to characterize so many developments in the late eighteenth century. Many seaside towns grew rapidly, and the forerunner of modern estates appeared for the first time, offering high-class dwelling for summer visitors, such as Kemp Town in Brighton. Yet in many cases, rapid development came at a price, with poor quality bricks and building materials used to cut costs and maximize profits; stucco was often used to cover up the cracks – literally – as well as lend an air of sophistication to higher-status terraces.

Terracing was an important feature of the next major phase of house building (PLATE 14), which took place during the Victorian period and incorporated the mass-construction of back-to-back workers' cottages in the industrial cities in the North and Midlands (PLATE 15). Where there was less space, courts were constructed where numerous families lived cheek by jowl in crowded conditions; later, tenements and blocks were also developed to serve a similar purpose. Yet among the middle classes, semi-detached and detached urban villas (PLATE 13) started to emerge where there was space to build, particularly in the suburbs that grew outside the crowded city centres; where there was less room, superior terraces were built with gardens to the front and rear. The houses tended to be built of brick, often with bay windows, but they would frequently incorporate a mish-mash of different styles from various former eras, giving rise to the phrase eclecticism to describe the period as a whole from 1840 to the turn of the century, as Neo-Gothic, Elizabethan and Jacobean styles would appear alongside one another. Yet towards the end of the period, from about 1870 onwards, there was a reaction to the appearance of mass-produced houses, and two linked styles of construction started to emerge – Arts and Crafts, and Vernacular Revival. Both looked back to the period before polite architecture, and encouraged the use of traditional building materials and techniques, and local building styles. The result was the appearance of mock-Tudor houses, mullioned windows and exposed timbers. Vernacular Revival continued through the Edwardian period at the start of the twentieth century until the early 1930s, and often incorporated Art Deco, characterized by curved lines, small round windows and rounded bay windows in semi-detached properties.

USING ARCHITECTURAL FEATURES TO DATE YOUR HOUSE

Having taken some time to investigate the architectural style of your house, the next step is to examine the materials from which it was built in more detail and attempt to assign a construction date to the property. It is best to start outside, with the walls that form the main structure of the property, and work your way indoors. Listed below are some of the main forms of building material that you will encounter, used in both vernacular and polite architecture.

The best place to start is with timber framed buildings, as wood is one of the oldest building materials known to man. There is a wide range of wooden framed buildings that you have to keep an eye out for during your research, and a few of the most common are described here.

Cruck frames

Cruck frame houses were constructed from large, curved timbers that formed both the walls and the roof structure, in essence created out of triangular wooden cross-sections at either end (an inverted V) with a long central tie-beam on top that formed the spine of the roof. Occasionally, raised cruck houses were constructed on a solid foundation, or even walls, to give more height to the house.

Box frames

Box frame (or timber frame) houses were constructed – as the name suggests – with vertical timber posts connected by horizontal beams that created a square or rectangular box shape. The four corner posts were joined at the top by tie-beams, with wall plates used to connect the intervening spaces.

Walls

Having examined the frame, the next step is to look at the walls. There are basically two types of wall that you need to consider in timber framed houses – mass-walling, where the entire wall is made up of the build material, or frame walling, whereby the wall space is broken up into smaller panels or frames by vertical and horizontal beams, the spaces being filled up with other material. In some parts of the country, the use of wooden frames became highly decorative (PLATE 5), with elaborate patterns appearing that varied from region to region, giving each a unique and identifiable vernacular style. Thus you can find ornamental framed magpie-work in the Midlands and the North West, and close-spaced vertical small frame beamwork in Wealden houses in the South East. Wood was also used increasingly to extend the space in houses, with jettying providing additional room through projecting upper storeys.

The most popular material to fill in the wood frames was wattle and daub, a type of wood-weave with vertical staves placed in the spaces that were then inter-laced with horizontal withies. A mixture of clay, chalk, mud, dung and horsehair was smeared over the top, and then covered with a coat of lime plaster (PLATES 4 and 6). Wattle and daub was gradually replaced by brickwork in the fifteenth century, with an increased use of patterning such as herringbone where it was to be left exposed. Yet many walls were further covered in cladding, such as weatherboarding, prevalent in the South East, in which overlapping boards were nailed to the exposed timbers. Many other materials were used to clad houses, such as tiles or slates, while rendering with an outer coat of plaster or cement increased a house's ability to withstand the elements.

Remember, though, just because you can see lots of exposed beams on the outside of your house does not necessarily mean that it is old. For example, the Arts and Crafts movement and Vernacular Revival of the late nineteenth and early twentieth century incorporated a lot of timber in the design of houses, often employing medieval house structures. However, the property could have been built as recently as the 1930s, so you also need to look for other evidence such as building plans, title deeds or maps – all of which are described later in this book.

Bricks were another important means of constructing walls, but were relatively expensive until the sixteenth century onwards and therefore only used in more high-status buildings. Due to the proliferation of local moulds and the influence of different craftsmen, bricks differed in size from area to area, so it is easier to spot an early property from the uneven or irregular size of the bricks. From 1571 the size of bricks was set by law at 9 inches × 4.5 inches × 2.25 inches deep (229mm × 114mm × 57mm) – known as the 'statute brick'; this was altered to 8.5 inches × 4 inches × 2.5 inches (216mm × 102mm × 64mm) in 1776, though to avoid brick tax larger bricks were often used. By the nineteenth century, bricks were being mass-produced to cater for the growing need for cheap housing brought about by the Industrial Revolution, and it is from this period that most houses for the lower ranks of society were constructed from this material. In the 1960s the Standard British size was set at 215mm × 102.5mm × 65mm (8.5 inches × 4 inches × 2.5 inches). As well as varying in size, earlier bricks had different colours according to the soil and clay type where they were made. Similarly, regional patterns emerged in the way bricks were laid to construct walls, giving rise to header bonding, stretcher bonding, English bonding and Flemish bonding, while bricks were often used in decorative patterns in timber houses, for example set as herringbone, or using different coloured bricks to achieve a similar effect.

Given the expense of firing bricks in the pre-industrial age, many regions found other uses for their loamy soils, and builders often constructed houses out of mixed clay and straw, known as cob. The practice of building walls out of cob was widespread throughout the South West, into the Midlands and across the North West, as well as in other parts of the British Isles, as it was relatively cheap to produce. Earth was mixed with water to produce a viscous paste, which had a range of materials added to provide strength. These depended greatly on the region, and included chalk, stones, gravel and even straw. To create the walls of the house, the mixture was layered in thick bands, often on top of foundations of rubble that gave added strength to the structure. Sometimes wooden frames were used to create clay lumps or bats, similar to bricks but much larger, which were then set on top of each other akin to modern masonry with clay mortar used to hold them in place. Regardless of the technique, most mud-based houses required an external layer of rendering, usually lime-based plaster or cement, often painted over.

Other important materials used for constructing walls included stone and flint. Much depended on the availability of local stone, and the varied geology of Britain means that stone-built houses will look remarkably different across the country, with a similar range of construction techniques adopted to accommodate the specific durability of the stone in question. Without wishing to embark on a geology lesson, there are three main types of rocks that feature in houses, namely igneous, sedimentary and metamorphic. The prime examples of igneous rocks are granites, hard stone found primarily to the west, while sedimentary rocks include limestones, which are more likely to occur from Dorset into the North East, and the somewhat softer sandstones, prevalent all over the country.

Metamorphic rocks that are commonly used for building are flints, cobbles and pebbles, which as you would expect proliferate in houses in coastal regions. The character of the stone often defines the way in which they can be used to build a house. Where possible, the best technique was to cut the rock into regular-sized blocks so that they could be laid on top of one another, much like bricks. The resultant rectangular block was known as ashlar, and was used more for expensive dwellings owing to the cost involved in cutting it to shape. Consequently, rough-hewn stone or rubble was more commonly used, with thick walls constructed with the largest stones at the bottom to help bear the load of the house. Where possible, the rubble was coursed according to size and shape, giving a more regular appearance, but in many places it was scattered randomly. The corners (quoins) of each wall were obviously important from a structural perspective, as were the sections above windows and doors, and so dressed stone or brick was often deployed here. Flint and pebbles were used in a similar manner to rubble as infill, but walls built of these materials on occasion incorporated layers of brick to add support; the size and shape of the bricks can give you clues as to when the house was erected. Higher status properties can be identified through the use of knapped flint, which had been split and flattened, while in cheaper houses they are usually left undressed. All houses using rubble or flint required plenty of mortar to keep them together, and thereafter the surface was commonly covered in limewash.

Roofing

As well as looking at the walls of your house, much can be learned about your property by examining the way the roof was constructed. Roofs consist of two basic elements, the raftering, which gives it shape and structure, and the covering, which protects the inside from the elements. There are a variety of shapes that you should consider –the standard gable, which looks like an inverted V with a single cross beam that stretched the entire length of the roof, creating a relatively steep slant; the hipped roof, which was V shaped but had a cross beam which ended before it reached the side walls, so that side beams extended down from the cross beam to the apex of each wall, creating a triangular incline; mansard roofs, either gabled or hipped, that were developed in the seventeenth century and incorporated two different inclines in the roof, with the lower one often steeper than the upper one; and indeed, any variation to or combination of the above, as fashion dictated. Thus Dutch gables were more elaborate than standard gables, and were commonplace in the seventeenth century, while many people chose to protect their gables with weatherboards placed on the end of the house. Inside the roof space, you can see the network of beams that were used to hold the roof in place – horizontal beams known as purlins that provided support, tie-beams running between pairs of rafters, supports such as crown posts used commonly up to the sixteenth century, king posts from the fifteenth century, and pairs of queen posts that rested on the tie beam and supported the side purlins.

In a similar manner, a wide variety of roof coverings have been used over the centuries. One of the earliest was thatch, of which Norfolk Reed to the east of the country and long-straw in the west were the most popular examples, the former being the more durable and the latter an easier and cheaper option that required more frequent replacement. Of course, the problems associated with a thatched roof were fire and waterproofing, and so it is no surprise to find other roof materials used. Stone was most commonly used where there was a good supply of raw materials, particularly in areas which were abundant in sedimentary rocks that could be split into layers more easily, predominantly across the central parts of the country. Tiles came to dominate roof coverings from the seventeenth century onwards, and two main types emerged – the plain or flat tile, made from either stone or fired clay, and the curved pantile from the seventeenth century onwards. In addition, and where it was in good supply, such as in Wales, slates were used as coverings. Indeed, slate proved to be so popular by the nineteenth century that Welsh quarries were exporting it across the UK.

Internal fixtures and fittings

Clearly, the most important part of dating your house relies on looking at the external building materials. However, you should also look inside, as there are important clues that can be found from the way the internal floor plan is set out, as well as from where fittings and fixtures are located. These include windows, doors, staircases and fireplaces, but care has to be taken when trying to date a property from such remaining fittings. Unlike external features, which tend to be more reliable as a means of dating a property, internal fixtures and fittings, including windows, have often been removed, altered or added for fashion purposes, and are less likely to be contemporary to the house. Just think of how often we redecorate our houses today, or fit new doors and windows. Therefore, it is best to examine internal architecture in combination – compare a staircase with the layout of the house, or check the style of the fireplace and its surround with any mouldings on the ceiling or walls, for example – so you are more likely to arrive at an accurate conclusion. Nevertheless, period features linked to the styles of polite architecture described above are a very good way of supporting the process of dating your house, and equally tell you far more about the life and times of those who used to reside there, or commissioned its construction in the first place. A list of useful publications is supplied at the end of this book that can help you with this process.

AVOIDING COMMON PITFALLS

The preceding sections have outlined the main clues you need to keep an eye out for when attempting to assign a build, construction or refurbishment date to your house, but in a volume of this nature, which concentrates on documentary sources, you should also seek out more specific reading material, and with this in mind a reading list has been provided towards the end of this book. It is important, though, to point out that an over-reliance on architecture can be quite dangerous, as there are pitfalls associated with the reading of buildings. Some of the most common ones are listed below:

As outlined above, many regions developed unique ways of building houses that remained unchanged for centuries, or 'bucked the trend' compared with building techniques employed in the rest of the country for the same period. Make sure you have not assigned an earlier build date than is actually the case.

• In contrast, to the untrained eye it might be tempting to attribute an early construction date to a rebuild in a retrospective style; for example, mock-Tudor houses were readily built in the 1930s.

- Salvage from older properties, or indeed an earlier house that once stood on the same site, can often provide misleading information as well. Roofs were expensive to construct, so they were often raised on props and new walls built underneath in a different style, or moved to a new building on a completely different site.
- Beware of partial rebuilds due to fire, which were especially prevalent when thatch was employed as a roofing material; this can also affect the way you date the construction of your house.

It is worth bearing in mind that properties built nearer the centre of a community or town are often older than those on the outskirts, or were at least constructed on the sites of earlier buildings. Also look at neighbouring houses and compare their architectural features with your own – they may be markedly different, which suggests that they were not constructed at the same time. It might be worth doing some research into their history as well, as you never know where you will uncover relevant clues; many houses are referred to in the title deeds of the properties on either side, or can be dated through sale catalogues of other houses that were built at the same time.

Research techniques   2.4

WHERE TO BEGIN YOUR RESEARCH

Bearing in mind the advice provided in section 2.2, the best place to begin your research is at the most 'local' level. This will often be a local studies centre, usually located at your nearest main library. This is where you will find many printed volumes that are directly relevant to your community, such as those listed in 'Useful publications'. Not only will these provide useful information about the area in which you live, but the experience will also ease you more gently into some of the research techniques that you will require later when you start work in an archive. Furthermore, printed local history studies will often (though not always!) provide document references to relevant material located in CROs or national archives. This will immediately give you a 'way in' to the records, saving you time and hopefully giving you a degree of confidence; you know that at least there will be something that you can look at. You will also find that the local studies centre will often have its own collection of photographs, maps, plans and newspaper cuttings that you can consult, giving you a good platform from which to build some knowledge. It is likely that staff at the local studies centre will be able to give you advice about further reading and where to go next to continue your research.

In all probability you will be directed to the next level on the archival hierarchy, the local record office. For most people this will be the relevant CRO, but residents in cities or large towns might also find that there are specialist record offices that collect and contain specific records that are equally relevant. London is a particular case in point, with the London Metropolitan Archives (LMA) and the Corporation of London Record Office to name but two, and a multitude of local record offices that also exist at borough level. It is at the CRO that you will find the largest collection of locally relevant documents and primary source material, plus a wider array of relevant publications for your local area.

This is where your local knowledge will be put to good use, as in addition to the thousands of private papers that were deposited by former residents of the county, you will find records generated by the various administrative bodies that existed through the ages – hence the need to know your parish, manor, Poor Law union and county division. Once again, there will be staff on hand to help you with this, but if you do have some pre-knowledge it will save you a great deal of time, and make searching for (and within) records much easier.

It might seem logical to look for material relating to your house in the CRO for the county in which it is situated, and most of the time this will hold true. However, your property might once have formed part of a larger estate, and the landowner may have resided in a different county. For a start, there is no guarantee that private records relating to your house were ever deposited in the public domain; but where such material *has* been made public, you are more likely to locate it at the CRO in the county where the landowner was resident. Be prepared – the detective trail can lead you to some very unexpected places, as the case studies in CHAPTER 15 prove.

At the top of the tree will be national institutions such as the National Archives and specialist archives. These will not necessarily be the best place to begin your research but will nevertheless contain crucial information. For example, as you will discover in the following chapters, the National Archives contains a wealth of information from the documents produced by the interaction between citizens and the state. More detailed information on the National Archives is contained below in section 2.6. If you live in Scotland, you should contact the National Archives of Scotland (NAS) in Edinburgh; the National Library of Wales (NLW), Aberystwyth, fulfils a similar function for the Principality, while the Public Record Office of Northern Ireland (PRONI) is located in Belfast. In effect, these four institutions hold 'government' papers created by various departments, but you will be surprised and amazed by how many will be relevant to your local community. After all, the responsibility of government was, theoretically, to look after people's best interests, and relevant and accurate information was required to fulfil this task. Tax assessments, land surveys, local correspondence, commissions and reports all survive to paint a far wider picture than the locally generated records found at CROs.

You will find that private papers, correspondence and other related material appear in other 'national' places of deposit that are slightly less accessible, such as the Bodleian Library, Oxford, and the British Library (BL), London. Other institutions such as the Family Records Centre (FRC) have been set up to make life easier for researchers embarking on a specialist line of research, and professional organizations also exist to offer guidance and advice. If you have a historic house, then you might find that it is listed in the National Monuments Record – there are separate institutions for England, Scotland and Wales. A full list of places, publications, organizations and websites that will enable you to locate where to start your research is provided under 'Useful addresses' and 'Useful publications'.

RESEARCH TIPS
The following research techniques are designed to give you some guidance about getting started. You will probably develop some of your own as you progress, but bear these points in mind when you do start to think about how and where to begin your research.

Realistic expectations
In BBC television's *House Detectives*, a different property was featured each week, focusing on a specific mystery that the owners wanted the team to investigate. After 30 minutes' screen time of architectural and documentary sleuthing, the mystery was invariably solved and the delighted owners discovered when, and by whom, the house was built. Be warned – this is never the case in reality! House history is a time-consuming process that requires a disciplined and methodical approach to research. Unlike the TV series, you have no time limits, so you should plan your research carefully. It may take you many months or even years of work to settle on a date of construction, and even then you may have only narrowed it down to a rough period, rather than a precise date. This can be highly frustrating, which is why it is important not to set your sights too high in the first place.

No evidence?
The houses featured in the TV series were chosen for a specific reason, as they had an interesting story to tell. Your house may not have such a grand past, or the documentary sources that you need to uncover its history might not survive; indeed, this is one of the most common obstacles facing every house detective. Even when the necessary documents do exist, they can be difficult to interpret or understand, particularly the further back you manage to research. However, it is not all bad news – sometimes the lack of evidence will tell you that your house had not yet been built, so you can search

later and perhaps easier sources. It is a bit like doing a jigsaw puzzle without the box lid to work from – you often have to sift through the evidence until the bigger picture slowly starts to emerge. Sadly, though, the jigsaw puzzle may have many pieces missing!

Following clues

One of the most common temptations in any line of research is to assume a link between clues just because it seems the most likely conclusion. It is far better to work backwards from known facts in a methodical manner than jump in feet first without any real substantive evidence. The research proforma in CHAPTER 14 contains a practical structure that details how to establish a framework of definite facts, which should then lead you to other lines of research. Never give up – if one line of investigation runs dry, go back to your framework, or indeed the earliest known fact, and pursue a different approach. You will probably need to do this many times during the course of your research, and as a result you may revisit an archive several times as new evidence comes to light.

Corroborating documentary evidence

Remember that no two houses will ever follow the same pattern of research, as they were constructed at different times; even houses built at roughly the same time in the same community may yield vastly different results, depending on the people who lived in them, and what records were generated and, more importantly, now survive. You may need to corroborate at least two or three separate sources before you can rely on the results with any degree of certainty. Don't be afraid to explore sources that you might not consider to be relevant – you never know where the detective trail might lead. The sources listed in this book are the most likely to yield results for the majority of houses, but you will find other sources that are of particular relevance to you, so don't be afraid to experiment.

Potential pitfalls

Not all properties will be described in the same way as they are today. House numbers are a relatively new invention, and many houses are described in documents by their physical location, or with reference to properties next to them that may not now exist. Indeed, house names and numbers, as well as street names, are liable to change; and much of your research will be about the people who lived there or the land on which the house was built, rather than the house itself. Finally, it can never be stressed too many times that architectural evidence should be used in conjunction with the documentary sources to prevent you 'discovering' that your house was built far earlier than it really was.

The Internet

More material is made available on the Internet each day, and the house historian can usefully access its growing resources to obtain advice and identify sources. Of particular use are the official websites that many archives and professional organizations maintain, as they contain information leaflets and contact details, plus online research services. Many also provide online access to their catalogues, and increasingly key word searches are available. However, you will need to exercise caution when using some of these online research tools, as it is tempting to rely on the results they produce as providing 'all' the information you will need. This is rarely the case, as many search engines scan document descriptions as opposed to document content, and will therefore not provide full access to place names unless they are specified in the document description. Furthermore, it is tempting to accept material posted on 'unofficial' websites, in particular name indexes or databases. Many are compiled by enthusiastic amateurs and will rarely be comprehensive; if you do obtain information that you think will be of use in your research, it is always wise to double check the facts against the original source material. One of the most essential skills that a house historian needs to develop is the ability to cast a critical eye over material and check information for accuracy and relevance. A list of potentially useful websites is provided under 'Useful addresses'.

Working in archives 2.5

GAINING ENTRY TO AN ARCHIVE

It is always a good idea to get in touch with a prospective new archive before you visit it. You may need to reserve a seat or microfilm reader, and in any case it is always wise to check opening times and document delivery restrictions. It is also likely that you will need to obtain a reader's ticket before you can gain entry, and at least one form of identification is usually required, which will vary from archive to archive. CROs usually require a document with your address on it, such as a recent utility or phone bill, plus another official document (passport, driver's licence or banker's card). Some CROs form part of a County Archive Research Network (CARN), and one CARN ticket will give you access to all archives on the network. Not all CROs have joined this scheme, so it is better to check than to assume. Some ways of getting in touch with your CRO or target archive are suggested in 'Useful addresses' and 'Useful publications', but these days many CROs have their own websites which provide access requirements, opening times and information pages about the material they hold. You may also be able to email for research advice.

RULES AND REGULATIONS: PRESERVING THE DOCUMENTS

Document preservation and conservation are important parts of archival work, and to ensure that documents are not damaged you will find that archives impose strict rules on what you can bring into the reading rooms with you, plus guidelines on document handling techniques. In general, the golden rule of archives is that you must work with pencils only – biros and pens are forbidden due to the potential harm they can cause to original material. Similarly, erasers and pencil sharpeners should not be used or placed near documents, as they can cause damage. There is usually a no eating or drinking rule in place for similar reasons, and this extends to cough sweets and chewing gum. If you are unsure about how you should be handling an item, or you feel it is delicate, please ask an archivist to assist you. Most archives have a store of foam wedges, supports and weights to help set the document out in a way that carries a minimum risk of harm. Try to limit your own contact with the item; for example, if reading a line of text, do not run your finger along the document, as grease from your skin can cause damage. Instead, place a piece of white paper under the line of text to help you keep your place. If you are having difficulty reading faded text, ultraviolet lamps can often help. Similarly, maps and plans are often covered under clear protective sheets, and you should always ask before you attempt to trace a document.

LANGUAGE AND OLD HANDWRITING

If you are fortunate enough to be able to trace back the history of your house beyond 1733, you may well encounter difficulties interpreting relevant material, as the language of official documents was Latin. So material such as manorial court rolls, a highly important source for a house historian, will need translating, as will any official record of deeds or land transfers that were enrolled in the central courts. The exception to this is the Interregnum period (1649–60), when the Parliamentary regime decreed that all official documents should be written in English, and in any case you will find that some types of document had already adopted the vernacular language before 1733.

Another potential problem will be that scribes tended to employ abbreviations when recording entries, so you will not necessarily be working from easily identifiable Latin words. Handwriting changed over the ages, and even if a document has been written in English, it may be difficult to decipher. Official sources can be easier, as scribal technique tended to change more slowly as writers adopted the handwriting of their predecessors. However, private hands varied widely, even within a relatively short period, often employing idiosyncratic shorthand techniques. Spellings also differed widely between authors, and it is not unusual to find variant spellings of the same word in a single piece of text. All of these problems can make interpreting documents difficult.

However, there are ways to make documents seem less intimidating. Most archives stock Latin dictionaries and aids to help you understand paleography, which is the technical term used to describe the handwriting and abbreviations employed in the documents. Furthermore, there are specialist volumes written for local historians that provide translations and explanations of the formulae for the most commonly used documents that you will encounter. You will find relevant material listed under 'Useful publications'. In addition, the National Archives has also produced its own online paleography course, available from the website **www.nationalarchives.gov.uk**.

If you are still unsure, try selecting a similar document from the Interregnum period, which will be in English. Most documents follow standard patterns, with only the details of individuals and places altering. This will enable you to decide where you should be looking in the document for key phrases, and assist with translation. In addition, some local history societies provide transcriptions and translations of important document series, with the added advantage that they are usually indexed. These too can be used to aid interpretation of difficult original material.

Finally, not everyone is familiar with the way documents are dated. Many dates are given in the form of a regnal year (for example, 15 Henry VIII covers 1523–4), and a large proportion of legal material also incorporates a legal term – namely Michaelmas, Hilary, Easter and Trinity – that signifies a particular part of the year in which business was conducted. Furthermore, you may come across dates such as 28 February 1700/01, which refer to the old-style dating technique employed by the Church that started the New Year on 25 March, rather than on 1 January as we do today. The practice was dropped in 1752, the same year that the Gregorian calendar was adopted. The best guide to the many and varied ways of writing dates is Cheney's *Handbook of Dates*, as this provides tables giving regnal years, Easter days and Saints' days, which also occur as a way of giving a date.

HISTORICAL CONTEXT
When looking at the material you have selected, it is very tempting to jump straight in to identify references to your house or house owners. This would be a mistake. Before you can usefully extract information from a document, you will need to understand why that document was created in the first place. If you do not do this, then you may be taking the information it contains out of its historical context and therefore run the risk of misinterpreting it. After all, documents were not initially created for the purpose of helping house detectives date their properties in the twenty-first century. The records might not easily lend themselves to modern research techniques

– for example, indexes may not survive, or you may need to identify names of people rather than the property where they lived. Ask yourself why the document was created, and what information it was originally intended to provide. This will allow you to read it in its own context, and thereby understand why it is arranged the way it is. It may therefore be necessary to corroborate the source with one or more others before you can extract useful information. Most archives provide information leaflets about documents and why they were created, so set aside some time to read these useful articles so that you fully understand why you need to look at the documents.

2.6 The National Archives

ARCHIVAL REFERENCES AT THE NATIONAL ARCHIVES

In this guide, document references will be provided to material located at the National Archives. Each document has its own unique reference, and the National Archives has adopted a coding system to allow you to identify which item you need. The coding system is primarily based around the government department, institution or body that created or maintained the documents in the first place, and usually consists of three separate parts. You will need to make a note of the document reference and order it from the repository floors before you can see it. This in itself can be quite a challenge, given that the National Archives holds an estimated 9.5 million individual items on nearly 200 kilometres (125 miles) of shelving, with approximately 2 to 3 kilometres (1 to 2 miles) of documents being added at the start of each calendar year. Indeed, the holdings are so large that some material is stored offsite in a secure cave system in Cheshire, which takes three working days to transfer and produce at Kew.

The first part of any document reference will always be a letter or series of letters that denotes the government department or institution that created or maintained the record. This is known as the Department Code. Hence, records created or maintained by the Inland Revenue are assigned the department code IR.

Over the course of their working lives, each department created thousands of documents, in some cases hundreds of thousands. Instead of listing them in one long sequence, they have been sub-divided into logical groups, each of which contains documents of a similar type or theme. For example, the records generated by a particular section of a department have been grouped together, as have documents of a distinct type, such as maps. A number is then assigned to this sequence, called the Series Number, and the combination of Department Code and Series Number allows an archivist to quickly tell what type of information is contained within that series. For example, the Field Books produced by the Inland Revenue for the 1910

Valuation Office survey have been assigned series reference IR 58. It is your task to identify the series that contains material relevant to your research.

Once you have located your series, your next task is to identify which individual item within that series is most relevant. To provide a unique reference, every document within a series is given a Piece Number, and this forms the third part of a PRO reference. Some pieces have in fact been listed at a more detailed level – for example, individual letters in a bound volume of correspondence. Numbers at this level are called Item Numbers.

THE *GUIDE*, CATALOGUE AND FINDING AIDS

When referring to a particular type of document, this guide will provide a series code such as IR 58. However, there are a number of additional aids that exist to help you with your research. One of the best ways to start your research is to access the catalogue. All document descriptions and references have been uploaded into an electronic database, which allows you to undertake keyword searches of document descriptions, although this does not search document content. Many documents do not have very good descriptions, but for a local historian the system can be of great use to identify references to places or people, especially in some of the more obscure parts of the catalogue. There is also access to the catalogue via the National Archives website (**www.nationalarchives.gov.uk**).

You will also find that the onsite *Guide* is a useful three part index to the records. Part Three, identified by a yellow spine, is a subject index that links topics with departmental series. Relevant series can be checked for potential use in Part Two of the *Guide*, which has a green spine and tells you the date range of each series, plus a brief description of the content of the documents. Part One of the *Guide* (which has a red spine) is not strictly relevant if you wish to find a document reference, but it contains useful information on the background history and function of the government departments listed in Part Two, and can be used to provide background context to the records. On occasion it will also provide relevant department codes and series numbers that are not always cross-referenced in Part Two.

Once you have identified a series that may contain useful information, you can then access the series list in the paper catalogue. These folders, arranged in alphanumerical order, contain the same information as the electronic catalogue, with two additional advantages. You will find introductory notes that provide information about the documents themselves, although not every series list contains them. You should also find a sheet of paper at the front of the series list that provides a worked example of a document reference, which is useful as not every series requires a simple three-part reference; sometimes a sub-series is required for particularly large series, such as the maps that accompany the 1910 valuation survey.

To help get you started, the National Archives has produced research guides that describe the most popular documents or topics that are researched. These are free, and are also available on the website. You will also find contemporary lists and indexes, published guides and other reference works available at each of the enquiry points. If you are in any doubt about what you should be doing, there are reader advisors at hand to point you in the right direction. Finally, if you are visiting for the first time, once you have registered as a reader you are asked to join a free induction that shows you how to find your reference and order documents via the computer terminals.

MAPS, PLANS AND LAND SURVEYS

3

Introduction

If you are unfamiliar with archival material, the best place to begin your research is with maps and plans, as they are relatively easy to interpret and allow you to see at a glance exactly where your house is – or should be! While they rarely provide details of owners or occupancy, they do at least give you a visual record of your local area. If you consult enough maps from a wide variety of dates, you can start to construct a chronological framework within which to base other documentary research. Maps that do *not* show your house can be just as important as those that do, as you can narrow down your search for a construction date to a period between the date of the last map that does not show your property, and the earliest one that does. However, you need to exercise some care with this approach; some maps may depict an earlier building that was subsequently demolished to make way for a later construction, and without architectural or corroboratory documentary evidence it can be very tempting to assume they are one and the same. Similarly, builders often submitted proposals to erect houses that were never actually carried out, and the appearance of building plots on a map does not necessarily mean that you can assume construction followed shortly afterwards. The lesson here is that you need to check other sources before leaping to conclusions based solely on one source – a lesson that serves well in any line of work, not just house history or maps.

The National Archives houses a vast collection of maps and plans, created as a by-product of the work of individual government organizations and departments. It is estimated that there are over 1 million maps and plans in the archive, but they are not fully catalogued, and new maps are discovered each day. In addition to these individual items scattered across a wide range of the National Archives series, there is a substantial, although incomplete, collection of OS sheets from various periods. Some of these form part of land surveys conducted by government departments, which are doubly important as they incorporate related assessment books. These can often give you names of owners and occupiers linked directly to property at a specific date.

However, it is important to remember that local archives will hold the majority of cartographic material that is relevant to your area, which often complements and usually supersedes the holdings at the National Archives. Therefore, if you are planning to start your research with cartographic material, your first port of call should be the local studies centre or CRO that covers the area in which your house stands, and use their resources to compile a list of maps that show your property. There are also specialist map collections, such as the BL's Map Department, which is a registered place of deposit for OS material (in contrast to the National Archives, which is not).

The following sources are the most appropriate and easily accessible at the National Archives, and are best researched having completed the preliminary map searches at a local level. However, if you have not had time to cover these local archives, not to worry; you can gain some familiarity with your local area by consulting some of the OS sheets on open access. You can then start to build up a more detailed framework of maps from some of the more complex sets of records held at the National Archives, focusing particularly on some of the national land surveys. Therefore the next step will be to examine the valuation survey and tithe apportionments, as they can provide a snapshot c.1910–15 and c.1836–58. The results you obtain will form a framework that can be filled in by the detailed census returns at the FRC that exist in ten-year intervals from 1841 to 1901 and are described in CHAPTER 9, section 9.2. If you have a rural property which you suspect formed part of a farm, then you can examine the records of the National Farm Survey from the 1940s. Once you have your framework, any of the other map searches listed below may yield useful information, especially enclosure awards, estate maps, military surveys and deposited plans that are often listed in the National Archives extracted map catalogue.

3.2   Ordnance Survey records

ABOUT THE RECORDS

The work of the modern OS department originated in the Board of Ordnance section of the War Office in the mid-eighteenth century, when the remit was to create a military map of the Highlands of Scotland. In 1791 a Trigonometrical Survey was commissioned to produce a military map and for the first time a map for general use. The first official map was published in 1801 at the scale of 1 inch to the mile. From 1841, under the Ordnance Survey Act, the OS became a separate institution, primarily creating maps and plans for ascertaining and recording boundary changes, as well as publishing county sheets.

COUNTY MAPS

Although the National Archives is not a registered place of deposit for OS maps, you will find many examples at the National Archives that can help you pinpoint your house in its locality. Their primary function will be to provide an overview of your area and allow you to identify changes in the community over time.

The earliest series of published OS maps at the National Archives date from 1801, and are on open access in the reading rooms. The scale is 1 inch to the mile, and therefore does not give a particularly detailed view of property in town and city centres. However, rural properties are easier to spot, and in any case they can provide an overview of an area and a point of comparison with later OS editions. The National Archives also holds 5 inch to the mile London maps from the nineteenth century on the open shelves, plus twentieth-century 6 inch to the mile maps, arranged by county. It is far easier to see individual properties on these maps, and they can be a useful reference tool when trying to locate your property for other searches. These maps are currently on open access in the Map and Large Document Reading Room, on the second floor of the building.

In addition to the National Archives, the BL is a registered place of deposit for published OS sheets, and most CROs have relevant county sheets for various periods. However, you might want to start with your local study centre, which is likely to be nearest to where you live and therefore a better environment in which to start your research. Most local study centres have a wide range of OS sheets, as well as copies of other potentially older maps and plans.

BOUNDARY RECORDS

Boundary records can provide some information about property, as they record changes in public boundaries in Remark Books (the National Archives series OS 26) and Record Books (OS 31 and 33). Property situated on parish boundaries can frequently be found marked in these books, which are arranged by county in alphabetical order. Parish name books (OS 23) can provide supplementary information about local administrative names, and evidence presented in disputed boundary cases were recorded in Boundary Reports (OS 32). Sketch maps (OS 27) and Journals of Inspection (OS 29) provided official confirmation of any changes before 6-inch Deposit Maps were published with the final decision marked on them (OS 38 for England and Wales, and OS 39 for Scotland).

These sources will be of limited use unless your property falls near a county or parish boundary. As such, they should perhaps not be the first ports of call, but can be used to supplement existing information.

3.3 Valuation Office survey

ABOUT THE RECORDS

The 1910 Valuation Office survey, also known as the Lloyd George Domesday, is one of the most useful sources for house history, but one that is often overlooked. Not only does the survey combine maps with assessment documents, but it also covers land and property in both urban and rural communities. The aim of the exercise was to assess the capital appreciation of real property that was attributable to the site itself, under the terms of the 1909–10 Finance Act (10 Edward VII c.8). Put another way, the government of the day wanted to find out the value of land and property across the country to raise money from tax (about which subject you can find out more in CHAPTER 10). A more detailed description of the history of the survey is provided in G. Beech and R. Mitchell, *Maps for Family and Local History*, which supersedes W. Foot, *Maps for Family History.*

Finding the records can be a little daunting, as there are various steps you need to take. Therefore it's important to understand the background to the creation of the records, as this will help you to understand all the procedures you need to follow before you can access the documents. As part of the assessment process, England and Wales were divided into 14 valuation regions (later reduced to 13) and further sub-divided into 118 valuation districts. Two sets of maps were compiled for each region and were used to detail all land or property that formed part of the survey. Each land unit – which varied in size from individual houses to large fields – was then assigned a hereditament (assessment) number, usually marked on the map in red, with the boundary for that property marked in red, or sometimes green, depending on the region. The official 'record' maps (*see* FIGURE 1) are deposited in the National Archives in series IR 121 and 124–35, while working copies, where they survive, are in the custody of the relevant CRO. The financial data compiled during the course of the survey was recorded in Field Books, which are at the National Archives in series IR 58; Revenue Books, often referred to as 'Domesday books' and which contain similar but less detailed information, are preserved in the CROs. It is the IR 58s that will be of most use to a house historian as they contain information about the property, while recording the names of the owners and occupiers, for the period *c.*1910–15.

Similar records for Northern Ireland and Scotland can be found in the PRONI or the National Archives of Scotland (NAS), respectively, and are described in more detail in section 3.3: Accessing Field Books.

ACCESSING VALUATION SURVEY MAPS (EXCLUDING LONDON)
Before you can view the Field Books at the National Archives, you will need

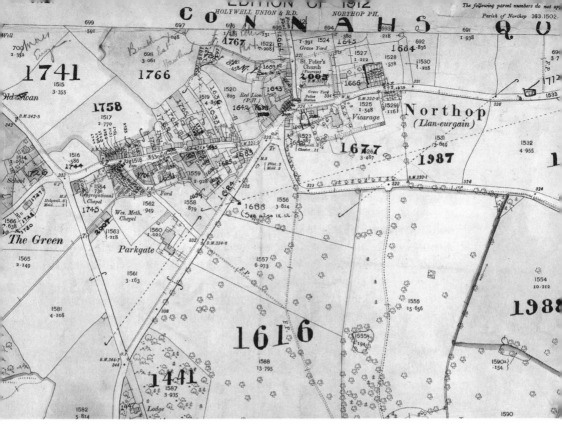

Figure 1 An extract from the valuation map for Northop, dated 1912. The property, formerly known as 'The Yacht Inn', is assigned hereditament number 1685. The distinctive shape of the property is discernible. (IR 131/10/85)

to identify and order the relevant valuation survey map on which your property is marked, as it acts as an index by providing you with the relevant hereditament number. There is a key sheet, or county diagram, for each county and they are arranged alphabetically in three folders, two for England and one for Wales; these are on open access in the Map and Large Document Room. Remember to look under Southampton for Hampshire, and be sure to consult the photocopied 'old series' index sheet for Essex (with the exception of the SW corner of the county, which uses the 'new series' index).

Each key sheet is divided into a series of numbered grids, which are in turn sub-divided into 16 smaller unnumbered rectangles, with each rectangle representing a map at the OS scale 1:2500 (or 25 inches to the mile). Your task is to identify within which of these smaller rectangles your property falls. At times this can be a tricky process; given the small scale of the key sheets, it is often difficult to identify the correct part of a township or city, and even some small villages might be hard to pinpoint with any degree of certainty.

Therefore you should start by making a note of the relevant larger numbered grid. You will need to convert the grid number from Arabic to Roman numerals, as the maps you will be ordering use this method of coding. To assist you in this conversion process, the National Archives has produced a research guide that shows the various Roman numerals used.

The next step is to locate within which of the smaller rectangles your property falls. This process sounds more complicated than it actually is when you come to do the search, and in any case there is more than one way to find the correct grid. For instance, you can make a judgment based solely on the key sheets, but if you are uncertain which rectangle is relevant there is an alternative method. As you have obtained the grid number (in this case IX), you can use this to search the 6-inch OS county maps that are on open access, as they contain individual maps that have exactly the same grid numbers, but at a scale that should allow you to locate your property with ease (1:10 560). It is then a case of comparing the OS sheet with the key sheet and judging which smaller rectangle is most appropriate. If you are still in some doubt, or think that your property might straddle the boundary between two rectangles, you should order both maps.

To find the document reference for your chosen map, you need to assign a number to the relevant rectangle. As you will see on the key sheet, the rectangles form a grid, four across by four down. Simply count from left to right, assigning a number to each rectangle as you go. Hence, the top row is 1 to 4, the second row 5 to 8, the third row 9 to 12 and the bottom row 13 to 16. (*See* DIAGRAM 1.)

Having established which grid your house falls within, the next stage is to assign a document reference to your chosen map so that you can order it for examination. The survey is not arranged by county but by Valuation Office region, and the maps for each region have been allocated their own National Archives series. A summary is listed in TABLE 3.1.

For administrative purposes, each region was sub-divided into separate districts, and each district has been assigned a National Archives sub-series number. You will find the maps listed in the relevant section of the series list. The name given to each district is meant to reflect a geographical area but can often be misleading, and you may need to search through several districts before you find your map. A summary of the districts for each region is provided at the front of each series list, and in Appendix 1 (pp. 70–2) of Foot's *Maps for Family History*. Furthermore, this publication also provides

1	2	3	4
5	6	7	8
9	10	11	12
13	14	15	16

Diagram 1 If your property fell within map grid 9, rectangle 16, your map reference would be Flintshire IX.16.

Table 3.1 List of Valuation Office districts and relevant National Archives series

REGION	TNA SERIES	REGION	TNA SERIES
South-Eastern	IR 124	East Midland	IR 130
Wessex	IR 125	Wales	IR 131
Central	IR 126	Liverpool	IR 132
East Anglia	IR 127	Manchester	IR 133
Western	IR 128	Yorkshire	IR 134
West Midland	IR 129	Northern	IR 135

a list of where you will find maps for each county (Appendix 2, pp. 73–9) and a list of map locations for a wide variety of places (Appendix 3, pp. 80–2). Copies are available on open access in the reading rooms.

You may find that the geographical area covered in your map crosses the boundary between two of these districts. In these instances duplicate maps were made, one for each district. You will probably need to order both copies, as they will contain information for the relevant district only.

In some cases you will find that the National Archives copies of the maps have not survived. If this is the case, there is a chance that the working copy has been deposited at your local CRO, and this may give you the information you need to order out the relevant Field Book. In general, the maps you will obtain are at a scale of 1:2500. To make it easier to mark properties in towns and cities, maps at scales of 1:1250 and 1:500 were also created. There are four 1:1250 maps for each 1:2500 map, representing the northwest, northeast, southeast and southwest quadrants. (*See* DIAGRAM 2.)

The 1:500 maps are even more detailed, and there are 25 for each 1:2500 map arranged in 5 rows of 5 (*see* DIAGRAM 3). Where they exist, a reference to more detailed maps is usually found on the 1:2500 map, and generally they are listed in the series list after the 1:2500 maps.

Once you have located the relevant map in the series list, note the

NW	*NE*
SW	*SE*

1	*2*	*3*	*4*	*5*
6	*7*	*8*	*9*	*10*
11	*12*	*13*	*14*	*15*
16	*17*	*18*	*19*	*20*
21	*22*	*23*	*24*	*25*

Diagram 2 If 1:1250 maps existed for Flintshire square IX.16, this is how they would be arranged. So if you wanted the southeast quadrant, you would need to locate Flintshire IX.16.SE in the series list.

Diagram 3 If 1:500 maps existed for Flintshire square IX.16, this is how they would be arranged. So if you wanted map 20, you would need to locate Flintshire IX.16.20 in the series list.

document reference for the map and order it out. When it arrives, you will see that each property or piece of land has been assigned a number, usually marked in red. Make a note of this, plus (if marked) the income tax parish (ITP) in which it falls. ITPs were created to group together small ecclesiastical or civil parishes, and are an important means of reference when locating the relevant Field Book that accompanies the map. Boundaries between ITPs are usually coloured in yellow on the maps.

You may notice that separate land parcels are given a coloured wash to distinguish them from their neighbours. Sometimes detached parcels of land that form one distinct hereditament are indicated by the note 'Part' or 'Pt' next to the hereditament number. This is usually accompanied by a brace (usually in red) that joins separated land parcels, or a hereditament that has been divided by a feature such as a road. Detached or separated hereditaments for large properties may stretch across several maps.

ACCESSING VALUATION SURVEY MAPS FOR LONDON
The procedure for locating a map for the cities of London and Westminster, and the surrounding suburbs, is slightly different. There is a separate series of key sheets for the London area that divide large grids into 100 smaller rectangles, rather than the usual 16. The key sheet folder on open access also contains larger scale inserts to allow you to identify your property in more detail, although the series is not complete. A good knowledge of London geography is perhaps advisable for this search, but there are various books on open access that provide you with modern maps of London and its suburbs.

The procedure is exactly the same as for other parts of the country – you should make a note of which grid and rectangle are most appropriate to your property, remembering to convert the grid number to Roman numerals. The maps for the London region are in the National Archives series IR 121, which is sub-divided into 19 districts, each with its own National Archives sub-series number. Once again, the names assigned to these districts can be misleading, and you may need to search through several regions to find the most relevant map. Remember to look for duplicate maps that appear in different districts and order both. The London region contains maps for property located in the surrounding counties, so you may need to search the relevant county key sheets as well to obtain map references. Further guidance is provided in Foot's *Maps for Family History*. London maps are at the OS scale 1:1056, while county maps are at the usual 1:2500 scale. You should be able to identify your property and make a note of the red hereditament number that has been assigned to it.

ACCESSING FIELD BOOKS

Once you have obtained the hereditament number for your property from the map, you are ready to locate the relevant Field Book. Each Field Book contains the information for exactly 100 hereditaments in numbered blocks, for example 1–100, 101–200, 201–300 and so forth, and each hereditament is assigned four pages in the book. This is where you will obtain crucial information about the property and its owner or occupier. Although the details will vary, you will be pleasantly surprised at what you uncover. You should at least get the names of the owner and the occupier, plus the full street address. It is not unknown for descriptions of the property to be included, with the possibility of finding sketch maps or inserts, descriptions of outbuildings, dates of previous sales, and even construction dates. These are all nuggets of information that can give you invaluable clues for later research.

Like the maps, the Field Books (*see* FIGURES 2A and 2B) are arranged in valuation districts, and identifying which region can be complicated. You should first check for any clues on the map itself, such as the name of the ITP in which your property falls; ITP boundaries are usually marked in yellow at the edges of the map. If these are not marked, or an ITP name is not provided, you will need to use several finding aids that are located on open access in the reading rooms.

With the series lists for IR 58 are place-name indexes that link a parish or place name with the relevant valuation district under the column headed 'Valuation'. Make a note of the name of this district, as the main series list for IR 58 is arranged by valuation district in alphabetical order, with the ITPs listed in alphabetical order under the main valuation district at the top of each page. There are separate indexes for London that are arranged by street name which then assign a valuation district and ITP. If the place you are looking for does not appear in the list, you should consult the Board of Inland Revenue's *Alphabetical List of Parishes and Places in England and Wales*, which is also on open access, in two volumes. This will assign an ITP to smaller parishes, hamlets or townships that were not large enough to be granted ITP status, for which you can then search in the place-name index for the IR 58 series list. Even with this guide, you may still have to use your local knowledge and judge which is the most relevant place.

These series lists can be difficult to use, and there is no guarantee that you will always find the ITP in the relevant valuation district. However, the National Archives online catalogue allows you to search document descriptions by keyword, while limiting your search to a single series. In this case you can often find your ITP by searching for it by name within series IR 58.

If you are still unable to locate your ITP in the IR 58 series list, then you may need to look at the relevant Revenue Book at the CRO, as they contain a list of parishes that made up an ITP and give the range of hereditament

3·3

Reference No.

Index Letter	Description of Buildings	Dimensions			Cubical Contents	Condition	Remarks
		Frontage	Depth	Height			
Bld.	Coach House					Old but fair order Brs.
	Shippon tie 3 loft over					" " " "
	Shippon tie 2 + Calf loft over					Very old but mod: fair. S Brs.
	Loose box stable					Very old but in mod: fair order. S Brs.
	Cartshed loft over.					" " — " " —
	3 Stall Stable loft over					" " — " " —
	2 Pigstys Brs. leanto					Old + poor order.

1685

Reference No. _____ Map. No. F 9. 16. B.

Situation Plymouth House, Northop

Description House & premises.

Extent

Gross Value { Land, £ ___ / Buildings, £ 20 } Rateable Value { Land, £ ___ / Buildings, £ 18 }

Gross Annual Value, Schedule A, £

Occupier Edward Foulkes

Owner do

Interest of Owner Freehold

Superior interests

Subordinate interests

Occupier's tenancy, Term _____ from

How determinable

Actual (or Estimated) Rent, £ 15

Any other Consideration paid

Outgoings—Land Tax, £ _____ paid by
         Tithe, £ _____ paid by
         Other Outgoings

Who pays (a) Rates and Taxes (b) Insurance Owner
Who is liable for repairs do
Fixed Charges, Easements, Common Rights and Restrictions

Former Sales. Dates
     Interest
     Consideration
     Subsequent Expenditure
Owner's Estimate. Gross Value
          Full Site Value
          Total Value
          Assessable Site Value
Site Value Deductions claimed

Roads and Sewers. Dates of Expenditure
           Amounts

Reference No. _____

Particulars, description, and notes made on inspection

House:- Stone Brick + Slated, roughcasted, Old but substantially built in fair order contains Hall, 2 Entertaining rooms, kitchen, 3 Bedrooms, +3 rooms in attic.
Wash house, Dairy + Bk kitchen Brs. fair order. Yard consist of yard + small garden in front + back of house. (Would be difficult house to let as there are a row of cottages in front) Area:- 1500 Sq Yds. Bld. as own.

Charges, Easements, and Restrictions affecting market value of Fee Simple

Valuation.—Market Value of Fee Simple in possession of whole property in its present condition

Act. Rent £ 15. 0 0
15y Purchase £ . 0 0
                 30. 0 0
                 Blt. 20
                          £ 400

Deduct Market Value of Site under similar circumstances, but if divested of structures, timber, fruit trees, and other things growing on the land

1500 Yds @ 1/6   Say £ 112

Difference Balance, being portion of market value attributable to structures, timber, &c. .... £ 308

Divided as follows :—
Buildings and Structures .... £ 308
Machinery .... £
Timber .... £
Fruit Trees .... £
Other things growing on land .... £

Market Value of Fee Simple of Whole in its present condition (as before) .... £ 420

Add for Additional Value represented by any of the following for which any deduction may have been made when arriving at Market Value :—
Charges (excluding Land Tax) .... £
Restrictions .... £
                  GROSS VALUE ... £ 420

Figure 2(a) The entry in the valuation Field Book for hereditament number 1685. The property is referred to as 'Plymouth House' and is in the possession of Edward Foulkes. (IR 58/94483)

Figure 2(b) A clue to Plymouth House's former use is given by the outbuildings, which include a 'Coach House'. (IR 58/94483)

numbers for each parish. Field Books for Southampton, Winchester and Portsmouth, and an area around Chichester, were destroyed by enemy action in the Second World War. Many records for Chelmsford and all for Coventry are also lost.

RELATED RECORDS

The National Archives holds Revenue Books for the City of London and Westminster (Paddington) in series IR 91. All other Revenue Books are at the relevant CRO, where you will also find the working maps. Where they survive, additional records created as part of the survey are largely stored at the relevant CRO as well. A summary of these is provided in Beech and Mitchell's *Maps for Family and Local History* and Foot's *Maps for Family History*.

The Scottish valuation survey is available at the NAS. Record maps are in series IRS 101–33 and Field Books are in IRS 51–88. Related valuation records are available for Northern Ireland at PRONI in a variety of VAL series. A survey of 1830 is available in VAL 1B, with maps in VAL 1A. A later assessment from 1848 to 1864, known as the Griffith's Valuation, is found in VAL 2B, with maps in VAL 2A; there is an index available on CD. A householders index is also available for consultation. Thereafter, annual valuations were conducted from 1864 until the early 1930s, with returns stored in VAL 12B. A general revision was undertaken in 1935, with returns in VAL 3B and maps in VAL 3A.

Tithe apportionments   3·4

ABOUT THE RECORDS

As with the Valuation Office survey, tithe apportionments can be a little tricky to access and so some background information about the documents, and why they were created, is important so that you get the most out of the records when you come to view them. Tithes were originally payments in kind of a tenth of the annual produce of land by way of crops and animals, payable to either the parson of the parish, or an entitled lay person, or both. Payment of tithes had been in existence for centuries, and during this time individual arrangements had been made to commute the payment to a fixed sum of money, or in some cases a grant of land. Enclosures hastened this process, in particular the Enclosure Acts of the eighteenth and nineteenth centuries; more details are provided in section 3.7.

By the 1830s tithes were highly unpopular amongst rural landowners, as they did not reflect the changing social and economic conditions of the dawning industrial age. Under the Tithe Commutation Act of 1836 (6 & 7

Will. IV, c.71), remaining payments in kind were to be commuted into fixed monetary sums based on a seven-year average of the price of wheat, barley and oats taken across the country. The process of commutation was primarily undertaken at a local level by negotiation, but a Tithe Commission was established to help parties reach agreement and arbitrate in disputed cases, in which case an award was produced. No matter which path was followed, the end product of the commutation process was a tithe apportionment that formalized the agreement or award. The apportionment consisted of a map that showed the properties that were liable to tithes, and an apportionment schedule based on the agreement or award that set out the liabilities for each landowner concerned. Under the terms of the Tithe Act an original and two copies of each record were made. The original was retained by the Tithe Commission, and subsequently these were deposited at the National Archives in two series, IR 30 (maps) and IR 29 (apportionment schedule). One copy was sent to the parish church and the other to the relevant register of the diocese, and where these copies survive they have been deposited in the CRO. In general the mapping process lasted until c.1856, although most agreements and awards were settled by the mid-1840s.

As a source for house history, the tithe apportionments provide vital clues about property ownership and occupancy, although you will not obtain details about the property itself. The maps should allow you to pinpoint dwellings that existed before urban expansion changed the landscape later in the century. Even if your house was not yet built, you can discover who owned the land and what it was once used for. Coverage is not complete for England and Wales, as no apportionments were created for areas where agreements had previously been reached through other means. Tithe apportionments will also be of limited use for properties in towns and cities, although where tithes were still payable, you will find detailed maps and assessments that provide an invaluable resource. Similar records for Scotland and Northern Ireland survive at the NAS and PRONI and are described in section 3.4: Related records.

Tithes are a complicated topic, and the process did not stop with the Tithe Commutation Act of 1836. Further Acts followed, including the 1936 Tithe Act, which produced related documents including District Record Maps in the National Archives series IR 90. These maps were compiled from more recent OS maps, and – where they survive – provide a useful point of comparison between the historic tithe maps in IR 30 and the modern landscape. For more information you should consult the relevant National Archives research guide on *Tithe Records*, and read some of the books listed under 'Useful publications'.

ACCESSING THE RECORDS

The best place to start looking for tithe maps and awards will be your CRO. In theory, they should have at least one of the deposited copies in their holdings. This potentially provides you with a choice of maps if one is of poor quality, and it may be possible to trace over the maps – something that is not recommended at the National Archives. Furthermore, later amendments that affected the value of the apportionment, such as the subsequent use of land for railway cuttings, were attached to the apportionment; these are not always to be found on the copies at the National Archives.

3·4

However, if you are planning to conduct some of the other searches mentioned in this chapter, or no copies are available at your CRO, there are approximately 11,800 maps and apportionment schedules available for you to consult at the National Archives. The documents are accessed via a combined series list for IR 29 and 30, as the maps and apportionment schedules share the same piece number for each parish. The lists are arranged alphabetically by county, and thereafter by parish. Each county has been assigned a number, as has each parish, and these numbers combine to form your piece number, prefixed by IR 30 if you wish to locate the map, or IR 29 for the apportionment schedule.

Kain and Oliver's publication *The Tithe Maps and Apportionments of England and Wales* provides an easier means of reference, and is available on open access in the reading rooms. This volume combines a similar county and parish listing, assigning piece numbers to each parish. The entry for each parish contains a brief description of the documents you will be accessing, such as the date of the map, features covered, scale and surveyor (if known), and the date of the apportionment. Furthermore, there

Example Days Farm, lies in the parish of Doddinghurst, Essex. The list informs us that the county number is 12 and the parish number is 109. The National Archives references will be:

IR 30/12/109 (map)

IR 29/12/109 (apportionment)

is an introduction for each county that provides a detailed description of tithe liability, with a map of the county that shows a general overview of how many parishes were liable to tithes and therefore produced documents as part of the survey.

Checking tithe liability is a popular line of research and is widely used for genealogical purposes. To help conserve these fragile documents, all agreements/awards at the National Archives have been copied and are now produced on microfilm, whereas the tithe maps for English counties, running alphabetically from Bedfordshire to Middlesex, are available only on fiche; thereafter, from Norfolk to Yorkshire and for all Welsh counties, you will need to order the original maps.

USING THE RECORDS

As with the Valuation Office survey, accessing the records involves several stages. The first step is to view the tithe map for your parish (*see* FIGURE 3). It can be difficult to identify property on the maps, and you will probably need to use local knowledge, make a comparison with OS maps, or order a map from series IR 90 if one survives for the parish in question. Furthermore, the scale, scope and content of the tithe maps will vary from region to region, despite the best efforts of the tithe commissioners to impose uniformity. Each plot of land that was liable to tithes was assigned an apportionment number on the map, which will be unique to that parish. The apportionment number corresponds to an entry in the apportionment schedule in IR 29 (*see* FIGURE 4). After a brief preamble that describes the means by which the apportionment was drawn up, you will find the apportionment schedule itself. It is divided into columns, listing the landowner, occupier, plot number (that corresponds to the plot number on the map), the name and description of the land and premises, the state of cultivation, quantities in statute measure, the names of tithe-owners, and other remarks. The schedules are usually arranged in alphabetical order by the name of individual landowners, rather than by plot number, but there is a key at the front of each apportionment book which you can use to find the page number on which each plot appears. You may need to ask for help in using the key, but it saves a lot of time.

Figure 3 An extract from the tithe map for Northop, Flintshire. The date of the apportionment for the parish was 1838, and the map dates from c.1839. The 'Yacht Inn' is plot b.38 in the centre of the village. (IR 30/50/32)

Figure 4 A section of the tithe apportionment schedule for Northop, Flintshire. It shows the lands owned by Benjamin Bellis, which include plot b.38 – 'Public house, yard etc. Yacht' – in the possession of Joseph Joynson. (IR 29/50/32)

It is the first four columns that are of most interest to the house historian, as you will find out the name of the owner or occupier and a description of the property, be it a cottage, house, outhouse, inn or shop. These names will allow you to conduct a search of other sources that exist for this period, such as the census returns discussed in section 9.2.

RELATED RECORDS

In addition to the maps and apportionment schedules in IR 30 and IR 29, a whole series of related records was created at the time that might contain some useful information, and the house historian should be aware of the following. Tithe files in IR 18 contain correspondence from commissioners who were investigating which areas had previously had their tithes commuted, and therefore can provide some information about places not covered in the apportionments. However, over the years these files have been heavily 'weeded' and thus survival of relevant material is not guaranteed.

				A	R	P		s	d	
	b 199	Arable do	do							
	b 207	Large do	do	12	1	18	2	11	9	A
	b 210	Field by Sandwell	do	3	2	28		14	5½	A
	b 361	Cae either	Pasture	3	1	9		11	4½	A
	b 362	Nant	do		1	15		1	1	A
	b 363	Caer Canol	do	2	3	1		10	6½	A
	b 366	Caer coed gellig	do	1	3	0		5	10½	A
	"	Pool in do	Pool			12	3			A
	b 364	Coal Waste	Coal Work	3	1	17		1	8½	A
				40	2	30		6	9	8
Webster Sarah	b 83	Part of the ddôl	Pasture	3	0	0	13	0½		A
	b 84	Part of Weirglodd y Tarn	do	1	3	1	7	6½		A
				4	3	1	1	0	7	
Williams Edward, Grocer	b 33	House yard and Garden in Northop	Homestead		1	8				
	b 111	Roft	Pasture	1	1	37		11	7½	A
				1	3	5		11	7½	
Cartwright Margaret & another	b 37	House garden & Smithy in Northop	Homestead & Smithy		1	7				
Davies Anne	b 51	House and Garden do	do		1	20				
Evans John	b 321	Garden near Sandwell	Arable			13				
Wynne Margaret	b 43	House and Garden	Homestead		1	7				
Williams John	b 21	House and Garden	do			14				
Foulkes Thomas	b 27	House and Garden	do			20				
				1	1	11				
Blackwell Robert	b 28	Croft	Arable		1	0		1	7½	A
Joynson Joseph	b 38	Public house yard & Gatch	Homestead		1	1				
	b 80	Orchard	Arable		1	25				
	b 112	Little field and road	Pasture & road	3	2	19		1	2	A
	b 119	Cae crwn	do	3	2	0		1	2	A
	b 120	Bottie pellaf	do	4	1	28		1	3	A
				12	0	33		3	7	1
Jones James & another	b 29	2 Houses and yard (Northop)	Homestead			14				
	b 113	Gardens	Arable		1	0				
				1	14					

Occasionally the commutation process brought to light disputes about boundaries, and where the commissioners were forced to make a judgment, you will find a boundary award in TITH 1, with schedules and plans that contain information about owners and tenants.

Altered apportionments reflect changes of ownership of individual plots of land. Those before 1836 are filed with the relevant records in IR 29, but after this date they were filed as Orders for Apportionment in series IR 94; the maps that accompany these alterations can be found in IR 90, mentioned above. These records can be of great use where later housing development took place in the area. Information about other records created under the 1936 Tithe Act can be found in the relevant National Archives research guide on *Tithe Records*.

In addition, your CRO will have duplicate copies of the tithe maps and apportionment schedules found in IR 29 and 30, so you may wish to start your research there (for details, see section 3.4: Accessing the records).

The equivalents to tithes in Scotland were known as teinds, and were payable by owners of heriotable property within a parish, as opposed to being attached to the land itself as in England and Wales. As such you will find that there was no 'snapshot' commutation; instead, an Act of Parliament in 1925 ended the system of teinds. Records of the Teinds Court and Commissioners are found at the NAS in several series, such as TE 1–6 (pre-1700) and TE 7–9 (post-1700). You may also need to look in private and estate records.

Tithe applotment books for Northern Ireland are primarily held at PRONI in the series FIN SA, with householder indexes on the shelves that provide surnames contained in the records. Some records are also held in the National Library, Dublin.

3.5 National Farm Survey

ABOUT THE RECORDS

Today many people have moved away from Britain's rural communities, but it is still possible to find out more about how our ancestors used to live if they resided on a farm. Indeed, you may well find it relatively easy to trace the history of a farmhouse, as you can use field patterns to follow the boundaries of the property with some ease. There is one set of records that can take your research into the middle of the twentieth century, which has fairly good national coverage.

In an attempt to assist the war effort, the Ministry of Agriculture and Fisheries (MAF) set up County War Agricultural Committees to increase food productivity and ensure that there were sufficient supplies to feed the country. In 1940 an attempt was made to survey all working farms in

England and Wales to identify the productive state of the land, assigning 'A', 'B' and 'C' grades.

A far more detailed survey was conducted in 1941–3, listing information on conditions of tenure, occupation, the state of the farm, fertility of the land, equipment, livestock, water and electricity supplies, weeds and general management. A plan of the farm, depicting boundaries and fields, was also produced as part of the process.

For the house historian, this is a particularly good source if you are tracing rural property, or suspect that your house once formed part of a farm. Not only will you obtain the name of the owner and the address of the farm, but also details of the number of employees and the nature of the farm's produce, and this can provide background information on the way people lived. It complements the valuation and tithe surveys and is obviously useful when the house in question was a farmhouse or building. However, the survey can also be helpful if you are researching an area that changed from farmland to housing after 1945.

ACCESSING THE RECORDS

The documents of the 1941–3 survey are found in two record series at the National Archives. The maps are in series MAF 73, and are arranged alphabetically by county. You will first need to consult a key sheet that is available on open access. Each county has been assigned a number, which forms part of the document reference and is stamped on the corner of the relevant county key sheet. Make a note of this number.

Each county map is sub-divided into numbered grids. Locate the grid in which your property falls, and make a note of this number as well. This forms the final part of the reference, and you will be provided with all the maps within this grid.

Once you have obtained your maps, you will need to find the one that relates to your property. The maps you are provided with will cover the entire area in the grid.

Example Day's Farm, Doddinghurst, Essex (see FIGURE 5) Essex has the county number 13, and the property falls within the numbered grid 71. Hence, the reference will be MAF 73/13/71.

There will either be 16 maps at the scale 1:2500, which adopt the same grid system as employed on the county key sheets for the valuation survey (*see* section 3.3: Accessing valuation survey maps (excluding London)), or four maps at the 1:10 560 scale. Once you have located your farm, you will see that the extent is marked using a colour wash, and has been assigned a reference; this usually consists of the abbreviated county code (a series of letters), the relevant parish number (the first number) and the farm number (the second number). The next step is to order the individual farm record that accompanies the map.

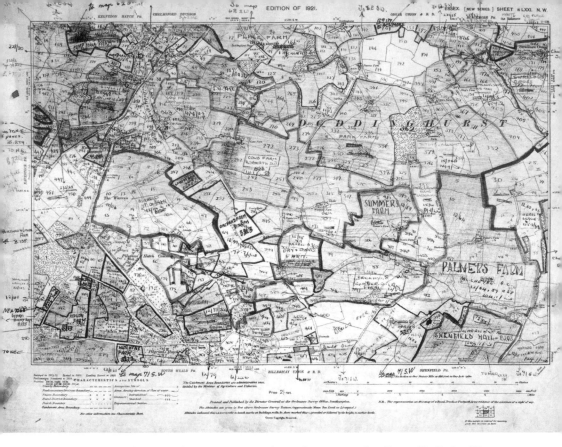

The records are contained in the National Archives series MAF 32 and are also arranged by county, and then alphabetically by parish. You should consult the series list, which contains an index that tells you where to find the records for each county. Work down the alphabetical list of parishes until you find the relevant one, and note the corresponding piece number in the left-hand column. Also note the code that has been assigned to the parish, as this also forms part of the document reference.

Figure 5 The National Farm Survey map for the parish of Doddinghurst, Essex. Property 15/18 is Day and Gent's Farm, in the possession of A. J. Harris. (MAF 73/13/71)

Example Day's Farm lies in the parish of Doddinghurst, which has been given the code reference 15 and is listed within piece number 837 in the left column (*see* FIGURE 6). The full TNA reference is therefore MAF 32/837/15.

You will be provided with an envelope containing the records for all farms that lie within the requested parish, and your farm can be identified by the number assigned to it from the map. The individual farm record consisted of four parts. The first was completed by the farmer, and contained details of small fruit, vegetables and stocks of hay and straw; animals are also listed. The second surveyed agricultural land, also completed by the farmer, while the third was a similar survey completed by inspection and interview.

The final part is the most useful for house historians, as it contains details of utility services, farm labour, motive power, rent and length of occupancy. It also bears the final grade assigned to the farm. All documents contain the address of the farm and the farmer's name, and taken as a whole can provide a great insight into the extent of farming communities in the mid-twentieth century.

Figure 6(a) Form B496 for Day's Farm shows that Gent's and Day's farms should be treated as one unit. It gives the name and address of the owner, Mrs Simpson Shaw, and mentions that two cottages form part of the farmstead. (MAF 32/837)

RELATED RECORDS

Similar local committees were established during the First World War to assess and improve food

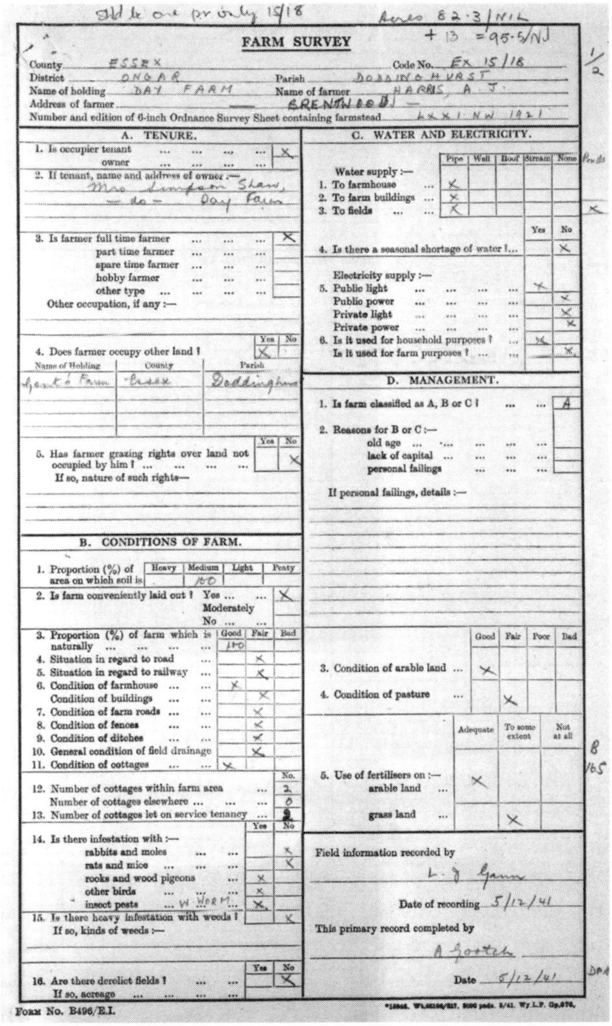

FARM SURVEY

County ESSEX — Code No. EX 15/18
District ONGAR — Parish DODDINGHURST
Name of holding DAY FARM — Name of farmer HARRIS, A. J.
Address of farmer BRENTWOOD
Number and edition of 6-inch Ordnance Survey Sheet containing farmstead LXXI NW 1921

A. TENURE.

1. Is occupier tenant ... X
owner ...
2. If tenant, name and address of owner:— Mrs Simpson Shaw, — do — Day Farm
3. Is farmer full time farmer ... X
part time farmer
spare time farmer
hobby farmer
other type
Other occupation, if any:—
4. Does farmer occupy other land? Yes X

Name of Holding	County	Parish
Gent's Farm	Essex	Doddinghurst

5. Has farmer grazing rights over land not occupied by him? No X
If so, nature of such rights—

B. CONDITIONS OF FARM.

1. Proportion (%) of area on which soil is: Heavy — Medium 100 — Light — Peaty
2. Is farm conveniently laid out? Yes X / Moderately / No

	Good	Fair	Bad
3. Proportion (%) of farm which is naturally	100		
4. Situation in regard to road		X	
5. Situation in regard to railway		X	
6. Condition of farmhouse	X		
Condition of buildings		X	
7. Condition of farm roads		X	
8. Condition of fences		X	
9. Condition of ditches		X	
10. General condition of field drainage		X	
11. Condition of cottages	X		

12. Number of cottages within farm area ... 2
Number of cottages elsewhere ... 0
13. Number of cottages let on service tenancy ... 2

14. Is there infestation with:—	Yes	No
rabbits and moles		X
rats and mice		X
rooks and wood pigeons	X	
other birds	X	
insect pests W. WORM	X	
15. Is there heavy infestation with weeds?		X

If so, kinds of weeds:—

16. Are there derelict fields? No X
If so, acreage

C. WATER AND ELECTRICITY.

Water supply:—	Pipe	Well	Roof	Stream	None
1. To farmhouse	X				
2. To farm buildings	X				
3. To fields	X				

	Yes	No
4. Is there a seasonal shortage of water?		X
Electricity supply:— 5. Public light	X	
Public power		X
Private light		X
Private power		X
6. Is it used for household purposes?	X	
Is it used for farm purposes?		X

D. MANAGEMENT.

1. Is farm classified as A, B or C? ... A
2. Reasons for B or C:— old age / lack of capital / personal failings
If personal failings, details:—

	Good	Fair	Poor	Bad
3. Condition of arable land	X			
4. Condition of pasture		X		

5. Use of fertilisers on:—	Adequate	To some extent	Not at all
arable land	X		
grass land		X	

Field information recorded by L. J. Gunn
Date of recording 5/12/41
This primary record completed by A. Gooch
Date 5/12/41

FORM No. B496/E.I.

MINISTRY OF AGRICULTURE AND FISHERIES.

THE DEFENCE REGULATIONS, 1939, AND THE AGRICULTURAL RETURNS ORDER, 1939.

RETURN WITH RESPECT TO AGRICULTURAL LAND ON 4th JUNE, 1941.

	CROPS AND GRASS	Statute Acres
1	Wheat	5
2	Barley	—
3	Oats	8
4	Mixed Corn with Wheat in mixture	—
5	Mixed Corn without Wheat in mixture	—
6	Rye	—
7	Beans, winter or spring, for stock feeding	—
8	Peas, for stock feeding, not for human consumption	—
9	Potatoes, first earlies	—
10	Potatoes, main crop and second earlies	6¾
11	Turnips and Swedes, for fodder	1
12	Mangolds	2
13	Sugar Beet	—
14	Kale, for fodder	1½
15	Rape (or Cole)	—
16	Cabbage, Savoys, and Kohl Rabi, for fodder	—
17	Vetches or Tares	—
18	Lucerne	—
19	Mustard, for seed	—
20	Mustard, for fodder or ploughing in	—
21	Flax, for fibre or linseed	1⅔
22	Hops, Statute Acres, not Hop Acres	—
23	Orchards, with crops, fallow, or grass below the trees	1
24	Orchards, with small fruit below the trees	—
25	Small Fruit, not under orchard trees	—
26	Vegetables for human consumption (excluding Potatoes), Flowers and Crops under Glass	—
27	All Other Crops not specified elsewhere on this return or grown on patches of less than ¼ acre	½
28	Bare Fallow	—
29	Clover, Sainfoin, and Temporary Grasses for Mowing this season	—
30	Clover, Sainfoin, and Temporary Grasses for Grazing (not for Mowing this season)	—
31	Permanent Grass for Mowing this season	46¼
32	Permanent Grass for Grazing (not for Mowing this season), but excluding rough grazings	22
33	TOTAL OF ABOVE ITEMS, 1 to 32 (Total acreage of Crops and Grass, excluding Rough Grazings)	95½
34	Rough Grazings—Mountain, Heath, Moor, or Down land, or other rough land used for grazing on which the occupier has the sole grazing rights	—

LABOUR actually employed on holding on 4th June. The occupier, his wife, or domestic servants should not be entered.

			Number (in figures)
35	WHOLETIME REGULAR WORKERS	Males, 21 years old and over	1
36		Males, 18 to 21 years old	1
37	If none, write "None"	Males, under 18 years old	1
38		Women and Girls	none
39	CASUAL (SEASONAL or PART-TIME) WORKERS	Males, 21 years old and over	
40		Males, under 21 years old	
41		Women and Girls	1
42		TOTAL WORKERS	4

Form No. C 47/S.S.Y.

M.(4050. 4/41. (52-4551)

	LIVE STOCK on holding on 4th June, including any sent for sale on that or previous day		Number (in figures)
43	Cows and Heifers in milk		19
44	Cows in Calf, but not in milk		2
45	Heifers in Calf, with first Calf		3
46	Bulls being used for service		1
47	Bulls (including Bull Calves) being reared for service		none
48	OTHER CATTLE	2 years old and above { Male	
49		Female	
50		1 year old and under 2 { Male	
51		Female	1
52		Under 1 year old:— (a) For rearing (excluding Bull Calves being reared for service)	6
53		(b) Intended for slaughter as Calves	
54	TOTAL CATTLE and CALVES		32
55	Steers and Heifers over 1 year old being fattened for slaughter before 30th November, 1941		none
56	SHEEP OVER 1 YEAR OLD	Ewes kept for further breeding (excluding two-tooth Ewes)	
57		Rams kept for service	
58		Two-tooth Ewes (Shearling Ewes or Gimmers) to be put to the ram in 1941	
59		Other Sheep over 1 year old	
60	SHEEP UNDER 1 YEAR OLD	Ewe Lambs to be put to the ram in 1941	
61		Ram Lambs for service in 1941	
62		Other Sheep and Lambs under 1 year old	no sheep kept
63	TOTAL SHEEP and LAMBS		
64	Sows in Pig		3
65	Gilts in Pig		—
66	Other Sows kept for breeding		
67	Barren Sows for fattening		1
68	Boars being used for service		
69	ALL OTHER PIGS (not entered above)	Over 5 months old	31
70		2—5 months	15
71		Under 2 months	
72	TOTAL PIGS		41
73	POULTRY	Fowls over 6 months old	16
74		Fowls under 6 months old	
75		Ducks of all ages	11
76	If none, write "None"	Geese of all ages	
77		Turkeys over 6 months old	
78		Turkeys under 6 months old	
79	TOTAL POULTRY		27
80	GOATS OF ALL AGES		
	HORSES on holding on 4th June		Number (in figures)
81	Horses used for Agricultural Purposes (including Mares kept for breeding) or by Market Gardeners	(a) mares	
82		(b) geldings	2
83	Unbroken Horses of 1 year old and above	(a) mares	
84		(b) geldings	
85	Light Horses under 1 year old		
86	Heavy Horses under 1 year old		
87	Stallions being used for service in 1941		
88	All Other Horses (not entered above)		1
89	TOTAL HORSES		3

Figure 6(b) Form C47 gives an indication of the way in which the farm operated. (MAF 32/837)

production. Surviving records are to be found deposited in the relevant CROs, but will not contain the same level of detail as the records described above.

Minutes of the County War Agricultural Executive Committees are held in MAF 80, some of which contain detailed indexes that include farm names. Furthermore, parish lists for June 1941 in MAF 65 provide the names and full postal addresses for the occupiers of all agricultural holdings in each parish. They are arranged in county order, and an index is provided in MAF 65/81. However, all records are closed for 100 years, and the MAF should be approached for access. A more limited survey was undertaken for Scotland. Farm boundary plans are stored at the NAS in series RHP 75001–285, but no individual farm records survive.

The National Archives extracted maps and plans catalogue 3.6

3·7

In addition to the OS material and the various land surveys and related records described above, the National Archives contains many thousands of individual maps. Some were deposited with central courts as part of legal proceedings, others were created by government departments through their daily work, and were filed with the main documentation, or indeed once formed part of private estates that came into the possession of Crown administrators. No matter what their origin or final location in the National Archives, whenever these maps have been discovered, they were noted and extracted from their parent documents, thus forming a rudimentary map catalogue. Each extracted map was then assigned a new National Archives reference, which usually consisted of the letter 'M' followed by a series of other letters to denote which part of the main catalogue it came from. A full list is available in several National Archives research guides that deal with maps, plans and architectural drawings.

In addition, there are a variety of printed volumes and catalogues in the reading rooms, principally the Map and Large Document Room, which allow you to search for a

Example A map depicting the hamlet of Cullercoats in 1757 is listed in Maps and Plans of the British Isles as MPH 322. To obtain this map, you will need to request MPH 1/322.

specific map by place. However, since these documents are also listed in the online catalogue, it is simpler to search by keyword to see what documents emerge, though it is always worth double-checking the older indexes just in case something has been omitted.

Although the range and diversity of cartographic material at the National Archives defy adequate description, you will find most of the maps described in sections 3.7 to 3.10 and listed in the various onsite and online catalogues at the National Archives to be amongst the most useful.

Enclosure maps and awards 3.7

THE ENCLOSURE MOVEMENT

Again, this subject is a rather vexed and complicated historical issue, and so a few words of introduction to the history of the enclosure movement are essential before describing the records, and how they work. The way in which land has been managed and cultivated in England and Wales has altered through the centuries, and one of the most important methods of change was the enclosure movement. The term 'enclosure' is employed by social and economic historians to describe a variety of mechanisms of change associated with the consolidation of smaller plots of land into larger units (engrossing or encroaching). However, it also covers land in communal use that was altered to a state of private property for the exclusive use of a single owner. The process of enclosure throughout England and Wales was piecemeal, gaining momentum from the sixteenth century onwards. Most early enclosures were arranged through private agreement between landowners and tenants, and have left no formal record, although you might find references in court cases or special commissions where the process was disputed.

RECORDS OF ENCLOSURE AWARDS

Enclosure awards are legal documents that record the subsequent ownership of land, and were commonly enrolled by decree of one of the equity courts, or were enrolled in other courts of law to provide a legal basis for the award. Advice about searching for legal material at the National Archives is provided in CHAPTER 8, but a brief summary of the most likely place to start looking is provided in TABLE 3.2.

Table 3.2 *Enclosure records at TNA*

PRIVATE ENCLOSURES	
Commissions of Enquiry	C 47/7, 205: Chancery commissions
	E 178, 134: Exchequer commissions and depositions
	DL 44: Duchy of Lancaster
Petitions to the Privy Council	PC 1, 2: Privy Council correspondence and registers
Licences to enclose	C 66: patent rolls

ENCLOSURE BY ENROLLED DECREE	
Chancery	C 78: decree rolls (with some place and name indexes)
Exchequer	E 159, 368: memoranda rolls
	E 123–31: entry books
Duchy of Lancaster	DL 5
Palatinate of Durham	DURH 26

OTHER SOURCES	
Extracts of non-enrolled awards	CRES 6: Constat Books, Crown Estate Commissioners; also CRES 2

ENCLOSURE BY ACT OF PARLIAMENT

From the mid-eighteenth century an increasing number of enclosures were effected by private Acts of Parliament; copies are now stored at the House of Lords Record Office, with some duplicates at relevant CROs. Their popularity prompted General Enclosure Acts to be passed in 1836, 1840 and 1845. Enclosure commissioners oversaw the process, and their records from 1845 survive in the National Archives series MAF 1. Parliamentary enclosure awards were also enrolled and can sometimes be found in the National Archives series CP 43, C 54, DL 45, DURH 26, E 13 and KB 122, although most awards and the accompanying maps are to be found in the CRO. A fuller description of these sources is provided in the National Archives research guide *Enclosure Awards*, and further reading has been suggested under 'Useful publications'.

USING ENCLOSURE AWARDS

In general, enclosure maps and awards will be of limited use to the house historian, as it is rare to find individual properties marked or listed in the documentation. However, they do provide a visual snapshot of the local area at a given time, as well as information on the names of local landowners involved in the process and the land they owned; furthermore, this land may even be where your house stands today. A typical award (*see* FIGURE 7) usually describes the boundaries of land that forms part

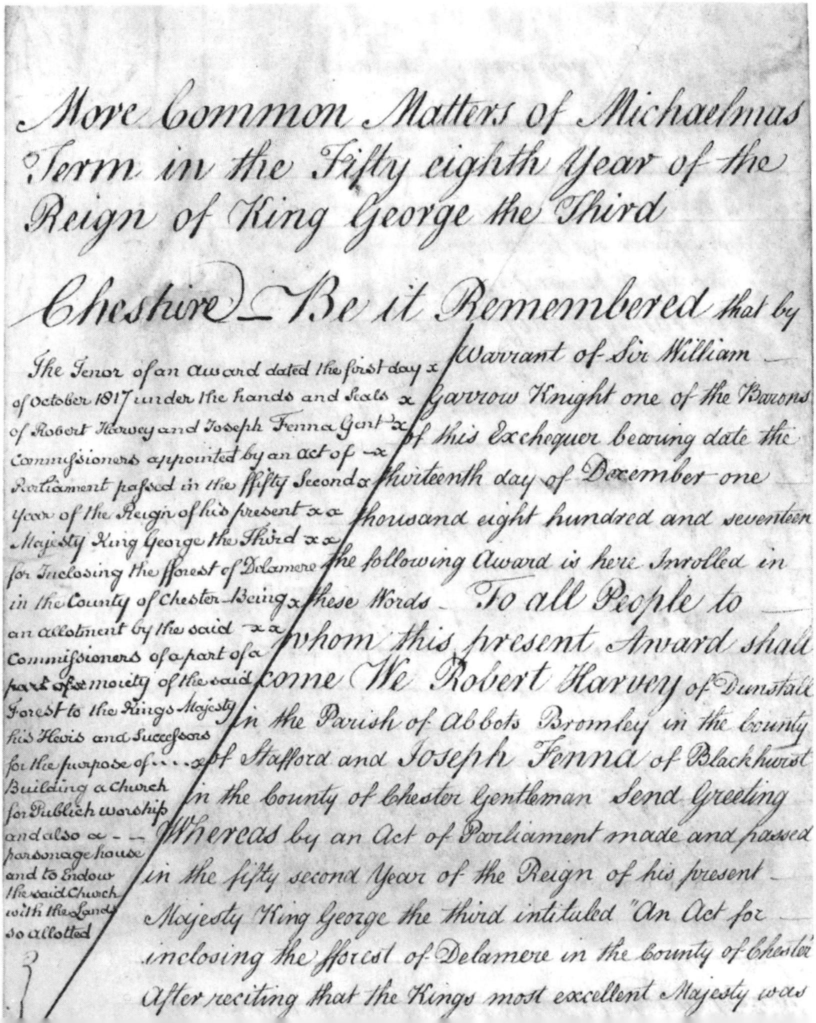

More Common Matters of Michaelmas Term in the Fifty eighth Year of the Reign of King George the Third

Cheshire Be it Remembered that by

The Tenor of an award dated the first day of October 1817 under the hands and Seals of Robert Harvey and Joseph Fenna Gent Commissioners appointed by an act of Parliament passed in the fifty Second Year of the Reign of his present Majesty King George the Third for Inclosing the fforest of Delamere in the County of Chester Being an allotment by the said Commissioners of a part of a part of a moiety of the said Forest to the Kings Majesty his Heirs and Successors for the purpose of … Building a Church for Publick worship and also a parsonage house and to Endow the said Church with the Lands so allotted

Warrant of Sir William Garrow Knight one of the Barons of this Exchequer bearing date the thirteenth day of December one thousand eight hundred and seventeen the following Award is here Inrolled in these Words To all People to whom this present Award shall come We Robert Harvey of Dunstall in the Parish of Abbots Bromley in the County of Stafford and Joseph Fenna of Blackhurst in the County of Chester Gentleman Send Greeting Whereas by an Act of Parliament made and passed in the fifty second Year of the Reign of his present Majesty King George the third intituled "An Act for inclosing the fforest of Delamere in the County of Chester After reciting that the Kings most excellent Majesty was

Figure 7 Enclosure award for Delamere Forest enrolled on the 1817 memoranda roll. It stipulates that a parsonage house should be constructed as part of the process. (E 159/704)

of the enclosure Act, followed by a list of changes to ancient rights (if applicable), and a description of the allotments to landowners made under the terms of the Act, distinguishing between copyhold and freehold tenure (for further information about the terms freehold and copyhold, and why it is important to distinguish between the two, see CHAPTERS 4–6). This in itself can be of great use if you wish to search manorial documents but require additional information on the layout of the local area. A detailed schedule then lists the owners and provides a number for each plot, and therefore acts as a means of reference to any surviving map.

Although enclosure awards are scattered across a range of archives and in a variety of sources, a volume entitled *A Domesday of Enclosure Acts and Awards* by W. E. Tate summarizes the details for the most common areas. The volume is arranged in county order and lists the type of award, the date the award was granted and where the documents can be found. As you will see when you examine this volume, the vast majority of all enclosure awards listed are now stored outside the National Archives, usually at the relevant CRO. A copy of this useful volume is available on open access in the reading rooms, along with a series of supplementary lists of awards that are deposited in the National Archives that also provide document references. Furthermore, a large number of enclosure maps (*see* PLATE 2) are separately listed in the extracted map catalogues, with links to the parent awards from which they were originally taken.

RELATED RECORDS: APPORTIONMENT OF RENTCHARGE

The term 'rentcharge' refers to rent that was charged on a particular piece or unit of land, and the need for apportionment of rentcharge arose when large land units were sub-divided into smaller units, usually a consequence of the enclosures of the eighteenth and nineteenth centuries. Under the terms of the Enclosure Act 1854, Law of Property Act 1925 and Landlord and Tenant Act 1927, it fell upon various government departments to equitably distribute the rentcharge between the new plots of land.

The records generated by these apportionments can provide information about how the charge was divided in a particular area, and will give details of individual streets and properties. There are three main types of record – orders (MAF 17 for the period 1854–1965, HLG 61 for 1965–7), certificates (MAF 19 for the period 1854–1965, HLG 62 for 1965–7), and certificates of redemption of rentcharge (MAF 21 for the period 1843–1965, HLG 63 for 1965–7). The records are fairly easy to access, and are arranged by the street or district that was affected. You should be able to obtain an idea of the individual who made the application for an apportionment, plus the person or persons who held the lease of the land.

Estate maps and plans

Private estate owners periodically conducted surveys of their property, usually to introduce new estate management procedures. Maps were often produced, sometimes linked to assessment books that can be cross-referenced to surviving manorial material. These provide an invaluable snapshot of landholding and property, and seem to occur most frequently when an estate changed hands, found amongst the collected individuals or with the accumulated paperwork of land or estate agents, or solicitors, who were responsible for the legal documentation. The most likely place to find such material is at the relevant CRO, but the National Archives does have a collection of estate maps that are listed in the various map catalogues. In addition, the National Archives is the logical place of deposit for maps, plans, rentals and surveys relating to Crown estates and property, plus areas of autonomous jurisdiction. These can be found among the papers of the Office of Land Revenue Records and Enrolments (LRRO) and the Crown Estates Office (CRES), with maps for the Duchy of Lancaster in DL 31. Estate maps and plans are described and listed in more detail in CHAPTER 6.

3.9

Deposited maps and plans for public schemes

RAILWAYS

Many public schemes involved the creation of maps and plans to depict the potential impact of the scheme on the local community, especially if compulsory purchase orders of land were involved. The most dramatic event that triggered large-scale map making was the construction of the railways from the 1830s, which changed the face of many local communities. With the arrival of the railways, construction of new dwellings often occurred, along with the removal of older properties that were in the way of the proposed routes. Many of these changes are depicted on maps that formed part of individual railway company archives, and are now deposited at the National Archives as part of the former holdings of the British Transport Historical Records section (BTHR). For the pre-nationalization period the records are arranged by local railway company, so you will need to identify which company operated along the line nearest to you. A National Archives research guide has been written to help you with this process, and there are finding aids available on open access in the reading rooms.

The records are primarily in series RAIL 1029–37 and 1071, plus some in MT 54. Photographs of railways are contained in AN 14 and 31, and RAIL 1057 and 1157. Other material will be located with the administrative papers of the individual railway companies, including papers on accommodation and other related property that may have eventually found their way into private hands, and are described more fully in Chapter 11. Other archives where railway maps and plans are deposited will include specialist railway archives, such as the National Railway Museum in York; the House of Lords Record Office, where many official plans were stored as part of the legislation that created the railway routes; and, of course, CROs where the railway companies were based.

ROADS

In a similar manner, road building through the ages necessitated the creation of maps, plans and associated documentation. One of the earliest methods of road management was via legally constituted bodies called turnpike trusts. These organizations, which were locally administered and funded, were responsible for the maintenance and upkeep of the roads in their care. Records of the trusts will be found either at parochial level, or among quarter sessions papers whenever the trusts failed to adequately maintain the roads and were therefore liable to prosecution. Where such cases were recorded, you may well find that the area of road that required repair was linked to the property or properties outside which it ran, and the names of the owners are sometimes listed. Quarter-sessions records are not stored at the National Archives, and are usually found at the relevant CRO.

Royal Commissions were often appointed to enquire into the state of roads administered by the turnpike trusts, and the maps produced as a result of this process can depict property. Relevant material can also be found in Ministry of Transport files – for example, series MT 27, which relates to the Holyhead and Shrewsbury roads – where many useful maps can be found. After the dissolution of turnpike trusts, the responsibility for road building and maintenance was passed to local authorities, and many road building or improvement schemes can be found among the Ministry of Housing and Local Government files in the HLG series. However, the most likely place to find maps and plans relating to turnpike trusts and roads will be the relevant CRO, where local authority maps and plans for road improvement schemes will have been deposited.

Private roads and streets developed out of the turnpike trusts, and in addition to the maps and plans referred to above, you may wish to explore various files on their maintenance and development. Earlier records can be located with material on turnpike trusts in MH 28, while more modern records are in HLG 51 and MT 149. Correspondence regarding conflicts of interest between private roads and railway companies can be found among the records of the individual railway companies, for example RAIL 1057. You will also find references to private roads in enclosure awards, although county archives will once again be the best place to begin searching.

REHOUSING PLANS AFTER PUBLIC SCHEMES

You will also be able to find references to planning or building proposals in a range of the National Archives series, in particular with regard to twentieth-century housing development schemes. Most of these schemes have plans attached to them, but these are not usually noted in the document descriptions. There is a wealth of cartographic material in a variety of HLG series that are described in detail in CHAPTER 12. Of particular use will be the records in HLG 24, which include rehousing schemes under the terms of statutory instruments, with sealed plans and schemes on the provision of accommodation for persons displaced from working-class dwellings as a result of undertakings including railway, gas, tram, school, harbour, road and other improvements, under the terms of the Housing of Working Classes Act 1903.

GEOLOGICAL SURVEY MAPS

You may also find some useful information from the records of the Geological Survey. Although their main work from 1835 was involved in geological science, many of the functions included survey work and map making, and will be of use if your property is situated on a place of geological value. Indeed, many geological surveys were conducted before building commenced, and therefore the maps and associated documents can provide information about when a property was built. Some records are at the National Archives in series DSIR 9 and ED 23 and 24, while the remainder will be found at the British Geological Survey. The Geologists' Association is also worth contacting (*see* 'Useful addresses').

Military maps   3.10

In addition to the early Ordnance Survey maps, the War Office maintained its own cartographic section, primarily for mapping military terrain. The house historian can often use military maps to locate houses that were formerly built as, or used for, military installations such as hospitals, barracks, fortifications or bases. The record series WO 78 is the best place to look for military maps and surveys, and these often include civilian property in the vicinity of a proposed military site. Maps in series WO 78 are listed in topographical county order in a series of folders on open access in the reading rooms. Most of these have been noted in the map catalogues, while the subject indexes to the unextracted map catalogue include many references to military installations.

It is also possible to locate Ministry of Defence buildings that later passed into private possession, and in addition to WO 78 there are Army establishment maps and plans in WORK 43, with Air Force establishments in

WORK 44. If you have the time, it might also be worth scanning through the files of the Board of Ordnance, who were responsible for the construction of many stores, barracks and depots. You will, however, need to be armed with some prior information, as there are few indexes available to the letter books and accounts that provide details of places.

Although the National Archives has a large collection of military maps, the best place to begin your research will be the Ministry of Defence map library at Tolworth, and you could also try the Imperial War Museum (*see* 'Useful addresses').

3.11 Maps and plans in the Office of Works

The remit of the Office of Works included responsibility for maintaining public buildings and national monuments in England and Wales. Although these will be of little use or interest to the house historian, it is not unknown for government property to eventually pass into the hands of private individuals. Indeed, the Office also maintained files on what it considered to be historic buildings, some of which were private residences. Included with the thousands of documents created or maintained by this department are two series of plans and drawings in WORK 30 (public buildings) and WORK 31 (ancient monuments and historic buildings). There are rudimentary indexes to these classes on open access in the reading rooms that list the buildings by place. If you do manage to find an item that is of use, registered files can be found in WORK 12 and 14 respectively. Miscellaneous plans and drawings are listed in WORK 38. Similar material for Northern Ireland can be located in WORK 42 (maps and drawings) and WORK 27 (registered files).

3.12 Architectural drawings

Most government departments made no differentiation between architectural drawings and other maps and plans. Where they have been identified or extracted, you will find them listed in the National Archives map catalogues, as described in section 3.6. However, the vast majority will be among registered files and papers, and still await discovery. The papers of the Office of Works (WORK), Office of Land Revenue Records and Enrolments (LRRO) and the Crown Estates Office (CRES) are rich sources, although they largely relate to public buildings. These may be of use if your property once formed part of a Crown estate, or was owned by a government department. However, you will find that files created by local authorities are of more use, in particular those that relate to building schemes. These are often listed in files created by the Ministry of Housing and Local Government (HLG), and are treated in more depth in CHAPTER 12.

In addition to the National Archives map catalogues, and the sources referred to above, a card index to drawings by individually named architects has been compiled, and is described more fully in a research guide. There is also a list of signed drawings found in the Office of Works. However, as with most searches for maps and plans, the best place to start will be at the CRO. The National Monuments Record holds plans, drawings and aerial photographs for buildings of historic value, including many architectural plans. There are separate sites for England (with a search room in London), Wales and Scotland. In addition, you may find relevant paperwork and plans in the Royal Institute of British Architects (RIBA) Library, while the Victoria and Albert Museum holds a collection of architectural drawings (*see* 'Useful addresses').

Photograph catalogue 3.13

In addition to the map catalogues, the National Archives has compiled a separate list of photographs that have been found among parent documents. Indexes, arranged by place and subject, are available for consultation in the reading rooms and will contain some images of houses and private property. In addition, there are distinct series that solely contain photographs, along with series of extracted photographs that begin with the prefix CN. The most relevant series include INF 9 (Dixon-Scott collection of towns and villages *c.*1925–48), INF 11 (British Council collection of London scenes, 1935–45), CN 1–19 (extracted photographs from various series), BD 11 (Welsh local authority files that include housing), BD 28–9 (Welsh local authority files, Town and Country Planning), and DT 21 (properties acquired by the General Nursing Council in London). COPY 1 also contains many photographs, and a surprising number are of individual properties. It is, however, important to remember that you may find related photographs of property almost anywhere in the National Archives holdings, and that these series will be of limited use to the house historian; in any case, the best place to begin your search for photographic material will be at your local studies library or CRO.

Other places to look for maps 3.14

The remit of this book is to highlight sources most likely to be found at the National Archives, but clearly there are many more cartographic sources deposited in archives across the UK. It is down to you to start your investigations at a local level, to see what you might uncover. Maps can be found in some of the most surprising places, connected to subjects that, on the surface, appear to have nothing to do with house history. For example, one of the most important cartographic collections relates to a survey undertaken by the nineteenth-century social reformer Charles Booth, who was interested in the living conditions of the poorest ranks of society. In 1886 he began to survey areas of London, and colour-coded maps according to the level of poverty that he found in each area. Booth's maps and associated papers are stored at the University of London Library, and the Library of the London School of Economics and Political Science; however, they can be accessed online at **http://booth.lse.ac.uk/**, where you can also purchase copies of the maps. Therefore you may find maps, plans, drawings and sketches that lift the lid on what life would have been like in your local community, even if your house is not directly featured; this is all part of the process of adding colour to your research work.

Black Ladies, Staffordshire

A rather grand medieval house stands in Brewood, Staffordshire, and is known by the name 'Black Ladies'. The origin of this name is fairly well known, as a Benedictine nunnery had been founded on the site in the 1140s and bore this name for centuries, before its suppression in the reign of Henry VIII. Yet the owners wanted to discover more about the building itself, in particular whether the fabric of the house was constructed on the site of the old nunnery, as the law of the day required, or whether the site was acquired by a new owner who simply adapted the nunnery to secular uses.

Crucial documents relating to the dissolution of Black Ladies were found at the National Archives among the calendared Letters and Papers, Henry VIII. From these, it was possible to put together the following chronology, which in turn allowed certain conclusions to be drawn about the fate of the old monastic buildings.

In March 1538, the order was given to suppress the nunnery, and a local gentleman called Sir John Gifford was asked to survey its possessions and assign a value to them so that they could be sold. Commissioners Sir Thomas Hennege and Dr Legh were then appointed to oversee the suppression of the nunnery; in October 1538, Hennege wrote to Legh to:

... inform him of the king's pleasure that Thomas Gifford, gentleman usher of the chamber, shall have the house and farm of Black Ladies of Brewood, Staffs., who has made suit for it for more than a year. At your now being there I shall put him in possession and he may at leisure apply to the Chancellor of Augmentations for the lease.

Thomas Gifford was the son of Sir John. Five days later the nuns surrendered the house to the commissioners, but a dispute arose over whether Gifford or another local called Littleton should take possession. Eventually the matter was settled in Gifford's favour in 1539, when Henry VIII granted him the site of the nunnery for the princely sum of £134.

Among the papers of Legh and Hennege was a survey taken after Gifford's initial assessment. This document was remarkably similar in layout to Gifford's original survey, and valued all possessions in the house, room by room. The rooms in the property and the way they were set out was exactly the same as the modern floor plan, with a few minor changes in description, which suggests that Gifford moved straight in without rebuilding. The rooms are listed as the hall, the parlour, the chief chamber, the bailiff's chamber, the buttery, the kitchen, the larder, the brewhouse, the 'color' [i.e. 'kiler' or kiln] and various other external rooms. Certainly, the house was left to his children and was subsequently passed down from generation to generation, still bearing the name 'Black Ladies'; for example, Thomas left 'the house and former site of the nunnery of Black Ladies' to his sons Humphrey and Robert. The history of the family is well known, and they remained staunch Catholics through subsequent reigns despite benefiting from the Dissolution. Indeed, Thomas bought up the vast majority of the fixtures and fittings of the chapel attached to the site, probably to ensure that they stayed with the house, and there is even further evidence to suggest that the Giffords looked after the former nuns in their new life on the outside.

Research at the Staffordshire Record Office provided further supporting evidence for the theory that Thomas Gifford left the basic structure of the house intact, as among the deposited papers of the

Gifford family was a further survey taken in October 1652. Despite being persecuted by the Crown for retaining their Catholic faith during the Elizabethan reformation, the Giffords had supported the Royalist cause during the English Civil War. Consequently, when the victorious Parliamentarians came to raise money to pay for the army, they sold off Crown lands and the estates of its supporters, including those held by the Giffords. The preamble of the valuation survey states that the lands were 'forfeited by the Giffords to the Commonwealth for treason', and in addition to a detailed description of all their lands there is a description of the house:

... all that capital messuage or mansion house called Blackladies with the site thereof consisting of a hall, a fair parlour wainscoted round, a kitchen, a buttery, a panthouse, a larder, a 'color', a brewhouse, with several lodging chambers above them, all built with timber, bricks and stone and covered with shingles and with cloisters between the said mansion house and chapel with a small courtyard behind the said mansion house and a garden before the said house both enclosed with a wall built in parts with stone and in part with brick, together with two orchards, a dairy house with a chamber over it, standing in one of the said orchards, containing by all estimation 2 acres worth. Total 2 acres. Value £8.

The description of the house is virtually identical to that of 1538 – it would appear that the basic structure remained intact over 120 years, although it is possible that 'improvements' had taken place internally and that additions had been made too.

Evidence survives from the 1680s and 1690s, when the owners of Black Ladies were involved in a court case with the vicar of Brewood. During the exchanges, the vicar of Brewood placed a series of interrogatories before local witnesses, in the hope that they would provide evidence to support his claims. These included the question:

Did you know that Peter Gifford, deceased, the late father of John Gifford, had his estate sequestered, his house plundered and made a garrison, his writing and estate papers burned or taken away, and thereby lost, during the civil war?

All witnesses agreed, suggesting that some repairs – possibly substantial – had taken place in the decades after the family re-covered their property. There were certainly substantial internal alterations made after 1710, the date when the aforementioned John Gifford died. According to documents in the Gifford family's collection at Stafford, John's widow Katherine converted part of the house into separate dwellings; she lived in one part that gave access to the chapel and hearths in the kitchen, while the remainder was leased out to other members of the family. John Gifford's will described Black Ladies as a 'capital messuage or hall' – a clear rise in the status of the building.

One final surprise was revealed while excavations were taking place in the grounds in the search for further evidence of external walls and buildings, listed in the sixteenth-century survey. Around the site of the old chapel, human bones were un-covered, buried facing towards the east and the Holy Land. Records at the Staffordshire Record Office showed that burials had taken place outside the parish graveyard, including Joseph Lloyd at Blackladies in 1719. It could be the case that these were his bones, but there is now no way of telling.

LAND LAW AND CONVEYANCING

4

4.1 Introduction

One of the most important sources for any house historian will be the records generated by the transfer of the property from owner to owner. Yet, conversely, this is also the most complicated area to research, as property transfers took many forms over the centuries and usually involved the creation of legal documentation, which can often be difficult for the beginner to understand or interpret. Collectively, these documents are known as 'title deeds', and their whereabouts are discussed in CHAPTER 5. However, it is important for the house historian to grasp the basic ways in which land itself was held, as the type of tenure determined the method of transfer. There were basically two main groups of tenure – 'free' (freehold) and 'unfree' (copyhold) – and this chapter should be regarded solely as an introduction to the common ways in which freehold property was held and transferred. One of the most important methods of transfer was by a process known as 'conveyancing', technically defined as the 'legal transfer of ownership of property from one party or parties to another'. The transfer of copyhold land was restricted by the regulations of the manorial system until the late nineteenth century, and is described in detail in CHAPTER 6.

The main period to be examined in this chapter runs from the Norman Conquest to 1925, when a series of statutes were passed to regulate land law and conveyancing. This guide is clearly not the place to describe the evolution of land law in great detail, as the house historian will need to know only the basic forms of tenure and associated legal terminology to understand the documents that were generated over the centuries; however, if you wish to explore this topic in greater detail, see the relevant section of 'Useful publications' (p. 248).

You will find that in this chapter reference is made to land rather than to houses as such. This is because in the eyes of the law the term 'land' included any buildings that were built upon it.

Landholding under the 'feudal' system   4.2

THE FEUDAL PYRAMID

The establishment of the 'feudal' system in England and parts of Wales in the aftermath of the Norman Conquest, in the eleventh century, shaped the way in which land was held for centuries to follow. In its simplest terms, the basic structure can be described thus: the king held all land, but granted some of this land to reward his followers, who held the land direct from the Crown as tenants-in-chief. In turn they granted land to their supporters, who continued the process to create a pyramid structure of landholding. This method of land grant was known as 'subinfeudation' and, with the exception of the Crown at the top, left everyone who held land as the tenant of an over-lord.

4·3

THE MANOR

The main unit of land was known as the 'manor', and was probably based on an Anglo-Saxon system of land division. It is important to grasp the concept that manors were not always compact geographical land units, but instead were often spread among the lands of other manors, and it was the unifying bonds of allegiance to a single lord of the manor that defined the unit in social and economic terms. Furthermore, the boundaries of the manor should not be confused with those of the local parish, as they were separate administrative units. A single manor might have stretched across several parishes, or conversely one parish might have contained more than one manor.

LAND TENURE

Each manor had a 'lord', who granted strips of land within the manor to tenants in return for service, usually a combination of rent, military obligation or work on the lord's land. Any surplus land retained by the lord was known as the 'demesne'. The terms by which tenants held land from the lord of the manor was called the 'tenure', and determined whether the tenant was free or unfree. Free tenants could hold land by either military or socage tenure. In the case of the latter, free tenants were required to perform an agreed amount and type of work on the lord's demesne each year. However, unfree tenants, or villeins, had only the amount of work set, and were instructed by the lord's representative as to the nature of the work when the time came. More information on manorial tenants can be found in CHAPTER 6.

Freehold land   4·3

TYPES OF FREEHOLD TENURE

As the previous section has demonstrated, in essence no-one 'owned' land since it had all been originally granted by the Crown. However, the terms by which land was granted throughout the feudal chain were of vital importance in determining how it could be transferred in future. The following are descriptions of the three main ways in which freehold land could be granted to an individual. They are technically known as 'estates', which means a period of time that the land would be held by the recipient.

In addition to the three freehold estates, a fourth type of estate, namely lease or a 'term of years', developed and is also considered here. As it was possible for leases to be made on copyhold land as well as freehold, the former was deemed a nonfreehold estate. There was a further important distinction between freehold land and lease. In the eyes of the law, freehold land was deemed as real property, or 'realty', and could not be 'devised' (or bequeathed to another) by will until the Statute of Wills was passed in 1540, and more specifically after the Tenures Abolition Act of 1660. However, leases were considered to be personal property, or 'personal', and therefore could be included in a will. This important yet often none too obvious distinction is considered in more detail in CHAPTER 7.

Fee simple

Land that was granted to an individual 'and his heirs' was deemed to be fee simple. In essence, this meant that on the death of the recipient it would pass to his immediate heir at law, unless the fee simple had already been granted (or 'alienated') to another by a previous agreement. When the line of heirs of the recipient finally died out, then the land would return to the original grantor or his heirs. Thus the word 'fee' indicates that the land was inheritable. However, as a fee simple was realty, it could not be devised by will to another until statutory developments in the sixteenth and seventeenth centuries.

Fee tail

Land granted in fee simple guaranteed only that it would be passed to the heirs of the recipient as long as it was not alienated. This was inconvenient to landowners who wished to keep their landed estates within the family for future generations. A solution was created by the 1285 Statute de Donis Conditionalibus, which stipulated that land granted to a recipient and 'the heirs of his body' would pass to all future issue of the recipient without the possibility of alienation. This was known as a fee tail, and only when all future issue had died out, would the land revert to the original grantor or his heirs.

Life interest

As the name suggests, the grant of a life interest in land would last only as long as the lifetime of the recipient, who became the 'life tenant'. This meant that the heirs of the recipient could not inherit the land. However, a recipient of a life estate could grant the land to others, but the new recipient was said to hold the property 'pur autre vie', or for the life of another. This meant that the interest of the new recipient could last only as long as the life of the original recipient, at which point it would revert to the original grantor.

LEASES

If an individual wished to grant land to another for a limited period of time but did not want to grant a life interest, since the recipient could live for an uncertain length of time, he leased the land for a 'term of years' (or 'demised' it). The following are the most common forms of lease that you will probably encounter, although you should bear in mind that it was possible to lease both freehold and copyhold land. This type of tenure was also referred to as fee-farm.

Fixed leases

Fixed leases were for a set period of time (for example, six months or ninety-nine years), and usually involved the payment of a fixed sum at the beginning. At the end of the agreed term the original lessor would reclaim the land, or renegotiate another lease with the tenant.

Periodic leases

Periodic leases were also for fixed periods (for example, weekly, monthly or yearly), but would be automatically renewed for the duration of another period of time unless either party provided a period of notice. Rent was paid on a regular basis (for example, per week, per month or per year).

Other forms of lease

In addition to these 'terms of years', other forms of lease were possible.

- Tenants at will were created when an agreement was made between the lessor and the lessee that either could determine, usually on the expiration of a fixed or periodic lease. Although no rent was payable, the tenant was due to pay some form of compensation to the lessor.
- Leases for life were tenable for the duration of the tenant's life; there were also leases that were curtailed by the marriage of the tenant.
- Tenancies at sufferance came into being at the expiration of a lease when the tenant remained on the land without the lessor's permission.
- Renewable leases contained a clause that allowed the lessee to request a new lease to be granted on the same terms as the old, as long as the request was made within a stipulated period before the expiry of the original lease. Perpetual renewable leases were possible before 1925.

TERMINOLOGY USED IN GRANTS OF FREEHOLD LAND

The following are the main terms with which house historians will need to familiarize themselves when attempting to decipher the types of grant of freehold land.

4·3

Possession, reversion and remainder

When a landholder, A, made a grant of land that was held as 'fee simple' to another individual, B, for life, B was deemed to be in 'possession' of the land. On B's death the land would eventually revert to A (or his heirs if he predeceased B), as the life interest in possession had thus ended. Therefore, during B's lifetime, A still held the fee simple 'in reversion', even though he did not actually possess the land.

However, if A had specified that the land should pass to a further individual, C, for life at the death of B, then C was said to hold a life interest in the land 'in remainder'. At the death of B, then C would take on the life interest in possession. Therefore, the grant would be 'to B for life with remainder to C for life'.

Conditional and determinable grants

If a grantor wanted to specify various terms to a grant, he would make it either conditional or determinable. A grant of 'conditional fee simple' meant that there was a condition attached to the grant. Phrases such as 'on the condition that', 'provided that' and 'but if ' were commonly used to frame such a grant. There were two types – a precedent condition, which stipulated the grant could not be received until the condition was fulfilled, and a subsequent condition, which would end the grant if the circumstances described in the condition ever arose.

Alternatively, a grant of 'determinable fee simple' meant that a limiting restriction was imposed, and this type of grant commonly contained the phrases 'until', 'during', 'while' and 'as long as'.

Conditional and determinable grants could also apply to grants of life interest, but were not permissible for grants of fee tail. If a grant was not conditional or determinable, then it was called 'absolute'.

Various types of interest

A future interest in a grant is one that has yet to be enjoyed by the recipient. As we have seen above, the grant of land, held in fee simple by A, to B for life, with remainder to C for life only resulted in B taking immediate possession of the land. C could claim to have a future interest in the grant, as it was dependent on the death of B.

A contingent interest was where a condition had yet to be fulfilled before the grant took effect, or when the identity of the recipient was still unknown.

Contingent interests were most commonly associated with future heirs to a property, either because they had not attained the age of 21, or were not yet born. If an interest was not contingent, then it was said to be vested, as no conditions had to be fulfilled before the grant could take effect, or when the identity of the recipient was already known.

Therefore a grant of land, held as fee simple by A, to B for life, with remainder to C for life when he attained the age of 21, gave B a vested interest and C a future contingent interest.

Trusts

Trusts, also known as 'uses', were originally designed to grant the legal possession of land to one individual while permitting another individual to enjoy the actual benefits of possession, such as any rents that were collected from the land. Usually two or more trustees were named in the original grant, and they were bound to hold and administer the land under the terms of the trust. Therefore, if A made a grant of land in fee simple to B and C 'for the use of D', then A would no longer be the legal possessor of the fee simple – it would now be the trustees B and C.

D also had an interest in the estate, but not in the eyes of the common law. Instead the interest was deemed 'equitable', as the law of equity compelled the trustees to carry out the terms of the trust for the benefit of D. Hence, if trusts were disputed, cases would be heard in the courts of equity, whereas property transfers made solely under the principle of common law ought, in theory, to end up in one of the common law courts. Advice about tracking down such disputes in the law courts is provided in CHAPTER 8.

The trust would end only when the trustees transferred the legal fee simple to D. Trusts were normally set up that transferred the fee simple to the trustees, but in theory they could hold either life interests or fee tail. The trust would end only when the legal estate was transferred to the beneficiary of the trust, provided he was of full age and that his equitable fee was not conditional or determinable.

Settlements

A settlement was the term given to a land grant that involved the creation of a succession of interests in the land, either by direct grants or via trusts. Settlements became especially important in the nineteenth century, when the owners of large landed estates created chains of inheritance that bound land to their families, known as 'strict settlements'. These are considered later in this chapter.

CHANGES TO LAND LAW UNDER THE 1925 LEGISLATION

In 1925 a series of statutes were passed that altered English land law. The main components were the Settled Land Act (1925 c.18), the Trustee Act (1925 c.19), the Law of Property Act (1925 c.20), the Land Registration Act (1925 c.21), the Land Charges Act (1925 c.22) and the Administration of Estates Act (1925 c.23). This guide is not the best place to investigate the impact of these pieces of legislation, but you will find that they have been referred to when relevant. Some suggested reading material on the subject is listed under 'Useful publications'.

4.4 Methods of transfer

The previous section has outlined some of the basic ways in which freehold land, and therefore the houses that were built on the land, could be granted or held by an individual. The way in which land was held therefore determined the method by which property could be transferred from one party to another. These are outlined below, with information on where to find relevant material within the National Archives. Don't forget, though, that in most cases listed below the original documents produced by the conveyance are likely to be stored elsewhere, most probably the relevant CRO; the records at the National Archives are likely to be strays, relate to Crown property, or records of the courts that were used to formally record the transactions. Consequently, advice about searching for title deeds – the combined record of previous transfers – is provided in the next chapter.

FEOFFMENT

Enfeoffment was the term used to describe the conveyance of land held by fee simple from one party to the other within the confines of a manor. In medieval times, the seller physically passed a sod of land taken from the property to the buyer, a process known as 'livery of seisin'. Once the transfer had been completed, the purchaser was then a tenant of the manor and subject to its rules and regulations. Although no written evidence of the transfer was legally required until the Statute of Frauds in 1677, both parties, as well as the lord of the manor, found it expedient to produce a record of the transaction. The result was a 'feoffment', known as a 'deed of gift', and was in effect a private charter that described the transfer from one party to the other. You will find that the format of the document tends to give the names of the people or parties concerned and a description of the property involved, with a summary of the feudal terms and conditions under which the property was held from the lord of the manor. The grant was permanent, signified by the Latin clause *habendum*, which in full usually reads *Habendum et tenendum … in perpetuum* (to have and to hold … for ever). The date of the transfer is usually provided at the foot of the text.

Feoffment originated in the eleventh century, and had lapsed as a form of conveyance by the mid-nineteenth century. No official enrolment in a court was required, and so there are no logical places at the National Archives to start looking. Feoffments will turn up as part of title deeds, but the best place to begin your research will be at the CRO, where you are likely to find a disparate collection of documents amongst the collected private papers and deposited archives of solicitors and estate agents, who historically acquired such material and held onto them for their clients. Many specialist institutions also hold feoffments, such as academic libraries and the British Library.

DEEDS OF LEASE

Documentation was also created when land was leased to individuals by one of the means described in 4.3: Leases. The *habendum* clause defined the period of the lease, and the rent is stipulated by a *redendum* clause ('yielding and paying'). Once again, the National Archives will not be the main place of deposit, and any surviving records will probably be stored in the relevant CRO, academic libraries or even private hands. However, you may well find deeds of lease for copyhold property enrolled on the official manorial court rolls, described in CHAPTER 6.

Of particular use will be leases that were used to convey building rights to a plot of freehold land. These allowed the builder to construct a property and then rent it out, while the freeholder enjoyed rent from the leaseholder. Building specifications can often be found in the terms of the lease, and may include a description of the intended property with measurements and proposed room layout.

FINAL CONCORD OR FINE

From the late twelfth century until 1833, one of the most popular methods of land transfer that generated an official record of the process was the final concord, or fine. The conveyance was achieved through a fictitious legal dispute between the purchaser, or querent, and vendor, or deforciant, which was usually resolved in the Court of Common Pleas. A final agreement, known as the concord or fine, was reached between the two parties. The concord was written in triplicate on a sheet of parchment, two copies side by side and the third along the foot of the parchment. This was then split into three parts by means of an indented or wavy cut as a preventative measure against fraud. One part was given to the vendor, another to the purchaser, while the court retained the final part, the 'foot'. This gave rise to the popular name by which surviving documents at the National Archives are known – the 'feet of fines'.

From the fifteenth century, fines were commonly used to convey land held in fee tail, as the process partially broke (or 'barred') the entail; a 'base fee' was created that was similar to a fee simple, except that it lasted only as long as the original fee tail would have done. Thus the new possessor of the land would need to check whether the original entailed interest had expired, as that was when the land would revert to the original grantor, usually the lord of the manor in which the land was situated.

The text of each fine is formulaic, beginning with the phrase 'this is the final agreement', followed by the date of agreement and the names of the judges. The document then provides the names of the parties, identified by the word INTER (between), with the querent listed first, followed by the deforciant. A description of the land or property in question is then provided, although you will find that there is no great detail given. A 'purchase price' is usually recorded, although this was a standard sum as early as the fourteenth century and did not reflect the actual purchase price. The documents were written in Latin until 1733, with the exception of the Interregnum period 1649–60, and if you are unfamiliar with the language, this standard pattern by which the documents were written will allow you to identify enough keywords and phrases to extract useful information about your property.

Feet of fines at the National Archives are in series CP 25/1 for the period 1195–1509, and CP 25/2 for the period 1509–1839. Many feet of fines for individual counties have been published, and a list is available on open access. The means of reference to feet of fines is through a series of contemporary indexes from 1509 to 1839 that are arranged by legal term and then by county or city in IND 1/7233–44 and 1/17217–68. These will provide you with the names of the county, querent and deforciant, and the location of the property.

Another series of contemporary repertories from 1623 to 1734 are kept in IND 1/7182–9, and annotated entries that correspond to numbers stamped on the fines can be found in IND 1/7191, 7192 and 7195–232. Indexes to these repertories that list entries by county and number are located in IND 1/7190 (1731–2), 1/7193 (1743–5) and 1/7194 (1745–7).

Supplementary material related to the feet of fines also survives. The concord of fine files, stored in series CP 24/1–13, and the notes of fine files, stored in series CP 26/1–14, contain legal documentation surrounding the compilation of the feet of fines themselves. You may find draft texts, annotations and background information on the agreements in these series, which are arranged in regnal years. There are indexes for the notes of fines in both IND 1/7233–44 and IND 1/17217–68, which double up as indexes to the feet of fines themselves, and can be used as a rough guide to the location of the concord of fines. However, it should be noted that some documents were filed in legal terms different from those described in the indexes.

A summary for feet of fines and related material for semi-autonomous jurisdictions is provided in TABLE 4.1.

Table 4.1 *Records of fines*

JURISDICTION	FEET OF FINES	CONCORD OF FINES
Palatinate of Chester	CHES 31 (1280–1830) CHES 32 (enrolments) (1585–1703)	CHES 31 (1280–1830) CHES 32 (enrolments) (1585–1703)
Palatinate of Durham	DURH 12 (1535–1834)	DURH 11 (1660–1834)
Palatinate of Lancaster	PL 17 (1377–1834) PL 18 (enrolments) (1587–1834)	PL 17 (1377–1834)

Feet of fines for Wales are in series WALE 2, 3 and 6, but have been transferred to the NLW.

COMMON RECOVERY

The common recovery was developed in the fifteenth century as a permanent means of barring entailed property, as long as the tenant in tail was in possession of the land, or had obtained the permission of the tenant in possession. In effect, it was another fictitious legal dispute brought in the Court of Common Pleas, designed to convert the fee tail to a fee simple.

The potential purchaser brought an action against the tenant in tail, claiming that the land was his all along and that he wished to 'recover' it. The tenant in tail appointed a third party, known as the common vouchee, to effectively represent him in court. The common vouchee was therefore required to appear in court to defend the suit on behalf of the tenant in tail. However, he would default, thereby providing the justices with the opportunity to make a judgment against the tenant in tail in favour of the original plaintiff. The entail against the land was thus broken through legal judgment and the land passed to the plaintiff as fee simple. In reality, the land would have been sold before the court case on pre-agreed terms.

The documents can appear quite complicated, given the complex legal process involved in effecting the conveyance. However, you will find that they tend to follow a fairly common format, and are once again in Latin until 1733, with the exception of the period 1649–60. As it was a court judgment, the record begins with a royal greeting, followed by the names of the justices and the relevant county. You will find that the description of the property is fairly brief, but you will obtain the names of the two main parties. Usually the name or names of the common vouchee relate to court officials, but occasionally they can refer to parties that had a vested interest in the case.

Until 1583 these judgments were originally recorded in the plea rolls of the Court of Common Pleas, which are in the National Archives series CP 40. Contemporary indexes exist in the form of docket books in CP 60, which will provide the names of the parties, the county and the relevant membrane number within the roll. The process proved to be so popular that from 1583 separate Recovery Rolls (*see* FIGURE 8) were kept, which are in series CP 43. Indexes for the period 1583–1835 again provide the names of the parties, the county and the membrane number, plus varying amounts of information on the property itself, and are to be found in IND 1/17183–216. Related material can be found in the Alienation Office entry books A 9, which record writs of entry intended for use in conveying land by common recovery.

A summary of locations for common recoveries and related material for semi-autonomous jurisdictions is provided in TABLE 4.2.

Table 4.2 *Common recoveries for semi-autonomous jurisdictions*

Palatinate of Chester	CHES 29	Plea rolls (1259–1830)
	CHES 30	Plea rolls (Flint) (1284–1820)
	CHES 31	Recoveries files (1280–1830)
	CHES 32	Recoveries enrolments (1585–1703)
Palatinate of Durham	DURH 13	Plea rolls (1344–1845)
Palatinate of Lancaster	PL 15	Plea rolls (1401–1848)

BARGAIN AND SALE

One of the most important developments for conveyances and land transfers came with the Statute of Uses (27 Henry VIII c.10) in 1536. As we have seen, realty could not be devised by will before this date. However, the tenant was able to set up a trust, or 'use', by making a grant of the land to trustees 'for the use and behoof' of himself for the duration of his lifetime, and then on trust to the use of whoever he designated in his will. This was possible because the trustees would be the legal possessors of the realty, while the tenant continued to enjoy the benefits and rents due from the land, which were considered personalty and thus could be devised. On the death of the tenant, the recipient would then direct the trustees to dissolve the trust and transfer the legal fee simple to him.

This arrangement benefited all except the lords of the manor in which the property was situated, as they were in danger of losing track of the rights and services due to them – the trustees legally owed these services to the lord, but as they were administering the land on behalf of another, they did not enjoy the benefits, and so could not perform the services; whereas the tenant was no longer under legal obligation. The Crown was one of the biggest losers under this system, and the Statute of Uses was designed to rectify this by giving the beneficiary the legal estate of the land, thereby restoring the lord's ability to exact service from him. One of the most important consequences was that tenants with a life interest in the land were often created. In response, a device called the 'bargain and sale' was employed to convey uses from one party to the next.

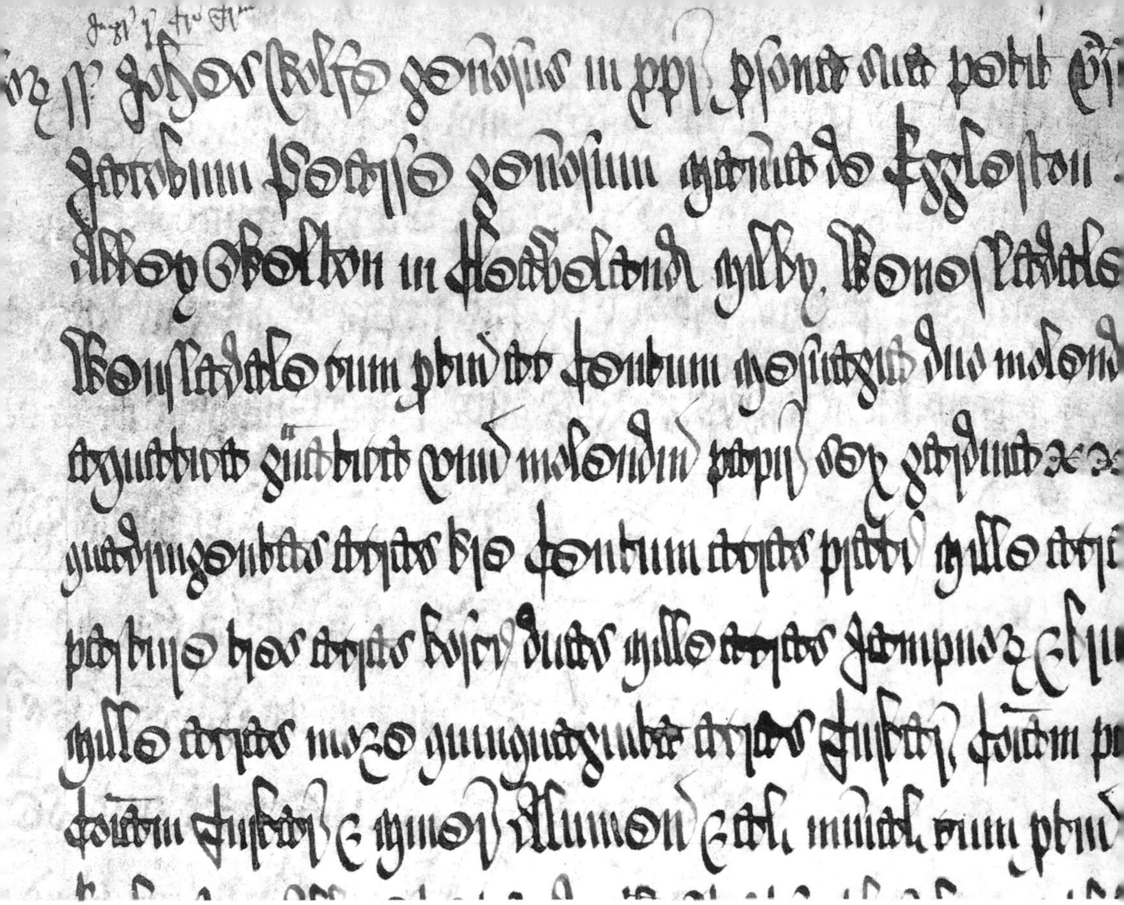

Figure 8 The transfer of the lands and possessions of Egglestone Abbey, Startforth, is recorded in an entry on the recovery roll from 1717. Its mill is described as a paper mill (molendini paperii). (CP 43/537)

In essence the bargain and sale was an indenture between two parties, whereby the first party bargained and sold property to the second. The first party remained the legal possessor of the fee simple, and conveyed the use of the land to the second party, who was liable to perform services to the lord of the manor under the terms of the Statute of Uses. To enable people to legally identify the correct person to perform these services, the Statute of Enrolments (27 Henry VIII c.16) was also passed in 1536 that required all bargains and sales of freehold property to be enrolled either with the county Clerk of the Peace in the quarter sessions, or with one of the central courts at Westminster. The National Archives does not hold quarter-sessions records, but where they survive, they will be found at the relevant CRO. However, a large number of bargains and sales were enrolled on the Chancery close rolls in c 54, and are described in the next chapter.

The documents will contain the following information that will be of use to the house historian. First, the date of the transaction and the names of the parties are given, followed by details of the financial transaction and, most importantly of all, a description of the property. The terms of the use are then defined, followed by the names of the witnesses. You may find that some enrolled bargains and sales contain recitals of earlier transactions, giving you a unique link to past transfers and the names of previous owners.

LEASE AND RELEASE

From the seventeenth century onwards, a new form of conveyance was introduced that developed the principle of bargain and sale and took advantage of the lease to create a means of conveyance that removed the need to enroll the transfer in court. The vendor drew up a bargain and sale of a lease of the property to the purchaser, usually for a term of one year, with the rent on the land being a nominal amount, typically one peppercorn. Under the Statute of Uses, the purchaser became vested in the lease without entering into possession, hence avoiding feudal dues. However, the lease was not enrolled, as only direct transfers of freehold property were subject to the Statute of Enrolment. The second part of the deed took place the following day and was a release that, on payment of a sum of money, removed the terms of the original lease and therefore vested the freehold interest with the purchaser.

As the requirement to enrol the transfer had been effectively bypassed, there are no court records in the National Archives. Surviving examples of deeds of this nature may survive in one of the places listed above, but you should start your search for surviving deeds by lease and release in the relevant CRO.

DISENTAILING ASSURANCE

Under the terms of the 1833 Fines and Recoveries Act, the need to undertake a fictitious lawsuit to bar the entail to land was replaced by a document known as a disentailing assurance. This permitted the holder of the fee tail to bar the entail as long as he was in possession of the land, or had the permission of the tenant who was in possession. It was a legal requirement to enroll these documents in Chancery, and examples can be found on the close rolls in c 54.

STRICT SETTLEMENTS

By the nineteenth century nearly half of all land was regulated by 'strict settlements'. To ensure that land was passed within a family, landholders had combined various forms of conveyance to establish a restricted, or 'strict', settlement of their land to certain named successors and 'the heirs of their body legally begotten'. At the heart of the settlement was a series of life interests for the current tenant and his son, followed by an entailed remainder to unborn future heirs, whose interests were known as 'contingent remainders'.

Since it was possible for an existing life tenant to destroy a contingent interest at any point, from the mid-seventeenth century onwards trusts were used to protect any contingent remainders. This was made easier after 1660 when realty could be devised by will. By the nineteenth century the format of a typical strict settlement was as summarized below.

4.4

- The first clause was the premises of the deed, which set out the date and the names and occupations of the parties involved in the settlement.
- This was typically followed by recitals of previous transactions that related to the current deed, which will allow you to trace the title of the property; this clause began with 'WHEREAS'.
- Next came the testatum, which outlined the purpose of the deed and began with 'WITNESSETH'. You will find out the reason why the deed was being created; a description of the property, introduced by the phrase 'ALL THAT'; and any exceptions to the property under settlement.
- The habendum clause, 'TO HAVE AND TO HOLD', set up the trusts contained in the deed, which related to the settler and often included an annuity for the heir until he inherited; pin-money to the settler's wife; jointures (money after the death of the husband) to his widow; and portions to any younger children. The property was then conveyed to the trustees for a term of years or in fee simple.
- The crucial section was the entail, which set up a series of life tenancies in the land for those already born, and a series of fee tail for those unborn. The trustees would be granted the fee simple, or a term of years, to protect the contingent remainders, and a final remainder was included to the settler and his heirs. This section would also include any conditions that might be attached to the grant to future heirs.
- The trustees were then given various powers that allowed them to administer the estate. Finally, the testemonium clause, 'IN WITNESS THEREOF', concluded the deed and stated that the parties had signed and sealed the deed in the presence of witnesses.

Under the terms of the 1925 Settled Land Act, two documents were required to draw up a strict settlement. The first was a vesting deed, which described the settled land, conveyed the legal estate to the tenant for life, and stated the names and powers of the trustees. The second was a trust settlement, which essentially described the trusts concerned in the settlement and appointed the trustees.

Strict settlements were therefore complicated documents, and this section has provided only a very brief introduction to their format and potential use. If you wish to explore this topic in more detail, suggestions for further reading are provided in the section on land law and conveyancing in 'Useful publications'.

TITLE DEEDS

5

5.1 Introduction

Today when you purchase a house, the legal documentation affecting the purchase will be added to the existing title deeds for the property, and a solicitor will assist with the formal registration of the transaction with the Land Registry – a process which is done online these days. To finance the purchase, most people apply for a mortgage, and the title deeds for the property are then deposited with the mortgage provider or solicitor acting on their behalf as security against the loan until the mortgage is paid off, or the property is sold on.

However, there was no systematic registration of land or property transfers until the formation of the Land Registry in 1862; and even then, registration remained a voluntary process for most areas outside inner London until late into the twentieth century. Before the creation of the Land Registry, transfers and title deeds were often enrolled in courts of law; but, as we have seen in CHAPTER 4, the rules, restrictions and regulations that governed land transactions and sales varied across the centuries, and subsequently resulted in different forms of transfer. This often presents the house historian with a myriad potential places in which to look for evidence.

It is also important to stress that the very nature of the records can cause confusion, as the documents contain legal jargon and can be lengthy and repetitive. Many of the legal terms are defined in the 'Glossary' at the end of this book, although relevant expressions will be explained in the context of the records they relate to. Furthermore, many records created before 1733 will be written in Latin, with the remainder in old-fashioned English or even French. Do not let this deter you, as you will be primarily searching for names of previous owners and dates of transfers, and therefore it will not always be necessary to transcribe the material in full.

Following the description of the various forms of freehold tenure in CHAPTER 4, the aim of this chapter is to present a summary of where to look for title deeds at the National Archives and elsewhere. However, it is important to remember that title deeds also contained transfers of copyhold and leasehold property, plus details of devises through wills. These are topics that are covered in more depth in Chapters 6 and 7 respectively.

Title deeds 5.2

A DEFINITION OF TITLE DEEDS

Defined in its strictest terms, a 'deed' is a legal document. Title deeds (*see* FIGURE 9), also known as muniments of title, are therefore the collected legal documentation for past transfers of a particular piece of land or property, and should perhaps be more accurately described as the 'deed package'.

In effect, they represent legal proof of ownership through previous transfers. As such, a variety of different types of document might be included in the deed package, such as indentures, mortgages, wills, manorial records and court papers. In theory, title deeds can stretch back for many centuries, and until 1925 this was often the case.

Figure 9 A selection of documents from the late nineteenth century – mortgage deed, contract of sale and indemnity – found among the title deeds for 'The Wilderness Club', Richmond, Surrey. (J 90/1711)

However, under the terms of the 1925 Law of Property Act, the requirement to prove descent of land as far back as possible was removed, with a new period of proof limited to only 30 years. This period was further reduced to 15 years in 1970. In consequence, older title deeds became redundant, and often no longer formed part of the deed package that was passed from one purchaser to the next.

Therefore, title deeds will differ from property to property, depending on how previous sales or transactions were conducted; this is the unique research trail that reflects the history of your house, and no other. You may find that there are no title deeds for your property more than 15 years old, or you may strike it lucky and find deposited deeds that stretch back many years, if not centuries. You will usually be able to identify from the documents the names of the vendor and purchaser; a description of the property in question, along with its boundaries and abuttals; the date of transfer; and the sums of money involved. Tenants and occupiers are also occasionally listed in the body of the text, and you may also find that the dates of previous sales are recited. If you are lucky, the date of construction may even be specified, particularly if the original building lease for the plot of land is included. No matter what form the paperwork takes, the house historian will be able to extract enough information to construct a detailed chronological framework.

WHERE TO LOOK FOR TITLE DEEDS

Trying to locate old title deeds can be a difficult process, as there is no logical place of deposit. Modern title deeds are usually retained by the mortgage provider as security, given that in technical terms a 'mortgage' is a pledge of land as security against a loan of money. Banks, building societies or solicitors acting on behalf of a mortgage provider are the logical place to begin your search, although you will find that most mortgage providers will charge a fee before they allow you to view the title deeds. Once the loan has been paid off, the need for this security ends, and you are entitled to claim your title deeds. This raises the problem that previous title deeds may well be in private hands, and consequently there is very little chance of tracking them down unless you can identify where the previous owners might now reside.

The alternative is that old title deeds were deposited in the public domain. When the 1925 Law of Property Act was passed, many solicitors and mortgage providers took the opportunity to dispose of title deeds that had accumulated over many years, and presented them to either current owners or, more usually, the relevant CRO. These are usually listed either by place or by the name of the family or business collection within which they were deposited.

However, a large proportion of old title deeds were simply thrown away and ended up in skips or rubbish tips, shocking as this may seem. Neverthe-less, it is still worth approaching solicitors that operate in your area on the off chance that they still have old title deeds squirrelled away in cupboards. It might also be worth talking to local estate agents, as they can often provide information about where and when previous sales occurred.

Deposited title deeds at the National Archives 5.3

Although your CRO will be the best place to begin your search for deposited title deeds, the National Archives also has a surprisingly large collection. The documents have accumulated for several reasons. Some properties had become part of the Crown estates through purchase or forfeiture, which meant that the legal proof of ownership was deposited with the relevant administrative body. Alternatively, property disputes that ended up in court often required the litigants to provide evidence of title; sometimes the doc-uments were left behind and remained within the holdings of the court.

However, there is no overall index to title deeds at the National Archives. The remainder of this section outlines some of the main areas where you should consider looking for existing deeds, and a full list of the National Archives series which predominantly contain title deeds is provided at the end of this book. Don't forget, though, that the vast nature of the National Archives holdings means that there are probably many other series where title deeds may be lurking, and await future discovery.

PRIVATE TITLE DEEDS
Large collections of title deeds for private properties have come into the hands of the Crown and can be found in a variety of the National Archives series, depending on which institution or government department handled the transfer. Similarly, in the aftermath of the suppression of the monaster-ies, many more deeds for monastic land and properties have also been col-lected. No matter what their origin or final location within the National Archives, the deeds are described as Ancient and Modern, depending on their date; Ancient deeds usually pre-date the seventeenth century, whereas Modern deeds date from the seventeenth century to the early nineteenth.

The list of National Archives series containing private deeds that com-mences on page 236 links them to any relevant finding aids and indexes that exist. In summary, the main series in which to look for deeds are C 146–9, E 40–44, E 132, E 210–14, 326–30 and 354–5. Deeds for areas that enjoyed semi-autonomous jurisdictions, such as the Duchy of Lancaster and the Palatinates of Durham, Lancaster and Chester, can be found in DL 25–7, DURH 21, PL 29 and WALE 29–31 respectively. Some of the deeds in the largest series, E 40, C 146 and E 210, have been transcribed and indexed in

A Descriptive Catalogue of Ancient Deeds in the Public Record Office, 6 volumes (HMSO, 1890–1906), which is on open access in the reading rooms. There is a key sheet in the front that provides the National Archives references for each deed.

These deposited deeds will be of most use if your property once formed part of a large private estate, as the vast majority of the material relates to principal landowners or tenants-in-chief who fell foul of the Crown and escheated their property. Most of the records will also be very early, so you will be highly unlikely to find title deeds to a specific modern property; most will relate to land on which houses were later built, rather than to the transfer of a building itself. Even if you are looking for earlier records of land transactions, the sources may be limited in use unless you know the names of the individuals who took part in the exchange. However, if you do not have this information, the indexes do include references to places, and most of the items are now available to search by keyword online via the catalogue.

TITLE DEEDS TO CROWN LANDS
In addition to private property deeds, there are also areas where you can look for deeds to Crown property that may later have been sold into private hands or which were leased out to private individuals. These are also listed at the end of this book but, in summary, you are most likely to find records in series CRES 38; LR 14–16; LRRO 13–18, 20, 25, 37 and 64; IR 10; TS 21; and WORK 7–8, 13 and 24. Many of these series have registers or card indexes that can aid identification of people or places, and these are also indicated in the list commencing on page 236. Furthermore, a keyword search of the catalogue will also yield results.

As with private deeds, it is important to remember that it will be unusual to find references to individual properties, and you will find that much of your research will focus on prior usage of a site, rather than identification of your current house. Records generated by the management of Crown estates should provide more relevant information about individual properties built on Crown land, and are described in CHAPTER 6.

DEPOSITED DEEDS AS EVIDENCE
In addition to title deeds that relate to private or Crown property, the records preserved by central law courts can prove to be a rich source for the house detective. In cases of disputed property ownership, litigants were required to provide evidence of title to support their case. Quite often the litigants failed to collect this evidence, and the courts retained these papers to form a wonderful archive that is rich with private records. This topic is covered in more detail in CHAPTER 8, but a summary of where to look is provided below.

The best place to begin your search will be amongst the Chancery Masters Exhibits, which contain evidence produced during Chancery disputes. The records are arranged in the National Archives series C 103–15 and 171, with a composite index in the series list for C 103. Masters documents, which contain similar records, are also contained in series C 117–26. Exhibits from Exchequer court cases can be found in series E 140, and later records from the Supreme Court of Judicature are in series J 90 (*see* FIGURES 9–10), which are stored in Cheshire and currently

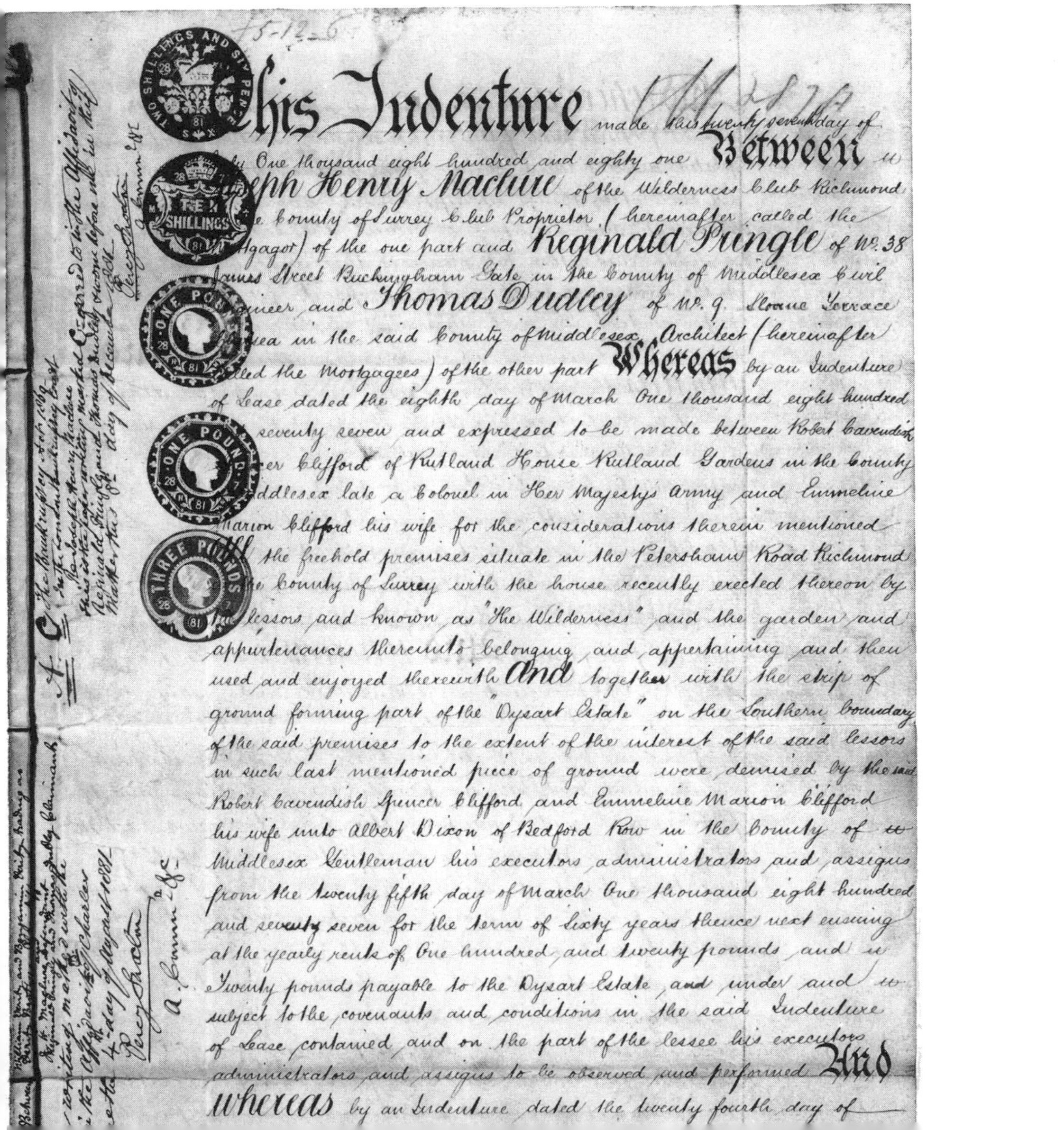

This Indenture made this twenty seventh day of … One thousand eight hundred and eighty one Between Joseph Henry Macclure of the Wilderness Club Richmond in the County of Surrey Club Proprietor (hereinafter called the Mortgagor) of the one part and Reginald Pringle of No. 38 James Street Buckingham Gate in the County of Middlesex Civil Engineer and Thomas Dudley of No. 9 Sloane Terrace Chelsea in the said County of Middlesex Architect (hereinafter called the Mortgagees) of the other part Whereas by an Indenture of Lease dated the eighth day of March One thousand eight hundred and seventy seven and expressed to be made between Robert Cavendish Spencer Clifford of Rutland House Rutland Gardens in the County of Middlesex late a Colonel in Her Majesty's Army and Emmeline Marion Clifford his wife for the considerations therein mentioned All the freehold premises situate in the Petersham Road Richmond in the County of Surrey with the house recently erected thereon by the lessors and known as "The Wilderness" and the garden and appurtenances thereunto belonging and appertaining and then used and enjoyed therewith And together with the strip of ground forming part of the "Dysart Estate" on the Southern boundary of the said premises to the extent of the interest of the said lessors in such last mentioned piece of ground were demised by the said Robert Cavendish Spencer Clifford and Emmeline Marion Clifford his wife unto Albert Dixon of Bedford Row in the County of Middlesex Gentleman his executors administrators and assigns from the twenty fifth day of March One thousand eight hundred and seventy seven for the term of Sixty years thence next ensuing at the yearly rents of One hundred and twenty pounds and Twenty pounds payable to the Dysart Estate and under and subject to the covenants and conditions in the said Indenture of Lease contained and on the part of the lessee his executors administrators and assigns to be observed and performed And Whereas by an Indenture dated the twenty fourth day of

Figure 10 First page of indenture concerning 'The Wilderness Club', Richmond, Surrey, mortgaged by Joseph Henry McClure to defendants Reginald Pringle and Thomas Dudley, who were trustees of settlement on his marriage to Miss Ellen Bottomley. The dispute concerned coal rights in Whiston and Huyton, Lancashire, plaintiffs being Joseph Crossland McClure and Elaine McClure, infants. (J 90/1711) require three working days' notice before they can be produced at Kew. You may also find deeds among the Court of Wards and Liveries records in WARD 2, as well as in the Chancery court of the Palatinate of Lancaster in PL 12, and exhibits in the Exchequer of Chester that include deeds and other land documentation relating to the city of Chester and surrounding villages are in CHES 11.

If you are able to identify relevant material within any of these areas, you should, in theory, be able to track down records of the court case itself, which should provide even more information about the litigants and potential owners. This type of research is described more fully in CHAPTER 8.

5.4 Enrolment of deeds

LAND REGISTRY

In 1862 the national Land Registry was established to provide a means of recording land transfers across England and Wales. Before this date, certain types of land transaction were required by statute to be enrolled in a variety of courts, depending on the type of transaction that took place.

Initially, there was no legal requirement to enroll land transfers at the Land Registry, and compulsory registration was introduced by the Land Transfer Act 1897 on only a gradual basis, county by county, with particular importance given to urban areas. Technically, compulsory registration for all counties has existed since 1990, although for most counties this has been the case since the 1970s. This means that presently only about 70 per cent of all eligible properties are actually covered by the records of the Land Registry, although this will increase as more properties come onto the register.

The records maintained by the Land Registry will contain information on the sale, plus maps or plans that depict boundaries of the land or property in question. The register of a property contains details of the current ownership only, as well as details of any registered mortgage or deed affecting the land, which might contain references to previous sales. Anyone can order a copy of the register and most documents referred to in it, as well as a copy of the title plan. Application should be made on the appropriate form to the office that deals with that area. There is a fee charged for this service. Copies of the application forms and further details are available from any Land Registry office, or via its website **www.landreg.gov.uk**.

The Land Registry may also hold historical records of an individual property from the time when it was first registered, though usually not the actual title deeds themselves. These limited historical records are only available at the discretion of the office concerned, and application should be made in writing, explaining why the records are needed. Again, a fee would be charged. Alternatively, you can normally purchase copies of any register in person at the headquarters of the Land Registry in Lincoln's Inn Fields, London, or at any district Land Registry, although it is advisable to telephone in advance of a visit. More information on the work of the Land Registry, including details of online registration of property transfers, the creation of electronic records, and the historic records that it holds, is available from its official website provided above.

LOCAL REGISTRIES

Before the Land Registry was set up, registers of deeds were already in existence in some parts of England. They were established by statute in an attempt to prevent fraud, given that the possession of title deeds conferred legal ownership upon the holder of the documents – hence the expression that possession is nine-tenths of the law. The statutes also defined the type of transaction that was eligible for registration in the local registries. Usually these were leases over 21 years; freehold transfers; mortgages and wills. They do not contain the actual deeds as such, merely a memorial or written record of the important sections of the deeds and the date of enrolment in the register. Details of the relevant archives that hold local registries are provided in Table 5.1.

Table 5.1 *Local deed registries*

Name	Date range	Location
Middlesex	c.1709–1940	LMA, 40 Northampton Road, London EC1R OHB
Bedford level	17th century onwards	Cambridgeshire Record Office, Shire Hall, Cambridge CB3 0AP
West Riding Yorkshire	1704–1972	West Yorkshire Archives Service, Newstead Road, Wakefield WF1 2DE
East Riding Yorkshire and Hull	1708–1976	East Riding of Yorkshire Archives and Records, The Chapel, Lord Roberts Road, Beverley *Correspondence to:* County Hall, Beverley HU17 9BA
North Riding Yorkshire (not including City of York)	1736–1972	North Yorkshire CRO, Malpas Road, Northallerton DL7 8TB

In addition, registration of property or land transfers for the City of London occasionally occurs on hustings rolls. A search of the records located at the Corporation of London Record Office at the Guildhall, Aldermanbury, might yield some results. Similar registration occurred for property in other cities or boroughs in municipal courts, and these records can usually be found in the relevant CRO or at municipal record offices. Some counties have collections of deeds enrolled under the Statute of Enrolments 1536. In addition, from 1715 to 1791 Roman Catholics and nonjuror Anglicans had to register their estates and changes of ownership. These records are to be found both in CROs and at the National Archives in series E 174 and FEC 1.

ENROLMENT OF DEEDS AND CONVEYANCES AT THE NATIONAL ARCHIVES

In addition to the deed registries described above, other statutes regulating the conveyance of land stipulated that the transfers must be enrolled in a court of law. Furthermore, many individuals voluntarily enrolled their title deeds so that it was clear who was the legal owner of the land. The National Archives holds many records of these courts, and the most useful series that contain enrolled transcripts of title deeds are listed below. However, it should be noted that a speculative search of these records is likely to be lengthy and ultimately fruitless, unless you have some idea that registration or enrolment did indeed take place, either through the antiquity of the property itself (from architectural evidence), or more precisely by reference in another written source such as personal correspondence, will or later title deed. Further advice is provided in section 5.5. Equally, the records described below are also rather technical and thus might not be the easiest to use.

Enrolments in Chancery

One of the most accessible places for deed enrolment was in Chancery. For a fee, private individuals had memorials of property sales or land transfers copied onto the back of the close rolls, contained in series C 54 (*see* FIGURE 11). From 1536 this practice gained in popularity when it was decreed that the enrolment in a court of law of a particular type of land conveyance known as bargain and sale was a statutory requirement (described in section 4.4: Bargain and sale). Once the Land Registry had been established and continued to grow in popularity, the close rolls were used less frequently as a place of enrolment. From 1903, when the close rolls were discontinued, the Supreme Court Enrolment Books in J 18 served the same purpose, although you are unlikely to find any title deeds enrolled much beyond the middle of

Table 5.2 *Indexes to Chancery close rolls*

DATE	FINDING AID	LOCATION
1227–1509	Calendar of Close Rolls	Open access (listed under C 54)
1509–1837	Index to grantees (buyers)	Open access (C 275/12–85)
1837–1848	Index to grantors (sellers)	Open access (C 275/86–8)
1573–1902	Index to grantors (sellers)	Open access (C 275/89–169)
1903–	General indexes (annual)	Open access (listed under J 18)
1559–1567	Calendar of enrolled deeds	IND 1/9455–7
1689–1820	Deeds enrolled for safe custody	IND 1/16936–7

98 | Title deeds

the twentieth century. Indexes to the enrolments in these sources survive in a variety of forms, and a summary is provided in TABLE 5.2. Close rolls are especially useful if the land was formerly owned under a charitable trust. There are separate indexes by place available in the reading rooms.

Grants of land made by the Crown were initially recorded in charter rolls in series C 53. You can find information about who owned a plot of land before your house was built, although they tend to be an earlier source (ending in 8 Henry VIII) and therefore less useful for a modern house historian. Later grants, along with enrolments of Crown leases and other methods of bestowing land onto individuals, were recorded on patent rolls in series C 66, and between 1483 and 1625

Figure 11 Plan from enrolled trust deed for the construction of a schoolhouse in Newbold, Derbyshire, in the close roll for 1872. (C 54/17354)

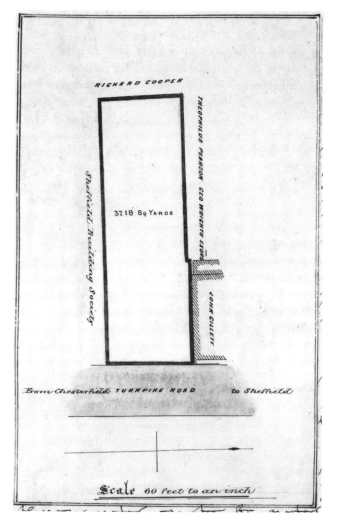

confirmations of previous grants were enrolled separately on confirmation rolls in series C 56. Patent rolls are of particular use in the Reformation period and beyond, when grants of land and property formerly belonging to monastic institutions were enrolled.

Published calendars to charter rolls exist for the entire period and are on open access. Patent rolls are also calendared for the period 1 Henry III–24 Elizabeth I, with a transcript in existence for 1201–16, and additional indexes in various Deputy Keepers Reports (DKRs). The *List and Index Society* has published later indexes for the remainder of Elizabeth's reign, and Palmer's Indexes, which also cover close rolls and other chancery series, continue the series beyond the Elizabethan period. These can now be found in the National Archives index series IND 1/17276–428 and are listed in the Catalogue of Index Volumes and Obsolete Lists and Indexes (*List and Index Society, vol. 232*).

Enrolments in the Exchequer

Although primarily a financial institution, the Exchequer served as a court of common law and equity where deeds and land transactions were also enrolled, and the house historian will find relevant records in one of three main areas.

Memoranda rolls originally developed to allow the officials of the Exchequer to make written notes about debts and financial issues. They were kept in duplicate, known as the King's Remembrancer in series E 159 (1218–1994) and as the Lord Treasurer's Remembrancer in E 368 (1217–1835). Enrolments of legal business, fines and conveyances developed during the sixteenth century as part of the Exchequer's equity jurisdiction, and from 1927 separate enrolment books, recording conveyances and associated plans, can be found in E 159 alone.

Finding aids for E 159 between 1543 and 1884 exist among the National Archives index series IND 1/17051–79 and 1/6724–32, the last two of which are called 'indexes to enrolments'; you will need to refer to *List and Index Society, vol. 232*, to determine which index you should consult for a particular period. Similarly, repertory rolls for E 368 have also been transferred to the National Archives index series and provide the name of the county, a brief note of the subject of the entry, and the rotulus number on which it is found. Relevant volumes are IND 1/6909–35, 6993–5, 7016–28 and 7031–51. Other indexes include Tayleure's in IND 1/16898, which covers various dates up to the reign of Charles I (1625–49); and an index of charters and grants in IND 1/17043.

The plea rolls in E 13 (1236–1875) are, as the name suggests, enrolments of common law pleas, often relating to land transfer and usually by private litigants, into the Exchequer of Pleas. Repertory rolls, which act as indexes, are in the series E 14 and cover the periods 1412–99, 1559–1669 and 1822–30.

There is also a selection of calendars in two series, one chronological and one alphabetical, to 1820 on open access.

Finally, miscellaneous books of the Exchequer in E 315 (1100–1800) cover a disparate range of material bound up in the 527 surviving volumes. A huge amount of information relating to land transactions after the Reformation is stored in these documents, including enrolled deeds and leases. An index to some of the enrolments of Crown leases in the series is in appendix 3 of DKR 49 (pp. 209–360), and there are a number of manuscript calendars and indexes on open access in the reading rooms.

Civil pleas in the Court of King's Bench

Apart from dealing with Crown pleas relating to criminal issues, the Court of King's Bench also heard civil pleas. Due to the documentation generated by the court, it proved a popular means of registering deeds or conveyances. Coram rege rolls exist from 1273 to 1702 in series KB 27. Lists of deeds enrolled during the reigns of Edward I and Edward II, and for 1656 to 1702, are in KB 173/1. Enrolled deeds from 1390 to 1595 and from 1649 to 1655 may be traced through the Docket Rolls (which from 1390 to 1656 are in IND 1/1322–84) or Docket Books (which from 1656 to 1702 are in IND 1/6042–96), and, from Michaelmas 1595 to Hilary 1649 only, via the special Remembrance Rolls in IND 1/1385–7. However, these are not searchable by place and therefore will be of limited use to the house historian.

After 1702, Judgment Rolls were maintained in series KB 122. A repertory of deeds and wills enrolled in the Judgment Rolls down to 1805 is available, although the series is difficult to use.

For earlier enrolments, you will occasionally find details of title deeds to land in the records of the itincrant justices, also known as eyre rolls, in series JUST 1, with the earliest coram rege rolls located in series KB 26.

Court of Common Pleas

One of the most popular courts where deeds and conveyances were enrolled was the Court of Common Pleas. Civil pleas were entered onto plea rolls, which are in CP 40 (1273–1874), which became used so frequently for a particular form of conveyancing, the common recovery, that a separate series of Recovery Rolls was created in 1583, in series CP 43 (1583–1838); these were also used to enrol deeds. Feet of fines were also stored with the records of the Court of Common Pleas, in series CP 25/1 and 25/2, and along with the common recovery have been described in more detail in CHAPTER 4.

The plea rolls were composed of distinct sections, one of which was usually reserved for the enrolment of writs, deeds and charters. There are no indexes as such, but you can obtain rotulus numbers of particular cases from the prothonotaries' docket rolls in CP 60 for the period 1509–1859.

Many means of reference survive for the recovery rolls, mainly removed to the National Archives index series. IND 1/17183–216 is a series of contemporary repertories from 1583 to 1835. From 1583 they are in the precise order in which the recoveries are arranged in the rolls, but from 1705 they are arranged alphabetically by county and then in entry order. You can use these rolls to obtain the county, the names of the parties, and the number of the rotulus on which the recovery is enrolled, although in some cases you may find additional details about the property involved in the case. A separate index to deeds enrolled in the recovery rolls between 1555 and 1629 is in CP 73/1, and from 1629 to 1836 in IND 1/16943–9.

Semi-autonomous jurisdictions

Enrolled deeds and records of conveyances can be found in similar court records for the semi-autonomous jurisdictions. The Duchy of Lancaster maintained its own chancery, and enrolments are in series DL 37. In addition, many title deeds and records of legal transfers were recorded in the Cowcher of the Duchy. Records are in DL 42, and an index to the series exists on open access. Plea rolls for the Palatinate of Lancaster can be found in PL 15, where conveyances and further deeds will be located. You can use Imparlance or remembrance books in PL 24 as a means of reference.

The Palatinate of Durham also operated a chancery, and the records of its main administrative official, the Cursitor, are in series DURH 3, which includes Chancery enrolments 1333–1854, plus registers of private deeds enrolled in Chancery 1544–1616. The Cursitor's and Registrar's miscellanea in DURH 8 also contain an enrolment book of deeds for 1879, and judgment rolls in DURH 13 contain material similar to the plea rolls in the Courts of King's Bench and Common Pleas.

The Palatinate of Chester maintained an exchequer, where deeds and other legal material were enrolled, which are in CHES 2 (1307–1830), although there are large chronological gaps in this series. Three alphabetical calendars exist in DKRs 36, 37 and 39 under 'Welsh Records'. Plea rolls for the Palatinate of Chester can be found in CHES 29, for which a calendar of the deeds, inquisitions and writs of dower on the rolls from Henry III to Henry VIII can be found in the appendices to DKRs 26–30. Similar material can be found in CHES 30 as well, although the rolls for the period after 1541 have been removed to the National Library of Wales.

Crown lands

Enrolments of deeds relating to Crown lands are usually to be found among the records of the offices and government departments responsible for managing the Crown estates. The most important areas in which to look will be LR 1 and LRRO 13–18, 20 and 25; LRRO 64 and 66 are indexes to enrolments.

Searching for a sale or property transfer   5.5

Unless you are in possession of title deeds that provide details of when a sale occurred, it can be difficult to track down how and when a property changed hands. However, there are various areas where you might start to look for property transfers, or even details of leases to tenants.

Local newspapers are probably one of the best places to begin searching for details. You will find that more and more papers survive from the eighteenth century onwards, and they usually carry details or notices that advertise property for sale, rent or lease. Searching the papers may be a time-consuming task, as there are no internal indexes. Some CROs have compiled their own indexes to names, events and places, but although they act as a good starting place, they are rarely complete. However, where advertisements do survive, you are likely to find a detailed description of your house, plus the name of the sale agent or vendor. It is then possible to approximate a date of sale, and then search for evidence for the method of transfer. The best place to start your research should be the local studies centre nearest to your house, and failing that the relevant CRO; you could also try the British Newspaper Library, Colindale, as they hold the largest national collection of newspapers in the UK.

Alternatively, sale catalogues and estate agents' prospectuses can be discovered among the deposited business records of the relevant company. These will also provide you with a rough date of the sale, and possibly information about the interior of the property. As with newspapers, the best place to start your research is at a local level, in all probability the relevant CRO. Nevertheless, the National Archives has a collection of estate agents' sale catalogues among records deposited as evidence with the Supreme Court of Judicature in series J 46. These are arranged by place and can be searched on the catalogue.

Documents such as electoral registers, census and rate books can also be consulted to determine a change of ownership or occupancy, as they can exist in a series for many years. These are described in more detail in CHAPTER 9. The valuation records of c.1910 might also be of use, as the Field Books can contain details of recent sales, and some books are known to record subsequent sales.

Scotland and Ireland   5.6

Although the main focus of this chapter has been on enrolled deeds and land transfers in England and Wales, there are different sources and methods of land transfer for Scotland and Northern Ireland as well. Furthermore, deeds for property in Wales can also be found at regional archives, and at the NLW.

5.6

Land transfers and registration in Scotland generated documents different from those in England. An important means of transfer of ownership of a piece of land or building was via sasines. A register of sasines exists from 1617 onwards, arranged in counties and by royal burgh; and detailed transcripts known as abridgements begin in 1781. The records are stored at the NAS in Edinburgh, where you can obtain further information about the nature of the records and the evidence for house history that they contain. The NAS also holds registers for deeds in the various courts, such as the Register of Deeds in the Court of Sessions known as the Books of Council and Session (NAS series RD, from 1554), the Sheriff Courts (NAS series SC, generally from the nineteenth century onwards), Royal Burgh Courts (NAS series B for varying dates), Commissary Court (NAS series CC), and Local Courts (NAS series RH 11, before 1748).

The Irish government passed an act setting up the Irish Registry of Deeds in 1708, which is located at the National Archives in Dublin. In addition, PRONI holds microfilm records in MIC.7. The registry contains memorials that are much more detailed than those in England and usually comprise a complete copy or a fairly full abstract of a document. Furthermore, copies of the memorials known as Transcript Books are also available on microfilm, from 1708 to 1929, in MIC.311. Indexes to these series also exist, and after 1832 the townland or street, the county, city or town, and the barony or parish in which the lands are situated are given.

Ark A

94

CULLERCOATS, NORTHUMBERLAND.

From the South.

Published by SHIELD & TURNER, Grey Street, Newcastle.

F.M.RICHARDSON.DEL.   J.JACKSON.SC.

[1845]

Wednesday. 10 Se

...sk mean. Th flea in my excuse — wh...
...n I do not look on those rocks and yell...
...nds. however my flean are settled today,...
...turday for 2 nights to C Howard — on Mon...
5 to London. then Chatsworth. all cong...
...e leave in the middle of October, y then if...

Cliff House, Northumberland

As its name might suggest, Cliff House is perched on top of cliffs that overlook the North Sea in Cullercoats, Northumberland. (The scene is pictured in the 1845 letterhead from the Duke of Devonshire, on page 105.) Today Cullercoats is a bustling township on the outskirts of North Shields, near Newcastle upon Tyne, but 250 years ago – when Cliff House was first built – it was little more than a small hamlet, relying on the sea to provide a living for its hundred or so inhabitants. The principal means of earning a living was fishing, although the rugged shoreline lent itself to smuggling, and consequently there was a never-ending struggle between government officials who sought to stamp out the illegal running of goods to shore, and the locals who were able to make money by assisting the smugglers land and distribute their goods.

Much about the history of Cliff House was already well known, as it had been an occasional residence of the Duke of Devonshire when he visited its owners, Robert and Fanny Arkwright, in the 1840s. Research at both the National Archives and the archives of the Dukes of Devonshire at Chatsworth House revealed correspondence from the Duke, including letters written on headed notepaper from Cullercoats that featured images of the hamlet, with a hand-written arrow marking the location of the property on top of the cliffs. As such, it was a house of some standing, well appointed with spacious rooms and a series of cellars, which had mysterious cages set into them. Other records, including census returns and local newspapers, showed that it was often let out to visitors during the nineteenth century, before passing to a solicitor and his family. Tragically, he died in the house in 1869, and his widow

resided there for at least a further 20 years. Various owners bought the property in the twentieth century, until the threat of demolition hung over it in the 1970s when the local council planned a £1m redevelopment of Cullercoats sea front. Its unique heritage and striking architecture won it a reprieve and Grade II listing status.

Much of the above was easy to track down from title deeds, census records and notes taken from local histories of Cullercoats. Yet the real mystery surrounded the builder and first owner of the house, Thomas Armstrong, in whose family it remained until 1837. Digging in the local studies centre revealed an article about the property in Tomlinson's 'Historical Notes on Cullecoats, Whitley and Monkseaton', which cited now-lost title deeds that stated 'on July 28th 1768, Benjamin Fleming of Newcastle, stationer, conveyed to Thomas Armstrong, North Shields, commander of His Majesty's cutter, Bridlington, "a piece or parcel of ground at Cullercoats where a cottage formerly stood"'. Other sources, such as land tax returns and later title deeds, confirmed that Thomas Armstrong then built Cliff House upon this site. This information would have sufficed most house historians, having established when the house was built and who constructed it. However, Armstrong's profession allowed further research to be conducted on his life and career, and revealed a truly astonishing story that in turn led to further discoveries within the house itself.

Thomas Armstrong was a customs officer, and had risen rapidly through the ranks. Correspondence files between the local customs house and the main Board of Collectors in London survive at the National Archives, and reveal what sort of a man he was. Armstrong entered the service on board the Bridlington in 1757, but within three years he had seized control of the ship by reporting his commanding officer for neglect of duty. He ruled with a rod of iron, often hitting his crew with ropes if they failed to obey him. Yet questions were often raised about his conduct, and in 1771 he was suspended from duty for letting smugglers escape, with the implication that he had aided their flight. He was eventually allowed to return to duty, but five years later the full story of his complicity emerged.

In summer 1776 two of the most notorious smugglers in the area, gentlemen called Lucas and Wallard, were sighted and the Collector of Customs in Newcastle ordered Armstrong and his men to seize them. A report sent to London explains what happened next. Having captured Lucas and Wallard's ship, the information sent to Armstrong from Newcastle relating to the notoriety of the smugglers

... should have excited the officers to double care and circumspection ... [but] seemed to have had a contrary effect – attempts to lock the two up were opposed by the officers, the smugglers were given leave to walk at leisure on deck between the three ships, and were on such goods terms with the officers that they breakfasted, dined and supped with the officers.

The smugglers made their getaway in a rowing boat, and the verdict on Armstrong was damning:

... we are therefore of opinion that there is the strongest reason to believe that the escape of Lucas and Wallard was concerted between them and the commanders of the cutters, and that captains Armstrong and Radley have been guilty of a great breach of their duty, and that Reay was instrumental in contriving the escape of the 2 smugglers. For these reasons we deem the aforesaid unworthy of any future trust or confidence, and have therefore dismissed them.

Armstrong's fall from grace, and complicity with the very smugglers he was paid to capture, explained how he had managed to afford his grand house, as well as shedding light on some of the more bizarre architectural features built into his house. On further examination, a secret cellar was found underneath the floor of his study, which in turn led to a tunnel which would have run right down through the cliffs onto the beach below. Although the beach entrance no longer exists, having been closed off by the local council some years before, the cellar section survives, and it would have been used to move illicit goods to shore, through Armstrong's house and into Cullercoats and beyond. Cliff House is a perfect example of why you should always try to research the people who lived in your house just as much as the bricks and mortar themselves, as the documents can often reveal a secret history that you never imagined possible.

6

6.1 Introduction

The aim of this chapter is to introduce some of the records that were generated by one of the oldest units of land in England and Wales – the manor. The National Archives has a wide collection of manorial material for manors that were already in Crown hands, or had fallen into the hands of the Crown through forfeiture, for example. In general, manorial records will be of enormous importance if your property was built on copyhold land, as the manorial court had sole responsibility for the transfer of copyhold land between individuals until the mid-nineteenth century.

The Crown was also the largest landowner in England and Wales, and generated administrative records for its many estates that were retained by a wide range of government departments, all of which can yield important information for the house historian. Records generated by private estate owners are also discussed, although the National Archives is not going to be the best place to start looking for relevant material; the relevant CRO will be a more appropriate location.

MANORIAL ADMINISTRATION

We have seen in Chapter 4 how land law evolved after the Norman Conquest, and that the manor was the basic unit of land. It was also stated that manors were not always compact geographical entities, and were often united only by the social and economic ties that bound each individual to the lord of the manor. Collectively these social and economic ties – the terms of tenure, various bonds of obligation and general rules of the manor – were known as the customs of the manor, and would vary according to each manor and region. It is, therefore, worth making sure that you know which manor your property is located in before you begin your research.

The administration of the rules and regulations of the manor generated many types of record. Some will be of greater use to the house historian than others. The most informative series are the official records of the manorial court, where the lord of the manor, through his appointed deputy, the steward, regulated tenants' entry into land and collected revenue generated by the feudal ties. These records are described in some detail, along with other documents generated by the day-to-day running of the manor, such as rentals, surveys and accounts. Survival of manorial records can be patchy, and advice about where to start looking is also provided, although if you are very lucky you may find records for some manors that stretch back from the twentieth century to the thirteenth century or earlier. It should also be noted that some parts of England and Wales were not subject to the 'feudal' system, and thus manorial records would not have been created.

ESTATE RECORDS

In addition, manorial documents formed part of larger collections of documents generated by the management of larger private estates, of which one or more manors may have formed an important constituent part. Aside from the court rolls, estate owners produced a variety of other documentary sources to assist them with the management of their financial arrangements. It is important to remember that these were private documents created for a private purpose. Sometimes this material has been deposited in the public domain, usually the relevant CRO. However, estate owners sometimes lived many miles from the property they possessed, in which case material would be deposited in another CRO. Indeed, there are no guarantees at all that family papers have been made public, or perhaps they are stored in private archives that have limited access. In either instance, you should exercise extreme caution and diplomacy if requesting permission to view material – after all, how would you feel if a stranger asked to look through your family's private records?

One of the largest landowners in the UK was the monarchy, owning vast swathes of land in its own right and often taking control of private estates. The National Archives is the natural place of deposit for records relating to the administration of Crown lands, as well as areas outside normal county jurisdiction, such as the Duchy of Lancaster and the Palatinates of Chester, Durham and Lancaster.

SEARCHING FOR HOUSES IN MANORIAL RECORDS

The principal house in the manor was the lord's house, known as the capital messuage. In theory there was one per manor (the 'manor house'); but if a lord held more than one manor as part of a larger estate, he would have required only one capital messuage at his main place of residence, so there may not even have been a 'manor house' in existence. It is also important to remember that it was the land on which a house was built that was usually recorded in the manorial records; and most plots of land did not have property built on them. Where houses are listed, you will find the dwellings of the main tenants described as messuages or tenements, which tended to be more substantial buildings that can often form the basis of modern property. At the lower end of the social scale, cottages were usually inhabited by the poorer members of the manor and are less likely to have survived in their original form.

A final note – many manorial documents were written in the official language of government, which prior to 1733 was Latin, so you may need to take a bit of time to interpret and translate the material, and you will also need to become accustomed to the different handwriting of the stewards who compiled the records. No matter how difficult the material may appear to be, it is worth sticking to your task, as manorial records can be a wonderfully rich source for house history, often providing a sequential link for many generations of occupiers of a plot of land or property

6.2 Manorial tenants

The following are the main forms of tenure by which an individual could hold land in a manor. It is important to determine which of these would have been applicable to your property, as each form generated different records.

FREEHOLD TENANCY

As we have seen, land held by a tenant on fixed terms was known as 'freehold'. In effect, this land could be disposed of without recourse to the lord of the manor, although freehold property could not be devised by terms of a will until restrictions were eased under the provisions of the Statute of Wills in 1540, the Tenures Abolition Act of 1660 and the Statute of Frauds in 1677. Freehold tenants were expected to attend the manorial court, where they were often enrolled as jurors. Furthermore, they were liable to pay certain dues to the lord. These included a heriot payable on the death of the tenant, and a relief when an heir or purchaser of land wished to enter into possession of the land. As rents were fixed and the lord had minimal involvement in land or property transfers, freeholders rarely appear in the 'official' records of the manor other than as a list of names when they acted as jurors at the manorial court (see below), so you will be less likely to find details of property transactions in manorial records. Instead, you should look in the areas described in CHAPTER 4.

COPYHOLD TENANCY

More accurately described as customary tenants, copyhold tenants formed the majority of manorial tenants and held their land under the terms of the prevalent customs of the manor. In return for land, the customary tenant was required to work for a fixed number of days on the lord's land. However, in contrast to freeholders, the nature of work was not fixed in advance, and would be decided by the lord's steward only when the appropriate moment arrived.

The lord of the manor regulated entry into copyhold land through the manorial court, a regular administrative and judicial session which produced a record of its business known as a court roll. This is where the origin of the name 'copyhold' lies, as the recipient of land was also given a copy of the relevant court roll entry as proof of title. Descent of land varied from manor to manor, depending on local customs, but there were two main types.

Land held by 'customary holders of inheritance' passed on the death of the tenant to an heir decided by the custom of the manor. There were various types of inheritance, such as primogeniture, partible inheritance or gavelkind (which was mainly found in Kent and parts of Wales). Alternatively, customary tenants who held land for life received only a life interest in the property. On the expiration of the interest, the land reverted to the lord. He was free to re-grant it to anyone he liked, although it was often the heir of the original tenant. Some manors accepted tenants for succeeding lives, a typical example being successive life interests for the tenant, his wife and one of his children. Copyhold land could be sold, but until 1815 was not regarded as inheritable and so could not be devised by will.

Copyholders were also required to pay a heriot, plus an entry fine when entering into a property. Default of payment could, and often did, result in loss of land. Other causes for default include the failure to repair the property or keep it in a good state, and such entries in the court rolls can often provide the house historian with crucial evidence about the date of rebuilds or extensions to a property.

LEASEHOLD TENANCY

Demesne land was the personal property of the lord of the manor, but it was frequently leased out to tenants at variable rates of rent, as it was not subject to the customs of the manor in the way copyhold land was. Furthermore, new land brought into cultivation – known as extents – was also leased out. Freeholders and copyholders alike were able to take advantage of leased land, while the lord benefited through the flexibility of a system that allowed him to review terms and conditions and set the lengths of the leases. You are more likely to find details of leases for demesne land amongst the private estate papers of the lord of the manor, or the steward who administered the land on his behalf. However, you may find some enrolments on the court rolls.

RELATED FORMS OF TENANCY

At the bottom level of society were the tenants at will, or cottars, who worked as labourers on the lord's land and held a cottage with a small strip of land or garden on which to cultivate food crops. They often occupied the waste of the manor, namely the land that was not under cultivation by any of the other tenants. They also rarely appear in official court records, unless they were subsequently charged rent to stay on the manorial waste.

Furthermore, tenants were allowed to sub-let their land, creating a situation whereby an official tenant might not be the actual occupier of a house or plot of land. However, the period of the sub-lease could only be 'pur autre vie', and would end with the death of the original tenant. Sometimes, 'uses' were employed to transfer land that created fictional legal tenants while the land was actually in the possession of other individuals. It is something that you will have to bear in mind if you do find names of individuals connected with your house in manorial documents, and you will probably need to consult corroborating sources, such as records of occupancy, described in CHAPTER 9.

6.3   Records of the manorial courts

MANORIAL COURTS

There were essentially two types of manorial court. The view of frankpledge and court leet were held twice a year to try minor offences and inspect tithings, which were groups of ten men who had mutual responsibility for each other's good behaviour. However, the most important type of manorial court was the court baron. The court was held on a regular basis to conduct and regulate the routine business of the manor, and court rolls are the written record of this process. The business varied from session to session, but generally included financial punishments for offences against the manorial rules; issues relating to the administration of the manor; the deaths of tenants and changes of occupancy since the last court meeting; and surrenders of land and admission of new copyhold tenants according to the custom of the manor. The lord of the manor's appointed steward or deputy officiated at the sessions. All free tenants were required to attend, and usually acted as jurors for the court. Customary tenants were also required to attend, and were amerced (penalized) if they failed to do so without paying an essoin (excuse).

COURT ROLLS

If your property was originally held as copyhold, then you can start your research within the manorial court rolls (*see* PLATE 9 *and* FIGURES 12–13), which can be the most useful series of documents available to the house his-

Figure 12 Part of the title deeds for a property in Thorpe-le-Soken, Essex, dated 20 October 1714. It is a memorandum from the manorial court that the copyhold property has been surrendered to the use of the possessor's will, so that it can be legally devised. (C 103/12/1)

torian. These are the written record of the court baron, and usually follow a standard format. The heading of the court roll details the type of court held, the names of the manor, lord and steward in question, plus the date of the session in progress. The names of the jurors will be provided, which can give an indication of who the freehold tenants of the manor were. Customary tenants who paid

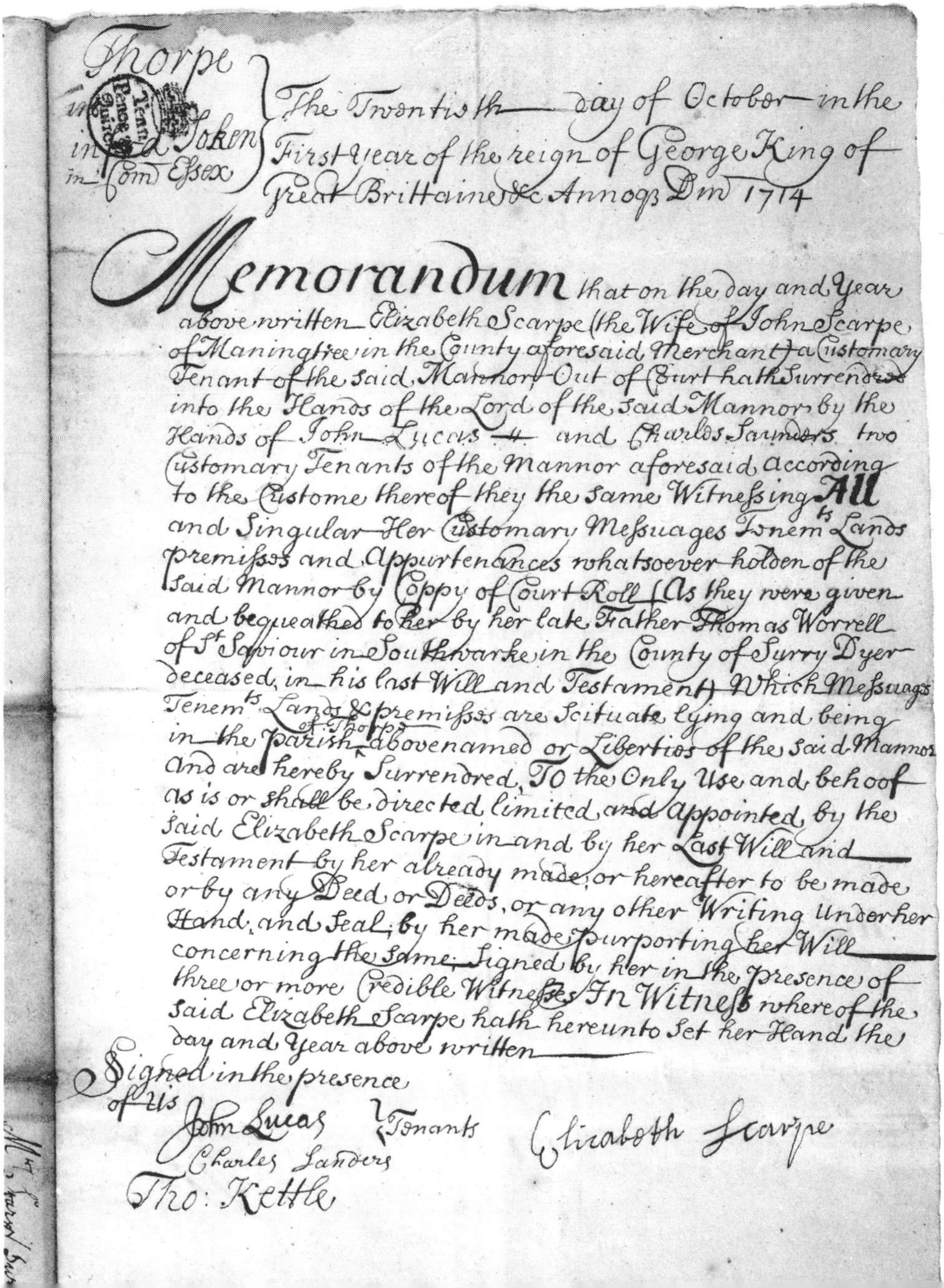

Thorpe in the Soken in Com Essex } The Twentieth day of October in the First Year of the reign of George King of Great Brittaine &c Annoq Dni 1714

Memorandum that on the day and Year above written Elizabeth Scarpe (the Wife of John Scarpe of Maningtree in the County aforesaid Merchant) a Customary Tenant of the said Mannor Out of Court hath Surrendered into the Hands of the Lord of the said Mannor by the Hands of John Lucas and Charles Saunders two Customary Tenants of the Mannor aforesaid according to the Custome thereof they the same Witnessing All and Singular Her Customary Messuages Tenemts Lands premisses and appurtenances whatsoever holden of the said Mannor by Coppy of Court Roll (As they were given and bequeathed to her by her late Father Thomas Worrell of St Saviour in Southwarke in the County of Surry Dyer deceased in his last Will and Testament) Which Messuages Tenemts Lands & premisses are Scituate lying and being in the parish of Thorpe abovenamed or Liberties of the said Mannor And are hereby Surrendred, TO the Only Use and behoof as is or shall be directed limited and appointed by the said Elizabeth Scarpe in and by her Last Will and Testament by her already made, or hereafter to be made or by any Deed or Deeds, or any other Writing Under her Hand and Seal by her made purporting her Will concerning the same Signed by her in the presence of three or more Credible Witnesses In Witness whereof the said Elizabeth Scarpe hath hereunto set her Hand the day and Year above written

Signed in the presence of us
John Lucas } Tenants
Charles Sanders
Tho: Kettle

Elizabeth Scarpe

		£ s d
	and one acre of land .	0. 15. 2
Richard . .	Crowther a Messuage .	0. 0. 8
Joseph . .	Cox 1 Messuage .	0. 0. 6
Elizabeth .	Crutchley seven eighths of eleven Messuages	0. 5. 6½
Edward .	Darell Esquire three acres of land .	0. 0. 6
Hannah .	Diamond 1 Messuage .	0. 0. 4
Roger . .	Dippie two Messuages .	0. 1. 0
Maurice and John	Dwyer half an acre of land .	0. 0. 1
Benjamin .	Dixon Esquire a Messuage Office and Garden .	0. 5. 0
Edward .	Davies Clerk three Messuages and Land .	0. 2. 0
Ann Hilliard Eyre a Mansion house called New Pallace farm Messuages ten acres called the Aldery and sixty seven acres and an half of land part of the Royal Gardens and thirty three running Lotts in New Meadows .		0. 12. 3
Jemima .	Eaton two Messuages .	0. 1. 0
William .	Ewer Esquire a Messuage Offices and Garden .	0. 3. 10
Thomas .	Ewer Esquire a rood of land in East Bancroft .	0. 0. 0¾
John Dillman Ingleheart seventeen Messuages thirty nine acres and an half of land Barnes and eight running Lotts in New Meadows .		0. 15. 5
Henry . .	Edmead eight Messuages .	0. 4. 0
Elizabeth .	Edmead now Wife of Crofton Ross three Messuages .	0. 1. 10
George . .	Ingleheart two Messuages .	0. 2. 4
John . .	Farnham three Cottages .	0. 1. 0
John . .	Fitzwater a Messuage .	0. 1. 0
Ann . .	Snelhurst a Messuage .	0. 0. 6
Mary . .	Farmer and for late Elizabeth Grantham six Messuages and a Stable .	0. 3. 4

Figure 13 An extract from the steward's rental for the manor of Richmond (alias West Sheen), Surrey, from 1786. The names of the tenants are provided, with a brief description of the property for which they were liable. (SC 11/1011)

an essoin not to attend the court are also listed.

The first section of the roll concerned presentments of all matters that the court would subsequently deal with. These were usually minor matters, such as disputes between tenants, but will occasionally feature repairs to property ordered by the lord of the manor, and references to property can be made in boundary disputes.

However, the most important section of the court rolls concerns the administration of the copyhold land. Land transactions concerning copyhold property were permissible only with the consent of the lord of the manor through the jurisdiction of the court. All new copyhold tenants were required to undergo a process of entry known as admission and surrender. First, the death of the old tenant would be announced in court and recorded in the court roll. Technically the land was 'surrendered' back to the lord, and the heir would then seek 'admission' to the property. A ceremony would be conducted in court whereby the tenant would grasp an official rod in the possession of the steward to mark his formal admittance to the property, and a record of the admittance would then be made in the court roll. A copy of the entry was provided to the tenant as proof of title. The entry usually contained a description of the property or piece of land in question, the name of the deceased tenant, the relationship with the new tenant, plus details of any longer terms of lives that might be involved. The property is usually referred to with reference to property on either side, or by the names of previous owners, although specific property names are occasionally provided.

Yet it is important to remember that the tenant might not be the occupier of a property. Tenants often leased their property, but required the permission of the lord first, and a written record is provided in the court rolls. Sales of customary land grew increasingly common, and were also recorded in the roll as an admission and surrender, the only difference being that the tenant was still alive.

Customary tenants increasingly followed the practice of freeholders by taking out mortgages on their property to raise loans, and these were entered into the court rolls. The practice was known as making a conditional surrender, as the tenant would surrender the property at court. The terms of the mortgage would then be entered onto the roll, so that if the mortgage was not repaid within the specified period then the tenant would default the property to the mortgage provider, who would become the new tenant and therefore be admitted. However, if the mortgage was paid in full, then the payment was recorded on the roll and the conditional surrender would be declared void.

'Surrender to the uses of a will' was a device used to bypass the descent of land through the customs of the manor. The land was surrendered to the court, and then the use, in this case defined by the terms of the tenant's will, was recorded in the court roll to be honoured on the death of the original tenant. This method of transfer became increasingly popular following a sale of copyhold land, to ensure that the purchaser retained the right to pass the land to his heirs without the restriction of the customs of the manor.

Many court rolls contain internal alphabetical indexes to admissions and surrenders, which will be of use if you already know the name of a tenant who possessed your property. These become more common in later court rolls, and in addition separate index books, or even registers of admissions and surrenders, sometimes survive. Where they do, they can provide the date of the previous admission, and can often instigate a chain search back to the earliest surviving court roll or book.

RELATED RECORDS PRODUCED AT THE MANORIAL COURT

In addition to the official court rolls, the steward created subsidiary documents to assist him with his duties. Minute books and draft court rolls usually contain notes taken during the court sessions, and provide details of admissions and surrender. As they were working documents, they were hastily written and contain many abbreviations, and as such they can be difficult to interpret. However, they serve as a useful substitute where official court rolls have not survived.

Estreat rolls contain records of amercements and fines made during the course of a court session. These can include financial penalties for not repairing houses, as well as details of entry fines for new tenants. You will usually find lists of names of the tenants who were due to pay, plus a note of the reason why they owed money.

Suit rolls and call books contain the names of all tenants who owed suit to the court, and in effect doubled up as court attendance registers. Although they will not contain details of property as such, they were amended and dated on the death of tenants and can serve as a useful means of reference to the court rolls themselves when trying to trace property descent.

6.3

LOCATING THE RECORDS
The majority of court rolls and related records will be found in the relevant CRO. The obvious place to start looking will be at the CRO of the county in which the manor is located, but this will not always be the case where the lord of the manor was not a local resident. To assist researchers to find court rolls, the Manorial Documents Register (MDR) was established from 1926 with the sole aim of listing the location of such records in the public domain and private hands. The MDR is maintained by the Royal Commission for Historical Manuscripts (HMC), now part of the National Archives at Kew. Furthermore, the list for some counties is now available online at the National Archives website **www.nationalarchives.gov.uk**. At present, the relevant areas covered are Hampshire and the Isle of Wight, Norfolk, Surrey, Middlesex, all three Yorkshire Ridings, and all counties within Wales. Plans to extend the online facility into other areas are in hand.

Secondary sources such as the *VCH* may provide clues as to the whereabouts of manorial material, and often give detailed descents of manors that can help you to locate relevant archives or collections. You may also like to examine the records in HMC 5/6–8 that provide lists of owners of manors in 1925, or try to track down the last known steward.

Court rolls at the National Archives are to be found in several series. There is a union index to manors in SC 2; and for properties within the remit of the Duchy of Lancaster there is DL 30, which is published as *Lists and Indexes VI*. There is also a separate union index covering (mostly) Crown manors in ADM 74; C 104–9, 111–16 and 171; CRES 5; DL 30/351–587; E 140; F 14; J 90; PRO 30/26; TS 19; SC 2/252–350 and 2/506–92; LR 3 and 11; and MAF 5. In addition, you will find references to material in E 315; DURH 3; WARD 2; E 36; SP 2, 14, 16, 17, 23 and 28; LR 11; DL 42; SC 6 and 12; E 137; C 54; and E 106.

ENFRANCHISEMENT OF COPYHOLD TENANTS
By the nineteenth century the conversion of land tenure from copyhold to leasehold meant that less land was subject to the customs of the manor, making the process of admissions and surrender increasingly obsolete. Where the practice still existed, changing ways of life, increasing urbanization and an increase in the number of tenants who resided many miles from

the manor itself meant it was inconvenient to perform the ritual admission via a court and to attend sessions that were increasingly irrelevant. In consequence, the enfranchisement of copyhold land was introduced in 1841.

Enfranchisement is the term used to describe the legal conversion of copyhold land to freehold. The process was started at the request of either the lord or tenant, but once it had been initiated, the other party was required to give his or her consent; compensation for loss of manorial income was granted to the lord, and where disputes arose the Ministry of Agriculture and Fisheries became involved as an arbitrator. The 1922 and 1925 Law of Property Acts abolished all copyhold tenure, and all outstanding copyhold land was made freehold from 1 January 1926.

The records of enfranchisement are now stored at the National Archives in the archives of the Ministry of Agriculture and Fisheries. Voluntary agreements and awards for compulsory enfranchisement from 1841 to 1925 are in series MAF 9. The records are arranged in county order, and thereafter by the name of the manor, and you will obtain the date of the award and the name of the tenant, plus evidence of title supplied from the court rolls by the lords from 1900; earlier evidences are in series MAF 20. Correspondence and papers can be found in MAF 48, while registers to enfranchisement records relating to MAF 9 are in MAF 76. It will also be worth investigating the records in MAF 13 and 27, which contain agreements and certificates of compensation.

Related manorial records 6.4

Aside from the records generated by the manorial courts, which tend to be of most use if your property was copyhold, there is a wealth of related material that can provide useful data for all forms of manorial tenure. The most common areas that will be of use to the house historian are described below.

MANORIAL SURVEYS

Various subsidiary documents were created to assist the steward with the administration of the manor, in particular to keep track of who owed manorial dues to the lord. Some of these can provide supplementary information for the house historian, even though properties themselves may not feature.

One of the most important types of manorial survey was the extent. This typically listed all the tenants for the manor, regardless of tenure, which meant that freeholders and leaseholders were recorded, as well as the copyhold tenants who appeared in the court rolls. The documents will typically provide the date that the extent was made, and then describe all land and its rent value to the lord, assigning the type of land to the name of a tenant, with a brief description of the property. However, extents were created only at the whim of the lord of the manor, usually when a manor changed hands. They became less popular by the fifteenth century, and were gradually replaced by rentals, which tended to be less detailed but still covered all types of manorial tenants. They were created on a far more regular basis, and were often annotated with details of deaths or changes of occupancy. You will find an increasing number of quit-rents included in the rental relating to labour services that had been commuted to monetary payments. These were the most prevalent form of survey until the sixteenth and early seventeenth centuries. You may also encounter custumals, which provided details of the customs of the manor. These may be of use if you are researching any customary requirements to maintain a house built on a plot of land, and you will also be able to identify the precise terms by which the tenants held their property.

Later surveys from the sixteenth century onwards (*see* FIGURE 14) took on new and varied forms, and included far greater detail than earlier list-based surveys. They were more formal, often the product of special manorial courts of survey, and conducted by survey commissioners. Tenants would be asked a series of questions so that the commissioners could compile a detailed assessment that commonly included a description of the boundaries of the manor; the customs of the manor; and a rent roll or rental. Boundary surveys can refer to property that lay on the outskirts of the manor, as natural features and fixed items such as large tenements were used as points of reference for the surveyors. However, the rent rolls are the most important section for the house historian. As with the earlier forms of survey, the rent roll will list all tenants who held property in the manor, plus a note of the rent they paid. Houses are commonly featured in the rent rolls, with any house names that might have been given, and outbuildings are sometimes listed too, although you are unlikely to find a detailed description or a location, unless it is with reference to neighbouring properties.

Maps were often produced to accompany survey documents. These provided a visual aid to the lord of the manor, and often contained a separate reference book that would list all the tenants for each holding. This can be an invaluable source, as not only are the properties depicted for a given date, but also they are linked specifically to the names of the tenants that were responsible for them. However, the survival rate of these associated reference books is not good, and the location of maps can be very diverse. They are usually found among CRO cartographic collections, or have passed into private hands and thus appear in some unlikely places, such as on the walls of offices or private houses.

Records of manorial rentals and surveys in the National Archives have been listed in a union index

Figure 14 An extract from a survey of the manor of Richmond, Surrey, *c.*1703–4. A full description of each property is provided, along with a note about the type of manorial holding (freehold or customary) and the amount of rent due. (LR 2/226)

S.ᵗ Wᵐ Brownlowes Estate formerly the
Lord Ancrams at Kew Viz:ᵗ Lord Plymouths
Acre & 52 Acres of Land and a Dwelling house
in the Occupacon of Widow Gorland and about
10 Acres of Orchard and Garden Two New
Built Houses Out Houses Orchards &c in
S.ᵗ Charles Eyres Possion 18 Acres by Kew
Green in William Cox's Tenure 18 standing
Lotts in Kew Meadowes and 18 more in one
Murdens Possion said all to be Freehold and
the Old Rolls Charge a Rent on this Estate
(But 'tis long since it was paid) ₰ Annñ — xxⅰ.ˢ 8.ᵈ

Mᵉ Edwᵈ: Allen for an Estate antiently
called Waylands Farme Pays a Quitt Rent
₰ Annñ — xⅰ.ˢ 8.ᵈ

Mʳ Mitchel a House Old Garden & part
of an Orchard and House in Possion of one
Gideon said to be Freehold of this Manor
but I have not Discovered whether any or
what Rent he ought to pay for the same

Mᵉ Robert Freeman holds some
Parish Lands which are said to be
Freehold of this Manor but Pays no Rent
for them

The Acc^tt of Clem^t Newsham Genl Steward to the most

Noble Henry Duke of Beaufort and the R^t hon:^ble the Lord

Woodstock of all moneys by him Rec^td & paid from Michas 1709 To L: Day 1710.

The charge is by Viz^t.

The Mann^r of Titchfield

Arreard there

			£	s	d
	P^d Robt: Pinke for Becking at Lady day 1709		005	15	00
	P^d Ditto for Ridge Lane then due		010	15	00
			16	10	00

Rents now due Viz^t.   Michas 1709

			£	s	d
	P^d Isaac Miller for the Corn mills		48	15	--
	P^d James Brown for the Bugle Inn		-6	--	--
	P^d Robt Bright for Posbrook farme		150	--	--
	P^d Tho: Brock for Locks farme		-16	--	--
	P^d Tho: Crowcher for Abshott farme		-45	--	--
	P^d Wm Hewatt for St Margaretts		-30	10	--
	P^d Arthur Taylor for the Demesnese		-22	10	--
	P^d Fran: Lunn for Cane Acre		--	15	--
	P^d Robt Pink for Becking		--5	15	--
	P^d Idem for Ridge Lane		-10	15	--
	P^d Wm Bright for Leeground farme		-34	10	--
	P^d farmer Wade for Whitely farme		-72	10	--
	P^d The R^t hon: the Ld Woodstock for Horny hills &c^a		--8	--	--
	P^d Idem for the Cutt of the upperside of the Brocks		16	12	06
	P^d James Atneve for the Deme Snese		-51	-2	-6
	P^d Tho: Houghton for the new broak ground		--5	-5	--
	P^d John White D^o		--2	16	--
	P^d R^t Lee D^o		--2	-9	--
	P^d Robt: Adams D^o		--5	12	-6
	P^d Wm Bright D^o		--5	-5	--
	P^d Arthur Taylor D^o		--7	14	--
	P^d Tho: Walcot for the Q^t Rents of his Lord^ble Man^rs		136	04	-5
			679	01	03

016:10:00
619:01:03
635:11:03

on open access entitled *Lists and Indexes XXV*. This includes material found in the following series: SC 11 and 12; DL 29 and 42; SP 10–18 and 46; E 36, 142, 164, 315 and 317; and LR 2. A key sheet in the front allows you to convert entries to a National Archives series reference. In addition, there is material in ADM 79, C 47/37, CRES 34, 35 and 39, F 17, LR 13 and LRRO 12, and you will need to search the series lists or undertake a keyword search on the catalogue to identify relevant material. Maps are scattered across a wide range of series, and the extracted map catalogue is the best place to begin your research. Two distinct series are DL 31 and LRRO 1. However, as with court rolls, you should probably expect to find the bulk of rentals, surveys and maps at the relevant CRO.

MANORIAL ACCOUNTS

In addition to surveys, the records generated by financial transactions can contain information about individual properties. Stewards' account books (*see* FIGURE 15) are a good place to begin looking, as they record money owed in rent and can contain information about property as well, especially if expenditure has been ordered on behalf of the lord. The records are arranged according to the 'charge and discharge' system, which first lists all revenue accruing to the property and then details expenses and payments made from this revenue. The balance was the amount paid to the lord of the manor. Collectively, these records are known as ministers and receivers accounts. Other material that can be of use will include rent rolls or rentals, not to be confused with the survey version, which provide lists of tenants who had paid money to the lord, as opposed to how much they owed.

Ministers and receivers accounts at the National Archives are listed in *Lists and Indexes V, VIII* and *XXXIV*, and *Supplementary Series II*. Most of the records of ministers and receivers accounts for private manors will be in the relevant CRO.

PRIVATE ESTATE RECORDS

Entire manors may once have formed part of far larger estates, and, in addition to the sources listed above, documents relating to the administration of private estates can yield even more information on individual properties. As most of this was once the personal property of the estate owner, the deposit of relevant material into the public domain depends entirely on chance; but where family estate papers do survive, they can provide supplementary evidence. Building accounts, correspondence and personal papers can contain crucial clues about the construction of estate property, and separate rent and payment books that

Figure 15 An extract from Clement Newham's book of accounts for the period 1709–10. The volume was compiled as part of his role as the steward for the Duke of Beaufort and Lord Woodstock, who enjoyed joint ownership of the manor of Titchfield. (C 108/45)

survived can add to our knowledge of who resided in the property. Once again, the National Archives is not the best place to start looking for such material, although surviving estate papers can be found listed under the names of previous owners. In particular, the series with the prefix PRO contains private documents deposited by gift, or acquired due to their national importance, many of which relate to the administration of private estates. Other collections, including abstracts of title, can be found among court exhibit series, described in sections 5.3: Deposited deeds as evidence, and 8.6; a particularly rich series is c 115, the Duchess of Norfolk's Deeds, which contain a huge array of correspondence, accounts, deeds and manorial material. You can also obtain information about private property descent from wills and death duty registers, which are described in the next chapter.

When looking for estate papers, it is important to bear in mind that they are likely to be deposited in the CRO of the principal seat of the family, and so you may find related material in surprisingly distant archives. The case study in CHAPTER 15 clearly demonstrates this, as estate papers for the manor in question are located in the Huntington Library at San Marino, California, USA.

6.5   Records of the Crown estates

One of the largest landowners in England and Wales was the monarchy, which, just like any private estate owner, generated administrative records as part of the management of its lands and manors. These can be a rich source of information for houses that were originally built on the Crown's extensive estates. The survival of records tends to be far more likely than for most private estates, as separate government departments were created to assist with the management, in particular relating to the financial aspects. Consequently, there are many more places in which to start your research.

In addition to the published finding aids for court rolls, rentals and surveys and ministers and receivers accounts listed above, records of Crown estate management (*see* FIGURE 16, *and also* FIGURE 24 on page 204) are to be found in three main areas – the Crown Estates Office (CRES), the Office of Auditors of Land Revenue (LR) and the Office of Land Revenue Records and Enrolments (LRRO). The most important series are CRES 2, 5, 6, 7, 34, 35, 39, 40, 45, 49 and 60; LR 1–3, 6–9 and 11–13; and LRRO 1–3, 5, 11, 12, 27 and 67. Most will contain leases, papers and correspondence, of which many will relate to domestic houses and buildings. If you are

Figure 16 A statement of claim from a bundle of papers relating to the enclosure of Delamere Forest, Cheshire, *c.*1796–1819. The forest formed part of the Crown estates, and was administered by the Office of Woods, Forests and Land Revenues. The department kept files on other administrative matters relating to Delamere Forest, such as abstracts of title, leases of lands and even the erection of workers' cottages. (CRES 2/127)

unsure whether your property once formed part of a Crown estate, then you can try looking at CRES 2/1613, which includes a list of Crown manors in 1827; and CRES 60 contains annual reports from all bodies that administered Crown estates between 1797 and 1942.

In addition to the administrative records listed above, certain Exchequer series will also contain records of forfeitures of land to the Crown, such as

Claims

···32···

No. of Claims as delivered.	In what Township or place.	Names of Proprietors.	Names of Occupiers.	No. of Acres claimed for.	Observations.
313	Willington	John Egerton	Joseph Reece	153 0 23	
do.	do.	do.	do.	33 2 4	
178	Woodhouses	Daniel Ashley		59 1 3	
204	do.	John Wrench	Elizabeth Gregory		
253	do.	Thomas Ashton	Samuel Yarwood	65 0 0	
255	do.	William Antwis	See this Claim in Frodsham Township		
271	do.	Earl Cholmondeley	Daniel Ashley	37 1 4	
		do.	Samuel Mason	20 2 39	
		do.	William Sandbach	0 1 0	
		do.	George Wilbraham	83 3 37	
284	do.	John Edwards, and others }	Thomas Norcross	23 0 0	
			Mary Jones	1 0 0	
29	On the Forest	George Rutter And right of Warren on 287 Acres	John Lewis	8 3 32	Called the Forest House.
31	do.	Samuel Wilkinson And right of Warren on 700 Acres	Samuel Wilkinson	23 0 0	Called Wilkinson's Lodge.
32	do.	George Pugh And right of Warren on 300 Acres	George Pugh	28 2 0	
34	do.	Joseph Janion, Claims the right of keeping 60	Sheep and 25		Lambs
72	do.	John Winpenny, ditto	ditto ditto 60	Sheep	
	do.		For Common Land	3 0 0	
108	do.	Mary Hornby And right of Warren on 1,270 Acres and 24 Perches	John Wright	73 2 32	Called Massey's Lodge, and Massey's Meadow,
117	do.	Samuel Hornby And right of Warren on 528 Acres and 2 Roods	John Bull	128 3 0	Called Hornby's Lodge
	do.	John Lewis, Claims the right of keeping 500	Sheep		
161	do.	Acres, and the right of keeping 300 Sheep			
164	do.	Robert Watson	Robert Watson, for Common Land }	2 0 0	
276	do.	John Arden	For Birkets Pool		
280	do.	do.	John Merrick for the Old Pale Lodge or the Chamber		
	do.	do.	William Brock for Eddisbury Lodge		
	do.	do.	John Burgess for Utkinton, or High Billinge Office		
	do.	do.	George Pugh for New Pale Lodge		
	do.	do.	Samuel Hornby for Hornby's Lodge		
	do.	do.	Peter Massey for Massey's Lodge		
	do.	do.	George Rutter for Clotton Office, or Walk		
	do.	do.	James Wright for Kelsall Walk, or Office		
		Ditto, for Young's Office	and Janion's Office.		
		Ditto, for all the Conies	and Pasturage of Conies,		
		and Sheep, and for all	Fishing, and the Titles of		
		Chief Forester, Bow	bearer and Forest Bailiff.		

ALL Persons are desired to take Notice, that a more particular Abstract of these Claims is left at the Swan Inn, in Tarporley, and another at the Bear's Paw, in Frodsham, for the inspection of all persons interested, their respective Agents or Attornies, and the Original Claims may be seen at the Office of Messrs. Leeke and Potts, in Chester, and that by the said Act, the Commissioners are empowered to settle, assess, and award such Costs, as they shall think reasonable to be paid, to the Party or Parties in whose favor any determination shall be made, by the Persons whose Claim or objection shall be disallowed or overuled, or against whom the said Commissioners shall determine.

ROBERT HARVEY, } Commissioners.
JOSEPH FENNA, }

Chester, 8th March, 1813.

Chester, printed by J. Fletcher.

leases, deeds and manorial material generated in the aftermath of the disso-lution of the monasteries in the Augmentation Office. Furthermore, the English Civil War also saw widespread forfeiture, this time from the Crown and its supporters to the new Parliamentary regime. The records generated by these events are described in more detail in CHAPTER 11. Other areas worth investigating include the FEC series, relating to forfeited estates, while WO 32/21803 contains a list of manors and deeds dated 1951 where the War Office had obtained manorial interests.

6.6 Records of semi-autonomous jurisdictions

Distinct series of manorial and estate records at the National Archives have been created for the Palatinate of Durham and the Duchy of Lancaster, and are summarized in TABLE 6.1.

Table 6.1 *Manorial records of semi-autonomous jurisdictions*

JURISDICTION	MATERIAL
Palatinate of Durham	DURH 3 court rolls
	DURH 20 estreats, ministers accounts and rentals
Duchy of Lancaster	DL 30, 42 and 49 court rolls
	DL 29 ministers accounts
	DL 29 and 42–4 rentals and surveys
	DL 31 maps
	DL 28 various accounts
	DL 32 parliamentary surveys
	DL 41 miscellanea
	DL 50 estreats

6.7 Scotland and Ireland

Scotland and Ireland developed a different system of landholding, and the best place to begin your research will be to contact the relevant national archives – NAS and PRONI. A brief summary of the type of material you will encounter is presented below.

In Scotland the feudal system took a form different from that in England. 'Retours', or services of heirs, were used to pass land from one individual to the next, and can be found in a variety of places. Retours for superior sub-jects, the equivalent to the English tenant-in-chief, were recorded in Chancery and can be searched from 1530. Further down the manorial chain, lower vassals were granted a simpler 'precept of clare constat'; these tend to be deposited in private or estate papers. From 1700 there are printed indexes to services of heirs, and some printed abridgements are available.

Legal challenges to this system tended to end up in the Court of Chancery and verdicts are recorded in the NAS series C 22 and C 28. The inquisitions themselves can appear before sheriffs or burgh courts and, between 1821 and 1847, can also be traced in NAS series C 27, if they appeared before the court of the Edinburgh sheriff on commission. From 1847 all inquest papers appear in NAS series C 29. In addition, records of large estates can be found in NAS series GD, to which there are several name and place indexes available. This is where you may pick up account books and rent details similar to the material for England and Wales. Further estate material will be deposited in the relevant regional archive.

PRONI has a wide collection of landed estate records, and a guide to the holdings is available, arranged by the name of the estate; an index to land-holders' names is also available. You will find rent rolls, rent ledgers, leases, wage books, maps and land agents' notebooks among the records. There are also records generated under the Encumbered Estates Acts of 1848 and 1849 that provide details of tenants and their houses through Encumbered Estates Rentals in PRONI series D.1201.

6.7

RECORDS OF PROPERTY INHERITANCE

7

7.1 Introduction

Chapters 4–6 have dealt with transfers of freehold conveyance, title deeds and copyhold land within the manorial system. Another important method of passing property, either within a family or alienating it to a stranger, was by making a legacy in a will. Similarly, death duty registers can also provide useful information about property descent, especially where the valuation of the estate was concerned. These sources are described below, and you will find them easier to search if you know the name of the owner, and have a rough idea of the date of their decease. Further reading on the subject is suggested in 'Useful publications'.

7.2 Property transfers in wills and administrations

THE LEGALITY OF BEQUESTS IN WILLS

Legacies made in wills that bequeathed property can be one of the most important ways of tracking the movement of houses within an extended family, and supplement legal sources for the transfer of land from one person to the next. However, the background to property transfers in wills is a little complex, but nevertheless very important if you are to grasp why a house is or is not mentioned in a will. Throughout history there have been restrictions on the type of property that could be transferred in a will – normally only the personal estate (personalty) of the deceased, such as cash, possessions and leases of property, could be devised, and freehold land was thus excluded as realty, along with the buildings and houses constructed upon it. For a long time copyhold was also excluded on the grounds that it was not inheritable under the terms of tenure described in the previous chapter.

To bypass this handicap, the 'use' or trust was employed by a landholder to establish trustees, who held the legal title to the land while permitting the landholder to enjoy the profits. As uses were considered personalty, the landholder could direct the trustees in his will to hold the land on behalf of another after his death, such as a widow, younger son or daughter.

The Statute of Uses in 1535 closed this loophole, but also prevented devises by wills. This proved so unpopular that in 1540 the Statute of Wills was passed to allow the limited devise of freehold land held in fee simple via a will. The abolition of military tenure by the Tenures Abolition Act in 1660 removed the last restrictions on what could be devised, and thereafter all freehold land held in fee simple could be devised. The 1677 Statute of Frauds stipulated that only written wills could devise real estate, and they had to be signed by the testator plus three or four witnesses.

People with copyhold property were still prevented from devising land until 1815, and consequently before this date you will need to check for descent in manorial records instead (*see* CHAPTER 6). The Statute of Wills in 1837 permitted the devise of all realty in a will, although all wills were to be written and signed by the testator in the presence of two witnesses who did not benefit from the will.

THE LACK OF A BEQUEST IN A WILL

There were many reasons why property was not mentioned in a will, one being that not everyone left a will in the first place. And even where one was made, it did not necessarily mention property.

As we have seen in CHAPTER 4, if land was held in fee simple and was not alienated during the lifetime of the holder, then it would automatically pass to his heir at law on his death, therefore removing the need for a specific bequest. A similar restriction was placed on land held in fee tail. In other cases, property might have been disposed of beforehand through a private agreement within the family, perhaps as part of a marriage portion for a daughter or as part of a strict settlement. In any case, the ecclesiastical courts had no jurisdiction over realty, as this was the preserve of the common law and equity courts. In effect, what we know of today as a will was in fact two separate bequests that were combined to form one document, with a testament covering the personalty and the will bequeathing realty.

Even if your property is mentioned within a will, it is rare to find street or house names specified; the usual format is to make a bequest of 'the house where I do dwell' to the relevant party. However, if you know the family was already in possession of a property, this can at least tell you who inherited the property next, and a new name can often prompt further searches in other areas. You may also find that names of occupiers are specified if a non-resident owner was bequeathing a leasehold property, and landowners with many houses can sometimes provide detailed specifications of where properties were situated and to whom they should next pass. Furthermore, if the occupier of a house was a leaseholder, the outstanding term of the lease could be bequeathed, and the name of the owner was also sometimes included.

Until 1925, if a person died intestate, left an invalid will or failed to make provision for any realty in a will, the property passed to the heir at law, which was the nearest blood relative starting with descendants. Personalty was passed to the next of kin, starting with a spouse. After the 1925 Law of Property Act, both realty and personalty passed to the next of kin. If the deceased was of sufficient wealth, letters of administration were then granted. Administrations will be of only limited use to the house historian, as they did not contain details of the individual's realty. However, if you know that an individual owned property and died intestate, you should be able to use administrations to determine the place of residence of the deceased and the name of the next of kin to whom the letters of administration were granted. It is possible that a search of their personal records – if they survive – might provide additional information.

PROBATE JURISDICTIONS BEFORE 1858

It is important to remember that wills were private documents and therefore can be difficult to locate and use. Where they have been deposited in the public domain, you are most likely to find them listed in local CROs, or diocesan record offices for the district that the property or owner was part of. They are often written in a difficult hand, and can be fragile. The National Archives has a large number of original wills in its collection and, aside from the probate records listed in section 7.3: Original wills, they can usually be found in private papers or exhibit series. However, they represent only a small proportion of the wills that passed through the various ecclesiastical courts.

Consequently, it might be easier to focus your attention on the process by which a deceased person's will was given official approval so that the executor or executrix of the will could begin honouring the bequests. This was known as the grant of probate, and until 1858 ecclesiastical courts were responsible for proving wills. However, there were various jurisdictions in operation, and the location and value of an individual's personal estate determined where probate was granted; to help you understand the pyramid system a little better, a summary is provided below.

- Probate for property held solely within an archdeaconry was granted in the archdeacon's court.
- Probate for property held within more than one archdeaconry but within one diocese was granted within the bishop's (diocesan) court.
- Probate for property over £5, held within more than one diocese or jurisdiction, was granted within the archbishop's court, known as the Prerogative court.

Plate 1 [left] Elsdon Tower, in Northumberland's national park. This 14th-century Tower house (or Pele tower) clearly reveals its defensive priorities in its castle-like details.

Plate 2 [below] An enclosure map (1817) for East Bergholt, Suffolk. As well as defining the allotments to be made, it serves as a guide to the type of holding (freehold, copyhold) for lands and property in the parish. Furthermore, names of owners are assigned to each plot, providing a virtual survey of the parish. This information can be crucial in determining how land was passed on. (MR 1/247)

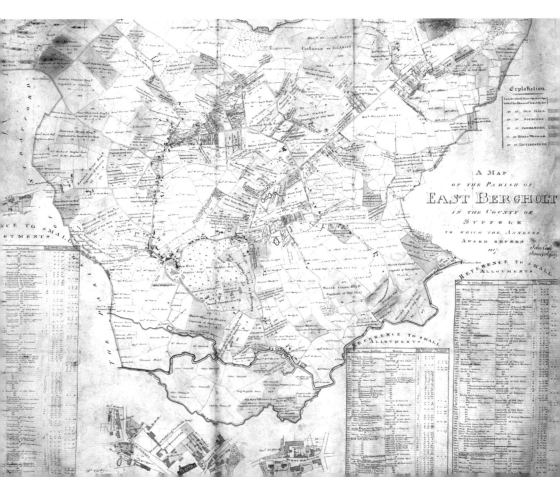

Plate 3 [above] A medieval hall house (13th century) in Stansfield, Suffolk. Now preserved by the Landmark Trust, it was once part of the village of Purton Green, which, like many former East Anglian villages, is no more.

Plate 4 [right] The Purton Green hall house interior, revealing its impressive timber framing.

Plate 5 [opposite, top] An attractive street of Tudor cottages at Bunyan's Mead, Elstow, Bedfordshire. The familiar black-and-white style inspired 'mock-Tudor' suburban architecture in the earlier 20th century, seen across Britain.

Plate 6 [opposite, below] Timber framing and wattle-and-daub walls. This house is in Lavenham, Suffolk, a village much celebrated for its vernacular medieval buildings.

Plate 7 [opposite, top] The distinctive golden hue of Cotswold limestone captures the sense of buildings in harmony with landscape. The village here is Stanton.

Plate 8 [opposite, below] Otley Hall, near Ipswich, Suffolk. The transition from wood to brick in building materials is reflected in the imposing chimney of this 16th-century moated house.

Plate 9 [left] An extract from the court roll of the manor of East Ham (now a London suburb), 1704. The entry relates to the discharge of a mortgage on a property in Church Street, originally made in 1639, worth £800. (SC 2/172/20)

Plate 10 [below] A robust North Country longhouse, complete with sandstone roof tiles, near Gunnerside, Swaledale, North Yorkshire.

Plate 11 [above] Georgian buildings may be the grand townhouses of London, Edinburgh and Bath; but often they are on a more intimate scale, as with these examples in Farnham, Surrey.
Plate 12 [right] Two elaborate Georgian doorways in Dublin, a city filled with architectural gems from the period.
Plate 13 [opposite, top] Victorian villas in Ealing, West London. They are testament to the suburban self-confidence of the expandiing middle class.
Plate 14 [opposite, below] These colourful terraced homes, in Appledore, Devon, were originally built for fishermen and ship-builders.

Plate 15 [above] An archetypal image of industrial Britain: terraced coal miners' cottages in the Derwent Valley, County Durham

Plate 16 [below] Old buildings, new uses. Reclaiming industrial spaces for living spaces, as with these apartments on London's dockside, gives new dimensions to house history.

- There were two Prerogative courts, one for the province of York and another for the province of Canterbury.
- Prerogative Court of York (PCY) covered the counties of Yorkshire (all ridings), Durham, Northumberland, Westmorland, Cumberland, Lancashire, Cheshire, Nottinghamshire and the Isle of Man.
- Prerogative Court of Canterbury (PCC) covered the rest of England and Wales.
- Probate for property held in both provinces was granted in both.
- Peculiars were also in existence that operated their own separate courts.

The records generated by archdeaconry, bishops (or diocesan) and peculiar courts were deposited at county or diocesan record offices, and those for the PCY are at the Borthwick Institute, part of the University of York. Records created under the PCC are deposited at the National Archives.

There are a number of books that can help you to identify the best place to begin your search for a will, and these are listed under 'Useful publications'. By the nineteenth century the PCC had become the main probate court for most wills in the southern province, as the £5 barrier (£10 in London) was rendered less of a restriction through inflation. However, you may well need to search in several different locations before you find an earlier will, if indeed one was made in the first place.

Searching for PCC wills and administrations   7.3

WILL REGISTERS BEFORE 1858

When a will was proved before the PCC, a copy was entered into a register. These survive for the period 1388–1858, in series PROB 11. The records for each year are arranged under the name of the principal registrar, and have been grouped in blocks of 16 pages. Each of these blocks is called a quire, and each quire was assigned a quire number. To provide a means of reference, basic initial alphabetical calendars of registered wills were created that assign quire numbers to wills. These are known as Register Books and serve as an index to PROB 11; they can be found in series PROB 12. However, the following finding aids have been produced based on information contained in PROB 12 and are, unless indicated, available on open access at both the National Archives and the FRC:

- 1383–1700 various printed indexes;
- 1701–49 printed/microfiche index (compiled by Friends of the National Archives);
- 1750–1800 printed index (compiled by the Society of Genealogists);
- 1801–52 no indexes – consult the 'calendars' in PROB 12 (printed volumes on open access at the FRC);

- 1853–8 alphabetically indexed calendars printed from microfiche, in PROB 12.

In most cases you will find a person's name under the year that probate was granted; this is then linked to the name of the registrar and the quire number in which the will is located. These can be matched in the series list for PROB 11 to obtain a document reference, although some of the indexes listed above provide this too. If you are unable to find a registered will, try looking a year or so after the date of death, as it could take some time for the registration process to be completed, especially if the will was complicated or contested.

However, with the introduction of documents online, the wills contained in the PCC registers can now be viewed via the National Archives website **www.nationalarchives.gov.uk** for a small fee – though users of the service at the National Archives or FRC can view the wills for free. Perhaps more importantly, there is a complete index, also available online, for all PCC-registered wills, based on the finding aids listed above, which you can search by name and date. This has revolutionized access to PCC wills, and provided you know the name of the person or people whom you suspect owned or leased your house, you can locate them very easily.

ADMINISTRATION BOOKS BEFORE 1858

Details of the letters of administration were recorded in Administration Act Books, which from 1559 to 1858 are in PROB 6. From 1796 the values of estates are also provided. These too can be searched by means of the Register Books in series PROB 12 and, as with the will registers, a series of finding aids is available:

- 1559–1660 various printed indexes;
- 1661–4 typescript indexes;
- 1665–1700 no indexes – consult the calendars in PROB 12;
- 1701–49 printed/microfiche index (compiled by Friends of the National Archives);
- 1751–1800 no indexes – consult the calendars in PROB 12 (there is a card index at the Society of Genealogists, which they will search for a fee);
- 1801–52 no indexes – consult the 'calendars' in PROB 12 (printed volumes on open access at the FRC);
- 1853–8 alphabetically indexed calendars printed from microfiche, in PROB 12.

ORIGINAL WILLS

Original wills that were brought before the PCC have been deposited in series PROB 1, PROB 10 and PROB 20–23. Where a probate act was granted and attached to the original will as evidence of probity, the grant was recorded in the Probate Act Book in series PROB 8 (where estate values are provided from 1796) and PROB 9. However, these will provide no additional information to the entries in PROB 11.

RELATED PROBATE MATERIAL AT THE NATIONAL ARCHIVES
In addition to wills and administrations, a variety of other records generated by the probate courts will be of passing interest to the house historian.

Probate inventories
Inventories were undertaken within a few days of death to protect the interests of any beneficiaries of the deceased, and the executors or administrators of the estate, against potential claims of fraud. Their purpose was to indicate the value of the deceased's personal estate, to ensure that there were sufficient possessions that could be sold to honour any legacies once all debts had been paid off. This process excluded realty, but the value of leases and mortgages would be part of the assessment.

Inventories would often comprise a list of the deceased person's personal effects, with a value assigned to each. The documents often took the form of a survey of all household contents, and can give an impression of the interior of a house, in terms of the number of inhabited rooms and the furniture, fixtures and fittings in each. Inventories can be found in the series listed in TABLE 7.1.

Table 7.1 *Locating probate inventories*

PROB 2 Inventories series I (1417–1660)	Index with series list
PROB 4 Parchment inventories (1661–1720)	Card index to names and places
PROB 5 Paper inventories (1661–1732)	Index with series list
PROB 32 Filed exhibits with inventories (1662–1720)	Index with series list
PROB 33 Indexes to exhibits (1683–1858)	Original indexes to exhibits in PROB 31 and PROB 37
PROB 3 Inventories series II (1702, 1718–82)	Index with series list
PROB 31 Exhibits, main series (1722–1858)	Index of wills; card indexes of names and places to inventories and other exhibits

You may also find inventories amongst the exhibit series in the law courts, as they were occasionally produced as evidence in cases. However, most inventories – where they survive – are likely to be held at the relevant CRO or diocesan archive; and most are now lost, since they were private documents.

Contested wills

Records of wills that were contested were subject to the ecclesiastical courts only if the material featured in the will related to personal effects, such as goods, chattels, cash and leases; freehold property that was under dispute was referred to the courts of equity (Chancery, Exchequer etc.), where a suit would be filed. Therefore, the records generated by contested wills in ecclesiastical courts will be relevant to the house historian only if the property in question was leased to another party.

If this is the case, you will need to identify whether there was a dispute, or 'cause', presented to the PCC. The best place to begin your search will be with the card index to the proceedings in PROB 18, covering the period 1661–1858; you may also find information in the will register itself in PROB 11, and annotations that a sentence in a PCC court, or decree in an equity court, was passed can be found in the Act Books in PROB 6–9 and the calendar to will registers in PROB 12. It is important to remember that the indexes will not be listed under the name of the deceased whose will was in dispute; as with the lay law courts, causes were filed and indexed under the name of the plaintiff, which you might not know. These annotations will give you the names of the contestants. The series listed in TABLE 7.2 will be worth examining for evidence.

PROBATE MATERIAL AFTER 1858

From 1858 the ecclesiastical courts ceased to register wills or grant administrations, and the civil Court of Probate took on this role. The Principal Probate Registry has copies of all wills and grants of administration that were made in England and Wales, and these can be viewed in central London at the Probate Search Room, First Avenue House (*see* 'Useful addresses'). A national calendar, which acts as a name index for the period 1858–1943, is available on fiche at both the National Archives and FRC.

SCOTLAND AND IRELAND

The method of disposal of a deceased person's estates in Scotland was different. All documents connected with the process were known as testaments, and included an inventory of the deceased's possessions. Where a will was included, the document was called a 'testament testamentor' – the equivalent to the English probate; and when no will was attached, a 'testament dative' was produced, similar to letters of administration. From 1515 to 1823 commissary courts handled the procedures, and indexes to the registers

Table 7.2 *Contested wills in ecclesiastical courts*

of testaments produced by these courts have been published up to 1801; other indexes are available at NAS from 1801 to 1823. From 1824 all commissary courts, bar Edinburgh, were abolished and the sheriffs courts handled the process. Indexes are available at NAS, but from 1875 a calendar of confirmations is the main means of reference, and records after 1984 are consulted at the Edinburgh Commissary Court. It is important to bear in mind that property could not be inherited through testaments until 1868, although trust dispositions and settlements did allow people to make provision for heirs. These are usually to be found recorded in the Court of Sessions register of deeds.

PRONI holds original wills from 1900 to 1994, and indexes to wills 1858–1984. Most original wills before 1900 were destroyed in Dublin in 1922, although local registries copied wills into bound books which can be accessed on microfilm in MIC.15C, and indexes to pre-1858 registers exist, as well as a card index to surviving original wills.

7.4   Death duty registers

From 1796 to 1805 death duty was payable on all legacies in a will worth over £20. After 1805 the liability was extended to include real estate, but until 1815 only if the terms of the will stipulated that the realty was to be sold to raise money to pay a legacy. Thereafter, all realty was assessed, which meant that a large number of house owners were liable for death duty and might be listed. However, before you can search the death duty registers, you will need to know the name of the deceased and the rough date when he or she died.

There are two series of records that you will need to consult. The first is series IR 27, which contains annual initial indexes to the registers themselves, arranged in date order by surname. Once you have located the relevant entry, make a note of the death duty reference number assigned to the individual, and then consult the series lists for the registers themselves in series IR 26. All indexes in IR 27 are available on microfilm, as are the death duty records themselves from 1796 to 1857; from 1858 to 1903 you will need to order the originals, which are stored offsite in Cheshire and take three working days to be delivered to Kew.

Death duty registers can be confusing at first glance, as a lot of information was entered in a series of columns. There is a National Archives research guide to help you to interpret the data, but the house historian should be able to extract the name of the deceased and his or her address plus details of the next of kin; details of any contests in law courts that delayed probate; plus notes made up to 50 years after the original entry about the beneficiaries and how the estate was actually distributed. For example, if a will stipulated that a house was to be sold on the death or remarriage of a spouse, then you will find its sale value in the register, along with the date of the distribution of the money and the amount of duty this incurred.

Death duty registers also serve as a means of determining where a will was proved or grant of administration was issued, and can therefore assist the process of locating the correct probate court.

Fife House, Brighton, Sussex

Fife House, Brighton, Sussex

Fife House (pictured on page 135 as it stands today), also known as No.1 Lewes Crescent, was one of the original houses built in the first decades of the nineteenth century in a high-class housing estate called Kemp Town, so named after its constructor Thomas Reed Kemp. As such, Fife House is of great architectural importance as one of only four intact Regency houses in the block, the remainder having been converted to flats or turned into office space. Yet little was known about its history, other than the fact that it was once owned by the 6th Duke of Devonshire, so further research in the archives revealed an astonishing amount of detail about the construction of the house and the life and times of its illustrious first owner.

Before 1823, when work on Lewes Crescent began, Brighton was a relatively small town, bordered to the east by open fields owned by Thomas Read Kemp. The town's popularity had grown in the early nineteenth century, but its development as a resort was hindered by a lack of adequate accommodation for its more 'fashionable' visitors. Encouraged by the success of George IV's architect, John Nash, who had built the Marylebone estate in and around Regent's Park to provide luxury accommodation in London, Thomas Kemp decided to cash in on the land that he owned by providing mansions for people of rank and wealth beside the sea, where many visitors decamped in summer to 'take the air'. In theory, his plans were spot on, but he was a poor businessman and in practice the enterprise crippled him financially.

The search for clues began in the local study centre in Brighton, where a great deal of information was gleaned from books and pamphlets. These, in turn, led to original newspapers, which were full of reports of Kemp's undertaking. Excavation for the foundations of the estate began in 1823, and most of the facades were completed by 1828. Yet the rest of the properties were left incomplete. This was standard building practice of the day, so that prospective buyers could then specify room size and layout. However, the construction of the estate met problems from the outset.

A series of mishaps befell the venture in the first year of construction, and fate dealt a particularly cruel hand to Nos. 1 and 3 Lewes Crescent. They were plagued by disaster in November 1824, when a fire and storm within five days of each other conspired to totally destroy the original facades erected by Kemp, leaving No.2 Lewes Crescent standing eerily alone. The local newspaper, the *Brighton Herald*, carried vivid reports of both calamities.

SATURDAY, NOVEMBER 20, 1824
Fire at Kemp Town. – On Thursday evening, about a quarter-past eight o'clock, one of the unfinished houses, at the extreme western end of Kemp Town, was discovered to be on fire. The alarm was given by some Blockade-men on duty near the spot; and, in the course of a short time, the town engines were at the scene of danger. The fire, which was supposed to have originated from the inattention of the workmen employed on the building, quickly reduced everything the interior presented of a combustible nature to a heap of ruins: leaving only the bare blackened walls as testimonial of its fury. At one time, the utmost apprehension was felt for the safety of the adjoining buildings, which were partially ignited by the heat and falling sparks; fortunately however, they escaped. Nothing could exceed the terrific grandeur of the scene of mischief. Situated on the verge of the cliff, it might have been observed for a considerable distance. – The house was of the largest class; and being a mere

skeleton as to its interior, the burning element could be plainly seen making the ponderous joints and rafters its prey. A few minutes after nine, the roof gave way with a tremendous crash. About half-past 10 o'clock, the fire had so far abated as to give every probability that its ravages would be extended no farther. A vast number of persons were present, who behaved extremely well on the occasion ... The house burnt was the third in the western wing of the Crescent, and was in a greater state of forwardness than either of the others in the wing; and in which the men were preparing the sashes, sash frames, &c. designed for the adjoining buildings: these, together with a quantity of deals, and some valuable chests of carpenters' tools, were totally burnt and destroyed. About midnight, when the fire was nearly extinguished, a portion of the 14-inch party-wall of one of the adjoining houses, (which was nearly red-hot) gave way; had this happened earlier, in all probability the fire would have extended to the other buildings. It was providential that the wind, which had fallen, carried the ignited embers in a contrary direction. A part of the back wall of the house which had suffered, has fallen; but the front wall, though cracked, is standing. The joiners, we understand, were in the practice of working in the house by candlelight. The only accident we have heard of is, that one of the watchmen (Haws) fell into a hole, dug out for the foundation of a house, and dislocated his hip-bone; but which was shortly after reduced. The High Constable, and several other persons, had similar falls; but without sustaining any serious injury. The house, we believe, belonged to Mr. Ingledew. – We are happy to state that the property was insured.

So not only did the newspaper report the fire, it also offered a fascinating insight into the construction process as well. Within five days, reporters were back at the scene.

SATURDAY, NOVEMBER 27, 1824
The Late Storm – It is our duty this week to record the appalling effects of the most severe storm that has visited these parts within the memory of the oldest inhabitant. On Monday evening, after a sharp and chilling day, a brisk gale sprung up from the S.W. and which, during the night, considerably increased. Towards daylight on Tuesday morning, it became calmer for a short time, when, again, increasing and joining its powers with the full spring-tide, the fury of the elementary alliance made the stoutest heart tremble. It was high water shortly after one o'clock, and the wind blowing directly ashore on the flood, and the rain descending in torrents. At this moment, the scene that the beach presented verified all those ideas that the most romantic fancy could see of seaside horrors ... We reached Kemp Town in time to become spectators of the destructive fury of the tempest. The first house, a large and elegant structure, at the western end, within one of the blocks at [the] scene of conflagration, had been partially unroofed by the wind before we arrived – a more violent gust came – the carapace wavered for a moment, and, in the next, [it became] a heap of shapeless ruins. Deprived of collateral support on the one side by fire, and the other by the tempest, the intermediate house now looked an unresisting and devoted victim to the storm. Contrary however, to the expectations of all, it survived the gale without sustaining serious injury. At the very instant that the house we have spoken of fell to the ground, Mr. Ingledew, the proprietor of that and the adjoining property, and his workmen, were on the roofs of the different houses, raising temporary securities of boards to prevent the entrance of the winds which threatened to unroof the major part of the new-built town. Their situation was one of imminent peril; but providentially their efforts succeeded without their receiving personal injury.

Building continued to struggle along unevenly, but Kemp continued to make no return on the venture. To reduce his losses, he sold many of the plots to the renowned builder and architect Thomas Cubitt. It is he who was credited with reviving the estate, as the *Brighton Herald* reported in 1892:

An old resident of Kemp Town has sent some notes about the earlier history ... Between 60–70 years ago Kemp Town was in a state of coma. The fine mansions that now exist were then carcasses only, with the winds howling through them, and so they would have remained for many a long day had not the late Mr Cubitt, that Prince of builders, seized hold of Kemp Town, roused it up and infused it with life and hope. Thenceforth for 30 years – until his death in 1855 – Cubitt's firm became an institution at the east end of Brighton.

Yet even Cubitt found the estate difficult to manage. In November 1827 the *Brighton Herald* reported the collapse of a scaffold on one of Cubitt's houses, when four men were plunged to the ground from the top storey, yet miraculously all survived. The end of the building phase was in sight, and on 26 July 1828 the *Brighton Herald* reported: 'We understand that most of the houses in Kemp Town, if not the whole of them, will, in the course of another year, be finished, and fit for occupancy.' Yet even with such an illustrious builder on board, there was still a very definite delay in taking up the houses; by the end of 1828 only 11 out of 105 houses were occupied, while the rest of the properties remained encased in scaffolding. Luckily, one of the first purchasers was William Spencer Cavendish, the 6th Duke of Devonshire. In 1828 he purchased the shell of 14 Chichester Terrace, and in January 1829 the adjoining No.1 Lewes Crescent was purchased from Messrs. T. & L. Cubitt for the sum of £3,650, the last payment being made in

November that year according to documents in the Chatsworth archives. The two houses were then knocked together and modifications made to greatly extend the internal space. Nevertheless, it must have seemed a rather forlorn property, as the Duke recalled in his private journal, even though he clearly appreciated its potential.

Are we to despise it because it is small? I have never reputed the selection of it, though surrounded by the shells and carcasses of houses that comprise Kemp Town. Much less smoke than at Brighton prevails here, and the healthiest air and the refreshing breezes compensate for the torment of wind that too often rages and nearly blows away the studious govern-esses, who constantly pace up and down with book in hand in the enclosure. The southeast aspect of the house is its greatest merit: it has every ray of sunshine in winter; and in summer, on the longest day, the sun has ceased to come into the rooms by two o'clock.

The Duke's journal is a remarkable document, as it describes in detail the contents of each room, as well as revealing how many of the rooms were decorated. Yet it was written in 1845, and within a couple of years he had spent a large amount of money improving the interior, sparing no expense. Paintings subsequently uncovered on the walls and ceilings are by John Dibley Crace, and were commissioned by the Duke. A letter survives in the Chatsworth archives from John Crace and Company to the Duke that includes an interior design, along with other written proposals for work on the property. Indeed, the Duke's account books at Chatsworth show that over £1,000 was paid to the Craces for work undertaken in 1848–9. The results were spectacular, and were reported in full in our trusty friend, the *Brighton Herald*:

SATURDAY, JANUARY 13, 1849
His Grace the Duke of Devonshire gave his first grand entertainment this season last night at his mansion in Kemp Town. The house has undergone considerable alteration since last year, His Grace having spared no expense to render it one of the most charming marine residences in the country. To attempt to do justice to the magnificence of the style in which the drawing-rooms are finished, would be impossible. In fact, all the arrangements are so complete, that a moment's glance attests the exquisite taste which has been displayed by the Noble Duke and the able manner in which his instructions were carried out by Messrs. Crace and Son, of London, to whom the task was delegated ...

Yet the extensive redecorations mask a far more tragic episode in the house's early history. 1 Lewes Crescent was the scene of a terrible accident in 1833, when the Duke's invalid nephew was dropped down a flight of stairs and died of his injuries. An inquest was held, which exonerated the poor servant responsible for the death, and an account was printed in the *Brighton Herald*.

SATURDAY, JUNE 3, 1833
An inquest was held at the Bristol Hotel on Monday, on the body of Hon. Charles Leveson Gower, aged 16 years; a son of Lord Granville. The deceased had long been severely afflicted with a paralytic affection, which had deprived him the use of his limbs. It appeared from the evidence, that on Thursday last as the servant was carrying him downstairs he accidentally stumbled with the deceased, whose head came in contact with the pavement of the hall. From the injury thus sustained the deceased languished till Sunday morning when death put a period to his sufferings. The Jury returned a verdict of 'Death from paralysis, accelerated by the fall.' and entirely exculpated the servant from blame.

Nevertheless, the house remained one of the Duke's favourite haunts right up to his death in 1858, after which it left the family and passed to other private owners.

LEGAL DISPUTES

8

8.1 Introduction

PROPERTY AND THE LAW

House owners have not always enjoyed undisputed possession of their land or property. The English legal system can be complicated at the best of times, and even more so when property or inheritance is concerned. Proof of ownership was vital, if land was to be sold or passed on without challenge, and contested successions, sales or transfers were frequent, especially when families disagreed with the terms of an inheritance, settlement or will. Furthermore, there were many statutes in place that regulated and controlled the erection of new properties and the extension of old ones, and failure to comply often led to prosecution.

Fortunately for the modern house historian, if a little less fortunately for the contemporary house owner who was embroiled in legal action, disputes and prosecutions have left a trail for us to follow. A great deal about property descent can be learnt from the deposited records of the various courts into which civil litigation could be taken, including the names of previous owners, dates of sales and even construction dates. This chapter describes the procedures and records of the popular courts that were used by litigants to register and settle property disputes, and how you can search the records they generated for information on your house. However, a cautionary note should be sounded before you think about using legal records. Unless you know that a property dispute ended up in court, legal records are not going to be the best place to start looking for clues about the history of your house; and you will probably need to have a rough date in mind, plus the names of the parties concerned. Without this information, to find your property via a random search of the surviving records would require an enormous quantity of luck, or patience, or probably both.

THE ENGLISH LEGAL SYSTEM

It is fair to say that, for the beginner, the English legal system appears incredibly complicated. Therefore it is worth taking a little while to sketch out the basic ways in which a case might come to court, and the various courts that were available for litigants to take their complaints. Before 1875 there were two main branches of civil litigation that you will need to consider. Common law courts, such as King's Bench and the Court of Common Pleas, dispensed justice according to the 'common law' and ancient custom of the land, and as such awarded compensation or damages but were unable to enforce contracts that had been broken. This meant that they were less effective at solving property disputes that involved breach of trusts or wills. In comparison, the courts of equity, primarily Chancery and the Exchequer, were able to make judgments on the grounds of justice and conscience as opposed to 'law'. This meant that they were in a position to force remedial action to be taken, although they were not allowed to award damages.

In 1875 all these courts were abolished and a Supreme Court of Judicature was created with five divisions – Chancery, Common Pleas, Exchequer, King's (Queen's) Bench and Probate, Divorce and Admiralty. In 1881 the Common Pleas, King's (Queen's) Bench and Exchequer were amalgamated to form the King's (Queen's) Bench. Although cases could be heard in any division, and common law or equity rules applied whenever needed, the King's (Queen's) Bench heard most actions relating to contract, and Chancery usually dealt with land, trusts and mortgages. A brief summary is provided in TABLE 8.1.

Table 8.1 *The structure of civil law courts*

PRE-1875	
Common Law	King's Bench
	Common Pleas
	Exchequer of Pleas
	Chancery (Plea side)
Equity	Exchequer
	Chancery
Applied equity principles:	Star Chamber
	Requests
	Wards and Liveries
POST-1875	
Supreme Court of Judicature 5 divisions:	King's/Queen's Bench and Divorce
	Common Pleas
	Exchequer
	Chancery
	Probate, Admiralty
POST-1881	
Supreme Court of Judicature 3 divisions:	King's/Queen's Bench (Contracts)
	Chancery (Land, trusts, mortgages)
	Probate, Admiralty and Divorce

As the table demonstrates, a property dispute could end up in one of many places, and it was not unknown for a single dispute to move between courts during the course of the action, or indeed for a case to be started in more than one court. However, local newspapers can often provide clues as to which court heard a dispute, and legal papers in private hands can also give an indication of where to begin your research. Furthermore, many of the indexes to the equity courts are available online and can be searched for names via the catalogue.

8.2   Equity proceedings in Chancery

Thousands of equity cases were brought before the Court of Chancery each year to resolve disputes between individuals or parties, covering a wide range of topics such as disputed wills, legacies, estate administration and property transfers (*see* FIGURE 17). During the course of a court case, many different types of documents were created, and the most useful are described in the following sections. However, it is important to remember that all documentation for a single case was not filed together, but rather in separate series determined by the type of document, making it difficult to accurately collate all material relating to a single case. Furthermore, documents were filed under the name of the first listed plaintiff, so it can be very difficult to locate multi-party cases where the principal name is unknown – though the introduction of the catalogue has partly rectified this, as document descriptions often include more than just the first named individual. Party names also changed over time, especially in long cases where plaintiffs or defendants died and were succeeded by their relatives and descendants.

Not all cases came to a judgment or recorded conclusion, as they were often initially brought into Chancery in an attempt to force the defendant to settle out of court. Consequently, it can be difficult to locate a definite outcome for many cases.

PROCEEDINGS

To understand the records you will be using, it is important to understand the procedures used in the court. When a plaintiff wished to start proceedings in the Court of Chancery, he would instruct a lawyer to file an initial 'bill of complaint' with the Lord Chancellor, who technically presided over the court. The bill of complaint stated the charges that the plaintiff wanted the defendant to answer, and a justification for bringing an equity lawsuit as opposed to a case under common law. It would commonly include the name, occupation and residence of the plaintiff. The body of the bill would then provide specifics of the complaint, and this is where you will find information about property or disputed transfers.

mplaint of Thomas Armstrong and also to the Exceptions taken by the said Complainant to the
already saved and reserved all manner of Benefit and Advantage of Exception for further
Complainant to her former Answer doth answer and say she hath been informed and bel...
is last Will and Testament in Writing of such Date Purport and Effect as in the said Bill
same but saith She doth not know the same of her own knowledge she leaves the Complainant
of her Belief except what arises from the length of time that has elapsed since her said
set forth And this Defendant saith she believes that at the time her said Husband went to sea
of such Particulars as in the Bill are mentioned but to what amount in the whole this Defendant is
Charles Allison's house at North Shields in the County of Northumberland then in this
situate at Cullercoats in the Bill mentioned And saith that she continued in the possess
as were lodged and deposited therein for near eighteen months after her said Husband
me she left the said house and locked up the Door with all the Furniture and personal Esta
der to go to London to make Enquiry after her said Husband and to learn whether he
ned and verily believes the Complainant or some other Person or Persons by his direction
the personal Estate and Effects of her said Husband therein and also of a considerable part
roperty of this Defendant which as this Defendant hath been informed and believes were sold
the last left her said Husband's house at North Shields as aforesaid she took away with her
a Policy of Insurance upon the Ship The Globe for two hundred pounds One Silver Sauce Boat One
air of Tea Tongs part of the personal Estate of her said Husband which are all now in this Defendan
set forth any other of the particulars of the Furniture personal Estate and Effects of her said
did not take any Inventory of the same before she left the said house and had not any mean
that according to the best of her knowledge Remembrance and Belief All the Furniture and Effects
nt to Sea on his said last Voyage consisted of six Chairs two Tables a Looking Glass a Tea Board
d Saucers two Basons a Pint and half a Pint a Tea Pot and two silver Spoons (which
llercoats) And this Defendant saith that the said Tea Kettle six Cups and Saucers two Basons
her said Husband taken from his said house at Cullercoats by her this Defendant or any oth
her said Husband's house at North Shields when she this Defendant quitted such last mentio
rooms above mentioned to be in this Defendant's Custody And this Defendant saith that some
particular she this Defendant doth not remember nor can set forth She this Defendant
with certainty say) of William Patterson of Cullercoats also four Shillings of Dinah Todd in th
neral Tenements part of the real Estate of her said husband but this Defendant doth

Figure 17 An extract from a Chancery proceeding brought by Thomas Armstrong against Jane Allison. The document shown is Allison's answer to Armstrong's bill of complaint, where she defends her actions in 'rescuing' personal possessions from her deceased husband's houses in Cullercoats. Armstrong is the executor of the deceased's estate – and also Allison's son-in-law. (C 12/2118/5)

Once a bill of complaint was filed, the defendant was required to provide a written 'answer' to the charges, and lay any counter charges against the plaintiff. The plaintiff might counter with a replication, and the defendant with a rejoinder. In essence this process, known as pleading, defined the limits of the case so that a recommendation could be made by one of the Masters of Chancery, who considered the case and reported back to the Lord Chancellor. Witness statements (depositions) were then taken and evidence (exhibits) brought into court to help the masters make a decision about the merits and legality of the case and pass this up to the Lord Chancellor. Once a verdict had been reached, a decree or order was issued settling the matter.

8.2

Chancery proceedings date from the late fourteenth century until 1875, when business was transferred to the Supreme Court of Judicature. The size, scope and detail of the documents varied over time, but you will find that, apart from the very earliest, they were written in English and should be legible. However, you may find that the repetitive nature of the legal language can be confusing at first, especially if the original bill was lost and you are left with later papers that contain unfathomable references to earlier documents. The records are arranged chronologically and are located in several National Archives series. From the mid-seventeenth century there were six clerks working for the masters, and proceedings for a single case could have been filed with any of them. To ensure that you have not missed any paperwork, you should search for the case within all six divisions. A summary of the National Archives series is provided in TABLE 8.2.

Most of these indexes are arranged by the name of the plaintiff, or the first listed plaintiff in a multi-party case, and unless you know this name, it can be virtually impossible to determine from the indexes alone whether a case is relevant or not.

The indexes to earlier cases in series C 1–3 are available in the reading rooms and provide a brief outline of the case, but still rely on names as a means of reference. However, the descriptions of each item in these series are fully listed online, so a keyword search of the catalogue can reveal not only the name of the principal plaintiff but also of the defendant, and any places listed in the lawsuit. Furthermore, the National Archives is involved with the creation of an Equity Pleadings database, at present focusing on records in series C 6. This is available online at www.nationalarchives.gov.uk and can be searched by name, place or subject matter.

DEPOSITIONS AND AFFIDAVITS

Once the pleadings had produced a final case to be answered, the Masters of Chancery collected evidence so that they could make an equitable decision. Depositions and affidavits played an important part in this process and are a good source of evidence about the background to the case and, in cases of

Table 8.2 *Chancery proceedings and relevant indexes*

The following series are available via the catalogue.

c.1386–1558	C 1	Early Chancery Proceedings	*List and Index, vols XII, XVI, XX, XXIX, XXXVIII, XLVIII, L, LI, LIV, LV*
1558–c.1640	C 2	Chancery Proceedings Series I	Printed calendars for Elizabeth and Charles I, partial indexes for James I
1558–c.1660	C 3	Chancery Proceedings Series II	*List and Index, vols VII, XXIV, XXX*
VARIOUS DATES	C 4	Miscellaneous Proceedings	Index to first 46 bundles

Indexes for these series available in the reading rooms, but not searchable online unless indicated.

SIX CLERKS PRE-1714	C 5	Bridges (1613–1714)	*List and Index, vols XXIX, XLII, XLIV, XLV,* searchable online
	C 6	Collins (1625–1714)	Indexes available, partial coverage in Equity Pleadings database
	C 7	Hamilton (1620–1714)	
	C 8	Mitford (1570–1714)	
	C 9	Reynardson (1649–1714)	Partially searchable on the catalogue
	C 10	Whittington (1640–1714)	

Indexes for these series available in the reading rooms, but not searchable on the catalogue.

VARIOUS SIX CLERKS POST-1714	C 11	Series I (1714–58)
	C 12	Series II (1758–1800)
	C 13	Series III (1800–42)
	C 14	Modern (1842–52)
	C 15	Modern (1853–60)
	C 16	Modern (1861–75)
	C 18	Miscellaneous (1844–64)
COURT OF JUDICATURE 1875 ONWARDS	J 54	Chancery Division

For the last row: Index for 1876–90 in IND 1/2218–26

property disputes, include detailed descriptions.

Depositions were written statements from deponents, namely individuals with knowledge of a dispute who were selected by both parties. A list of pertinent questions was compiled, known as an interrogatory. Sworn, signed and dated statements were then made in answer to the interrogatories and were used as evidence in the case. Affidavits were voluntary statements made on oath during the case. TABLE 8.3 provides a summary of the National Archives series, broken down in terms of Town Depositions (sworn in London) and Country Depositions (sworn elsewhere).

It is important to remember that the depositions were listed by the name of the plaintiff, rather than that of the deponent. If you know only the name of the deponent, then the Bernau Index is a good place to start looking. This is a composite index to the names of many parties in Chancery equity cases, including deponents. It can be consulted on microfilm at the Latter Day

Table 8.3 *Chancery depositions, affidavits and interrogatories and relevant indexes*

EARLY DEPOSITIONS	
C 1 and 4 (1386–1534)	Indexes available (with proceedings)

TOWN DEPOSITIONS	
C 24 (1534–1853)	Indexes IND 1/16759 and 1/9115–21
C 15–16, J 54 (1854–80)	Indexes available (with proceedings)
J 17 (1880–1925)	Indexes IND 1/16748–52

COUNTRY DEPOSITIONS	
C 21 (1558–1649)	Indexes available, searchable online
C 22 (1649–1714)	Indexes available, searchable online
C 11–14 (1714–1880)	Indexes available (with proceedings)
J 17 (1880–1925)	Indexes IND 1/16748–52

AFFIDAVITS	
C 31 and 41 (1611–1875)	Indexes IND 1/14545–67; entry marked with a cross – original affidavit in C 31; no cross – copies in C 41 (1615–1747)
J 4 (1876 onwards)	Various indexes in IND 1

INTERROGATORIES	
C 25 (1598–1852)	Mainly relating to Town examinations, and separated from the relevant depositions

Saints Family History Centres and at the Society of Genealogists, and publications that offer guidance on interpreting references obtained from Bernau are listed under 'Useful publications'. However, you need to copy the Bernau reference accurately, in full, to assist conversion into a modern National Archives reference.

DECREE AND ORDER BOOKS

During a case the court might issue an order to one party or another, and when it reached a final decision it would issue a decree in favour of the victorious party. Before 1544 decrees and orders were sometimes enrolled on the back of the bill of complaint; between 1544 and 1875 they were recorded in Decree and Order Entry Books, in series C 33, and thereafter in J 15. Decrees and Orders are usually written in English, and will tell you the outcome of the case; this will be of use to determine where the property ended up after the verdict. You should also be provided with the date that the hearing took place, plus information on when depositions or affidavits were recorded.

There are two sequences known as A and B books listing suits by plaintiff, and until Trinity term 1629 both A and B books list suits from A to Z. From 1629 entries for plaintiffs A–K are in the A books, and entries for plaintiffs

L–Z are in the B books. In 1932 the A and B books were amalgamated. Indexes to these volumes, from 1546, are available on open access.

Decrees could be enrolled at extra cost, and are more likely to survive in cases involving property so that a permanent record was preserved. Decree rolls (1534–1903) are in c 78 and are indexed in IND 1/16950–61B; supplementary rolls are in c 79, with indexes in IND 1/16960B. A place-name index exists in IND 1/16960A. Appeals against enrolled decrees and orders take the form of petitions and are in c 36 (1774–1875, indexes IND 1/15029–47) and J 53 (1876–1925, indexes IND 1/15048–51 and 1/15282).

However, before starting a search of these records, it is important to bear in mind that the majority of cases (approximately 90 per cent) never reached the stage where an order or decree might have been issued, and therefore the pleadings and depositions might be the only surviving evidence.

ARBITRATION AND APPEALS

Occasionally, the Masters of Chancery acted as arbitrators, and you may find reports on such decisions in series c 38 (1544–1875) and J 57 (1875–1962). Indexes are available between 1606 and 1875 (IND 1/1878–2028, 10700–41 and 14919–73), with many other IND 1 volumes for the post-1875 period. Awards were also enrolled in c 33 (1544–1694), and un-enrolled awards are in c 42 (1694–1844), although there are no indexes to this series.

Equity cases in the Court of Exchequer   8.3

Another court where property disputes could end up was the Exchequer, which dealt with equity cases from the mid-sixteenth century until 1841, when such actions were transferred to Chancery. The procedures were the same as in Chancery, namely that a process of pleading, based on bills and answers, created a simplified case that then required the presentation of evidence to allow a final decree to be made. In theory, the plaintiff was a debtor of the Crown, but this was usually a fiction designed to allow the action to be brought before the court.

Although the records of Exchequer equity cases are similar to those in Chancery, the means of reference are much harder to use. Fewer indexes exist, and far less material is available online for keyword searching. If you suspect your property once formed part of a case in the Exchequer, the series described in this section might contain relevant material. However, one of the main ways of picking up information is through the country depositions in E 134, which were thoroughly listed and are readily available to search online as they contain not only the names of the parties concerned, but also detailed descriptions of the case and mentions of any disputed property.

Many National Archives series contain information relating to equity

Table 8.4 *Exchequer proceedings and relevant indexes*

Bedford, Buckingham, Cambridge, Cheshire, Cornwall, Cumberland, Devon, Essex, Hampshire, Hereford, Hertford, Huntingdon, Kent, Lancashire, Lincoln, Middlesex, and all Welsh counties	Elizabeth I	1558–1603	IND 1/16820
	James I	1603–1625	IND 1/16822
	Charles I	1625–1649	IND 1/16824
	Interregnum	1649–1660	IND 1/16826
	Charles II	1660–1674	IND 1/16828
		1669–1685	IND 1/16830
	James II	1685–1688	IND 1/16832
	William & Mary	1688–1694	IND 1/16834
	William III	1694–1702	IND 1/16836
	Anne	1702–1714	IND 1/16836
	George I	1714–1727	IND 1/16838
	George II	1727–1760	IND 1/16840
	George III	1760–1801	IND 1/16842
		1776–1820	IND 1/16844
		1779–1820	IND 1/16846
	George IV	1820–1827	IND 1/16848
	William IV	1827–1837	IND 1/16850
	Victoria	1837–1841	IND 1/16852
Berkshire, Derby, Dorset, Durham, Leicester, Monmouth, Norfolk, Northampton, Northumberland, Nottingham, Oxford, Rutland, Shropshire, Somerset, Stafford, Suffolk, Surrey, Sussex, Warwick, Westmorland, Wiltshire, Worcester, York	Elizabeth I	1558–1603	IND 1/16821
	James I	1603–1625	IND 1/16823
	Charles I	1625–1649	IND 1/16825
	Interregnum	1649–1660	IND 1/16827
	Charles II	1660–1674	IND 1/16829
		1669–1685	IND 1/16831
	James II	1685–1688	IND 1/16833
	William & Mary	1688–1694	IND 1/16835
	William III	1694–1702	IND 1/16837
	Anne	1702–1714	IND 1/16837
	George I	1714–1727	IND 1/16839
	George II	1727–1760	IND 1/16841
	George III	1760–1801	IND 1/16843
		1776–1820	IND 1/16845
		1779–1820	IND 1/16847
	George IV	1820–1827	IND 1/16849
	William IV	1827–1837	IND 1/16851
	Victoria	1837–1841	IND 1/16853

cases and proceedings in the Court of Exchequer, but the most useful are listed in TABLE 8.4. You should consult the relevant research guide prepared by the National Archives for further information on the subject.

PROCEEDINGS

There are two series of bills and answers. E 111 mainly contains strays from other courts, and covers the reigns of Henry VII to Elizabeth I; but it is listed and available to search online.

E 112 contains the main series of bills and answers, and dates from Elizabeth's reign to the cessation of the court's business in 1841 (4 Victoria). The documents are arranged by the reign of the monarch in which the action was first filed, and grouped into counties. These are then indexed by means of contemporary bill books.

Replications and rejoinders that have strayed from E 112 can be found in E 193; there is a partial index post-1700 in OBS 1/752.

DEPOSITIONS AND AFFIDAVITS

Exchequer depositions taken in London (the equivalent of Chancery town depositions) are stored in series E 133. There is an original calendar for pieces E 133/1/1 to E 133/10/1071 in E 501/10, which covers the period 2 Elizabeth I to 45 Elizabeth I and is arranged in chronological order. This is on open access, and will provide the county, date and legal term where the deposition was made, the suit number, the names of the plaintiff and defendant, and most importantly the subject of the deposition. The document reference is obtained by adding the bundle number and suit number to E 133. The period 1603–1841 is not so well served, but there is a list on open access that provides the bundle number, piece number and the names of the plaintiff and defendant for pieces E 133/11/1 to E 133/164. The list is arranged alphabetically by name of plaintiff. However, the descriptions are available online, which will enable you to search for defendants as well as plaintiffs through the catalogue.

However, Exchequer country depositions are perhaps the most informative and easily accessible documents. These were taken by Exchequer commissioners, and are now stored at the National Archives in series E 134. There are topographical calendars available on open access, which provide the names of the plaintiff and defendant, plus an outline of the case. The commissions themselves are in E 178, and can also be found via the indexed calendars for E 134; they provide the interrogatories on which the depositions were taken. Both series are available for searching online, and are probably the quickest way to find a case that might be relevant to your property.

Once you have identified a case, the documents will provide a list of statements in answer to the interrogatories. They often provide detailed descriptions of property, property boundaries, owners and occupiers; local events that impacted upon property; and disputed trusts, wills and property transfers.

E 111 is another area in which you should look, as it contains special commissions, interrogatories and depositions, and can be usefully searched via the catalogue. Affidavits can be found in E 103 (1774–1841) and E 218 (1695–1822). There are partial indexes for E 103, but none for E 218. Some affidavits relate to surveys requested by either party following an Exchequer commission, and can contain details of property boundaries.

DECREES AND ORDERS

At each stage of the case, an order was made so that the next stage could proceed. An order was entered in a minute book (E 161), written out (E 128 and

131) and registered (E 123–5 and 127). Sometimes the orders can provide additional information about the case.

Where a final judgment was reached, a decree was produced. As with orders, they were first entered in a minute book (E 162), written (E 128 and 130) and registered (E 123–4 and 126). A summary of surviving indexes to these series is provided in TABLE 8.5.

Table 8.5 *Exchequer decrees and orders and relevant indexes*

E 111/56	Entry book, decrees and orders (Philip and Mary)	No index
E 123	Entry book, decrees and orders series I (1559–1605)	Manuscript index; also IND 1/16897
E 124	Entry book, decrees and orders series II (1603–25)	Manuscript index to 1610
E 125	Entry book, decrees and orders series III (1625–61)	IND 1/16854–60
E 126	Entry book, decrees and orders series IV (1604–1841)	IND 1/16862–6
E 127	Entry book, decrees and orders series V (1661–1841)	IND 1/16860–1 and 16867–91
E 128	Decrees and orders files (1562–1662)	OBS 1/424 (1634–42); thereafter use the indexes to the entry books
E 130	Original decrees files (1660–1841)	IND 1/16862–6
E 131	Original orders files (1660–1842)	IND 1/16860–1, 16867–91

In 1819 Adam Martin published an alphabetical index to entry books from 1558 which covers some of the material contained in series E 123–7. The details of this publication can be found under 'Useful publications'.

8.4 Other equity-based courts

In addition to Chancery and the Exchequer, other courts developed that followed the principle of equity when reaching decisions. The main two are described below; both the Court of Requests and the Court of Star Chamber were offshoots of the King's Council. Furthermore, the Court of Wards and Liveries may contain some information about contested administrations of the estates of Crown tenants-in-chief.

COURT OF REQUESTS

The court was established in 1483 with the aim of providing the poor with access to justice. Relevant cases heard by the court, from this date until its records end in 1642, cover disputes over title to property and contracts, including assignments of dower. The procedure of the court was very similar to that of Chancery, with a process of pleading producing a simplified case. Evidence in the form of depositions and affidavits was collected for the judges to consider; they determined an outcome on equitable grounds, and issued orders and decrees. Documents produced in this process were predominantly written in English.

Proceedings can be found in the series REQ 2, along with attached depositions. There are some indexes, usually by the name of the suitor and by place for the Elizabethan period, but a large number of documents after 1603 are unlisted, and trying to find relevant material can be time consuming and ultimately fruitless. A summary of the series is provided in TABLE 8.6.

Table 8.6 *Court of Requests proceedings and relevant indexes*

1485–1547	REQ 2/1–13	Listed in *List and Index XXI*, index in *List and Index Supplementary, VII, vol. 1*
1547–1553	REQ 2/14–19	Listed in *List and Index XXI*, index in *List and Index Supplementary, VII, vol. 1*
1553–1558	REQ 2/20–25	Listed in *List and Index XXI*, index in *List and Index Supplementary, VII, vol. 1*
1558–1603	REQ 2/26–136	Listed in *List and Index XXI*, index in *List and Index Supplementary, VII, vol. 1*
	REQ 2/137–156	Listed in *Aitkin's Calendar*, index in *List and Index Supplementary, VII, vol. 1*
	REQ 2/157–294	Manuscript list, index in *List and Index Supplementary, VII, vols 2 and 3*
	REQ 2/269–386	None
1603–1625	REQ 2/295–311	Manuscript list, index in *List and Index Supplementary, VII, vol. 4*
	REQ 2/387 424	Manuscript list, index in *List and Index Supplementary, VII, vol. 4*
	REQ 2/425–485	None
1625–1649	REQ 2/486–806	None
Various dates	REQ 2/807–829	None

All other relevant material will be in REQ 1, although it will be of limited use to a house historian. Decree and Order Books are in REQ 1/1–38 and 209, with drafts in REQ 1/39–103. Affidavits are in REQ 1/119–49, with contemporary indexes in REQ 1/118 and 1/150.

COURT OF STAR CHAMBER

The court was established in 1485 and abolished in 1641, and was named after the stars that decorated the ceiling of the room in which the court sat at Westminster. Aside from its judicial work, it heard cases that involved land enclosures and contested property rights, in particular boundary disputes. As with the Court of Requests, it used the principle of equity to reach a decision, and therefore pleadings, evidence, orders and decrees were produced, mainly written in English.

Proceedings are arranged by the reign of the monarch in which they were first filed in court. They can be found in the series listed in TABLE 8.7.

Table 8.7 Court of Star Chamber proceedings and relevant indexes

Henry VII Records: 1485–1509	STAC 1	Series list, index in *List and Index Supplementary series IV*
Henry VIII Records: *c.*1450–1625	STAC 2	Series list, index in *List and Index Supplementary series IV*
Edward VI Records: Hen VII–Eliz	STAC 3	Series list, index in *List and Index Supplementary series I*
Mary Records: Hen VII–Eliz	STAC 4	Series list, index in *List and Index Supplementary series IV*
Elizabeth I Records: 1558–1601	STAC 5 STAC 7	Four manuscript lists, index in *List and Indexes* *Supplementary series IV* Manuscript list
James I Records: 1601–25	STAC 8	Manuscript list, index in *Barnes index* (three coded volumes by party and place)
Charles I Records: 1625–41	STAC 9	Manuscript list

A large amount of supplementary material has now been lost. For example, no Decree and Order Books survive, although very rare endorsements on the proceedings have been found. You may find some relevant items in court miscellanea in STAC 10, but this has not been listed and so can be difficult to use.

COURT OF WARDS AND LIVERIES

When a tenant-in-chief died, an inquisition post mortem was conducted to determine whether the Crown was entitled to feudal dues from the land, estate or property that the tenant held. When an heir was found to be under age, the Crown was legally entitled to administer the estate until majority was reached, which was usually 21, and enjoy the profits. The right to these profits could be, and often were, sold by the Crown, and if they fell into private hands, disputes could arise. To settle issues, a Court of Wards and Liveries was set up, and operated between 1540 and 1660. Like the Court of Requests and Star Chamber, it operated under the rules of equity, and therefore documents were written in English. If your property once formed part of a large estate of a tenant-in-chief of the Crown, these records are worth investigating for evidence.

Pleadings are in WARD 13, and there are indexes in IND 1/10218–21; supplementary pleadings are in WARD 22; depositions can be found in WARD 3; and decrees, orders and affidavits are in WARD 2. Of particular value will be the surveys of tenants' lands in WARD 5. The miscellaneous books of the court are in WARD 9, and there are several published volumes relating to the miscellanea of the court available on open access.

Equity courts of semi-autonomous jurisdictions 8.5

The Palatinates of Chester, Durham and Lancaster and the Duchy of Lancaster operated their own equity courts where property disputes could be heard. The records are summarized in TABLE 8.8.

8.6

Table 8.8 *Equity records of semi-autonomous jurisdictions*

Palatinate of Chester	Pleadings CHES 15 Depositions CHES 12 Decrees and Orders CHES 14 and 13 (originals)
Palatinate of Durham	Pleadings DURH 2 Depositions and Interrogatories DURH 7 Decrees and Orders DURH 5 and 6 (drafts)
Palatinate of Lancaster	Bills PL 6 Answers PL 7 Replications PL 8 Depositions PL 10 Decrees and Orders PL 11
Duchy of Lancaster	Pleadings DL 49 Depositions DL 3, 4 and 48 Decrees and Orders DL 5 and 6 (drafts)

Equity court exhibits 8.6

In addition to the official records created to support each party's case – such as the depositions and affidavits described above – other evidence was often required, and was brought into court to help the officials reach a decision. In property disputes, this meant proof of title to land or evidence of prior legal agreements. However, at the conclusion of the case the litigants sometimes failed to retrieve this evidence, and the courts thus accumulated a vast collection of title deeds, legal papers, family trees, manorial records, maps, plans and other such material. These have been deposited at the National Archives and are an amazing source for the house historian. Furthermore, they can (in theory) be linked to the cases that generated them, providing even more information about the litigants concerned.

CHANCERY MASTERS EXHIBITS

Once the pleadings were complete, documentary evidence was presented to the Chancery Masters for consideration. During the eighteenth and nineteenth centuries the masters preserved a vast amount of this private material, and the documents themselves date from the twelfth century onwards. These are known collectively as the Chancery Masters Exhibits series (*see* FIGURE 18). The records are stored in C 103–14, and are primarily listed by the names of the parties concerned. A composite index to the parties exists

The Manor of Thorpe *Whereas* upon the fourteenth
within the Soken ——————— day of June in the year of our Lord
one thousand seven hundred and forty
five Henry Burton and Mary his wife
Copyhold Tenants of the said Manor in right of the said
Mary *Did* (she the said Mary being first solely examined by
William Mayhew Gentleman Deputy Steward of the said Manor
according to the custom thereof and consenting) Surrender into the
hands of the Lord of the said Manor *All that* Messuage or Farm
called Bernards Farm with the Lands Hereditaments and
Appurtenances holden of the said Manor by Copy of Court Roll *And*
also all that Tenement or Cottage with the Appurtenances holden
of the said Manor then in the occupation of Samuel Negus *And*
the Reversion and Reversions Remainder and Remainders thereof
And all the Estate right Title Interest property Claim and demand
whatsoever of them the said Henry Burton and Mary his Wife of in
and to the same and every part and parcel thereof *To the* only
use and behoof of Hannah Dyer of Colchester in the County of Essex
Spinster her heirs and Assigns for ever *But* upon Condition that
if the said Henry Burton and Mary his Wife or either of them their
or either of their heirs Executors Administrators or Assigns should
pay or cause to be paid unto the said Hannah Dyer her Executors
Administrators or Assigns the Sum of two hundred and fifty
pounds of lawful money of Great Britain with Interest for the same
at and after the rate of four pounds and an half per Cent: on or
upon the fourteenth day of June then next ensuing the date
thereof without any Deduction or Abatement then the said
Surrender to be void or Else to remain in full force *And Whereas*
the said Hannah Dyer hath since the making and passing the
said Surrender intermarried with John Nuthall of the City of
Norwich Esquire *But* before her Marriage by Indenture Tripartite
bearing date the Second day of October one thousand seven hundred
and fifty three And made between Hannah Dyer of Colchester
Spinster of the first part John Nuthall of the City of Norwich
Esquire of the second part Abraham Caley of the City of Norwich
Merchant Samuel Harvey of the City of London Mercer Stebbing
Sherman of Colchester Linen Draper of the third part for the
Consideration

in the c 103 series list, although some supplementary indexes are also available; so it will be essential to have prior information before you start a search, such as the names of individuals involved in the case. However, you should also be able to pick up additional information, such as place names, occupants or previous owners, via a key word search of the catalogue, although some documents have perfunctory descriptions and may give only the names of the parties concerned. The Duchess of Norfolk's Deeds are in c 115, and manor court rolls extracted from c 103–14 are in c 116. Similar exhibits collected by the Six Clerks are stored in c 171.

Chancery Masters Documents are similar to exhibits, and they can be found in c 117–29. The records are arranged by the name of the master who presided over the case, and so to search the records you will need to locate the relevant master's name from an index in c 103. Work is proceeding on a more comprehensive index, including enhanced document descriptions, which will eventually appear on the catalogue.

Later exhibits and documents can be found in j 90, which has its own indexes with the series list. Most of the documents derive from the Chancery Division of the Supreme Court of Judicature, but there are also examples from the King's (Queen's) Bench Division, the Exchequer Division and the old Court of King's Bench. Records in j 90 are stored offsite in Cheshire and currently require three working days' notice before they can be produced at Kew.

EXCHEQUER EXHIBITS

The Equity Court of Exchequer also required evidence to be collected, and there are a few areas where you can look for surviving exhibits. The best place to start is series e 140, which contains documents dating between 1319 and 1842; there are several manuscript calendars and indexes available, and the series is well listed and searchable online. Stray documents from Exchequer cases can be found in c 106, but you will also find other series such as e 219 (Clerks Papers, 1625–1841), e 163 (Miscellanea, 1154–1901) and e 167 (Papers of the Clerk to the Deputy Remembrancer, 1689–1877) contain exhibits as well, many of which will be of use to the house historian. Later series from the Supreme Court that include Exchequer exhibits are j 90 and j 17.

EXHIBITS FOR SEMI-AUTONOMOUS JURISDICTIONS

The equity courts of areas under semi-autonomous jurisdiction also retained exhibits. These can be found in CHES 11 for the Palatinate of Chester, with cause papers in CHES 9; DURH 21 (Palatinate of Durham);

PL 12 (Palatinate of Lancaster); and DL 49 for the Duchy of Lancaster. Exhibits from the Court of Wards and Liveries are in WARD 2.

8.7 Civil litigation in common law courts

COMMON LAW COURTS

Before 1875 there were four main central common law courts where litigants could enter a case. They are best summarized as in TABLE 8.9, although in reality all courts took cases between subjects.

Table 8.9 *The common law courts pre-1875*

Chancery	Cases between Crown and subject regarding royal rights
Common Pleas	Cases between subjects
Exchequer	Cases between Crown debtors
King's Bench	Cases between Crown and subjects

Property disputes between individuals that were settled under the auspices of the common law were less frequent than in the equity courts, unless the plaintiff was seeking compensation rather than restoration of land or enforcement of contract. However, cases can appear in any of the above areas, although many were dropped or a private agreement was reached before a judgment could be made. In these instances it will be difficult to extract much information about the process, as surviving records are difficult to use; the records of a single case can be scattered across many areas, and at present less is known about common law records compared to those of the equity courts. As such, it is easier to focus research on the main series of documents that were generated – the plea rolls – and then attempt to look in other areas, such as judgment books, for information. However, these tend to record the later stages of a case, and many disputes that were dropped at an early stage will simply be impossible to locate. It is also important to remember that the common law courts were used to record fictitious legal disputes as part of a conveyance, and it is necessary to distinguish between a genuine dispute and an enrolled deed or land transfer. In fact, the growth of conveyance in the Court of Common Pleas by 'common recovery' led to a separate series of records, the recovery rolls, being created in 1538.

In theory, cases relating to property disputes might appear in any one of these courts; however, you are more likely to find pleas of cases between private individuals entered in the courts of Common Pleas or King's Bench. The Exchequer of Pleas was usually reserved for revenue cases, especially those that impinged on royal revenue-generating rights, although many land disputes found their way into this court. Chancery was also used primarily for cases that involved royal rights, but among the most important areas of litigation were the division of lands between joint heiresses, including assignment of dower, and challenges to inquisitions post mortem and feudal incidents payable on land and property.

8.7

PLEA ROLLS OF COMMON LAW COURTS

Plea rolls record the formal processes in a common law court: until 1733 they were written in Latin, and were formulaic in the business they recorded. The details you would expect to find on a common law court plea roll include a description of the action concerned (where you will pick up details of the property or settlement under dispute); how the case proceeded within the court; and a final judgment, if one was actually made. A summary of the plea rolls for the various courts, plus a list of finding aids and indexes, is provided in TABLE 8.10. You may need to look in a series of courts to find the records of a case.

Table 8.10 *Common law plea rolls and relevant indexes*

COURT	DATE	INDEXES
KING'S BENCH		
KB 26	1194–1276	Various printed calendars
KB 27	1273–1702	From 1390: docket rolls and books in IND 1/1322–84 and IND 1/6042–96
KB 122	1702–1875	Docket books In IND 1/6097–372
COMMON PLEAS		
CP 40	1273–1874	From 1509: prothonotaries docket books in CP 60, usually three books per term
CP 43	1583–1837	Pleas of land; indexes in IND 1/17183–216
EXCHEQUER OF PLEAS		
E 13	1236–1875	Selective calendar in IND 1; for details consult *List and Index Society, vol. 232* Index of places in E 48/1–18 Repertory rolls in E 14 (only periods 1412–99, 1559–1669, 1822–30)
CHANCERY PLEAS		
C 44	1272–1485	Series list
C 43	1485–1625	Series list
C 206	1558–1901	Series list

RECORDS OF JUDGMENT

Judgments of cases were usually recorded on the plea rolls, but by the late eighteenth century many of the cases were not filed. To find out information about the names and dates involved in a case, plus a brief outline of the

Civil litigation in common law courts | 157

issues involved, various rolls exist that record judgments and orders. These can assist in filling in missing information for later cases, and various indexes to these records are set out in TABLE 8.11.

Table 8.11 *Common law records of judgment and relevant indexes*

COURT	SERIES	DATE/INDEXES
KING'S BENCH		
Entry Books of Judgment	KB 168	1699–1875; series includes indexes KB 168/129–263
Specimens of destroyed documents	J 89/13/286	Index in J 89/13/287
COMMON PLEAS		
Entry Books of Judgment	CP 64	1859–74; series includes indexes
Specimens of destroyed documents	J 89	
EXCHEQUER		
Entry Books of Judgment	E 45	1830–75
CHANCERY		
Remembrance Rolls	C 221	1565–1785
	C 222	1638–1729

SUPREME COURT OF JUDICATURE (KING'S/QUEEN'S BENCH)
Following the reorganization of the judicial system in 1875, all courts were amalgamated into the Supreme Court of Judicature, with five divisions. Each division could apply common law or equity according to the case it heard (*see* FIGURE 19), and it can therefore be difficult to locate papers of common law cases. The main place to look, though, will be among surviving King's (Queen's) Bench papers. Nevertheless, many of the records have been destroyed, and so you are likely to encounter great difficulty in finding information. Cause books are in J 87 (Green Books, from 1875) and J 168 (1879–1937), which provide the names of parties and a brief description of the cause; indexes to the Green Books from 1935 are in J 88. You may also find specimens of destroyed documents in series J 89.

CIVIL LITIGATION IN ASSIZE COURTS
Records of property disputes were heard in civil assize cases by itinerant justices, if a writ *nisi prius* had been issued from one of the central common law courts in London. This enabled parties to transfer the case from the central court to a more convenient local assize court, which was held twice a year. The records generated by the assize courts were similar to those of the central courts, and are stored in a variety of National Archives series; a leaflet summarizes the best place to begin your research, as the records are

In the High Court of Justice / *Chancery Division* **A**

In the matter of the Companies Acts 1862 & 1867
And
In the matter of the Patent Cocoa Fibre Company limited

This is the Exhibit marked "A" mentioned and referred to in the affidavit of Frank Lewis sworn before me in this matter the 10th day of October 1878

In the High Court of Justice.
CHANCERY DIVISION.

In the Matter of THE COMPANIES' ACTS 1862 and 1867,
AND
In the Matter of THE PATENT COCOA FIBRE COMPANY, LIMITED.

KINGSTON-ON-THAMES, SURREY.

Particulars and Conditions of Sale

OF A

VALUABLE

FREEHOLD PROPERTY

Situate about a Mile from the New Kingston Station, and a Mile-
and-a-quarter from the Surbiton and Kingston Station,
on the South Western Railway,

COMPRISING, A COMPACT

MILL, KNOWN AS "THE MIDDLE MILL,"

WITH A COMFORTABLE

DWELLING HOUSE, OUTBUILDINGS, GARDEN,

AND

RICH MEADOW LAND,

CONTAINING ALTOGETHER ABOUT

Nine Acres and Three-quarters,

Which, pursuant to an Order of the Chancery Division of the High Court of Justice, made in the above
matter, will be

Sold by Auction,

With the approbation of the Vice-Chancellor SIR JAMES BACON, by

MR. FRANK LEWIS,

(Of the Firm of FRANK LEWIS & KEMP),

The person appointed by the said Judge,

AT THE MART, IN TOKENHOUSE YARD, BANK OF ENGLAND,

On FRIDAY, the 27th day of SEPTEMBER, 1878,

AT TWO O'CLOCK PRECISELY.

Particulars, with Plans and Conditions of Sale, may be had of Mr. JOHN B. BALL, the Liquidator,
1, Gresham Buildings, Basinghall Street, E.C.; Messrs. FRANK LEWIS & KEMP, Auctioneers, 95, Gresham
Street, E.C.; and of Mr. A. PULBROOK, 28, Threadneedle Street, E.C.; and on the premises "The Middle
Mill," Kingston-upon-Thames.

Figure 19 The sale particulars for Kingston Mill, to be sold by auction on 27 September 1878 by order of the Chancery Division of the Supreme Court. The case originally commenced in 1877, and related to the liquidation of the Patent Cocoa Fibre Company. (J 46/342A)

arranged according to the relevant judicial circuits. Crown minute books will record the basic details of the case, such as the names of the parties, and are usually arranged chronologically. However, there are no indexes, so you will need to have some prior knowledge of the date when the case took place, perhaps from examining a local newspaper report.

The courts of King's Bench and Common Pleas kept note of cases that were removed under *nisi prius*. These were known as *posteas*, and can be found in the National Archives series listed in TABLE 8.12.

Table 8.12 *Common law posteas*

COURT	DESCRIPTION	DATE
COMMON PLEAS		
CP 36	Entry books of *nisi prius*	1644–1837
CP 57	Early *postea* books	(unsorted)
CP 41	*Postea* books	1689–1837
CP 42	*Postea* books	1830–52
KING'S BENCH		
KB 146	*Panella* files (early *posteas*)	Pre-1522
KB 20	*Posteas*	1664–1839
KB 146	Notice of trial books (under *nisi prius*)	1698–1842

8.8 Quarter sessions records

It is important to make clear that the National Archives holds no quarter sessions records at all. Where they survive, they will be found in the relevant CRO or amongst the deposited private papers of serving Justices of the Peace (JPs).

The quarter sessions were so named because they were held four times a year, and were courts presided over by JPs. Their remit was to undertake routine judicial and administrative functions in the shires, with the power to prosecute certain types of offence. More serious matters were usually – but not always – referred to the itinerant assize judges, who toured county circuits twice a year.

Quarter sessions records tend to enjoy a mixed survival rate. As with all court records, prosecutions involved the creation of many different types of document, including personal working papers generated by the JPs. However, the main stages of a session that produced relevant records were indictments for an offence, recognizances to ensure appearance at a session, and summary convictions. The formal court sessions generated quarter-session rolls, which include writs to appear, lists of attendees, recognizances, indictments and jury lists; session and process books to record proceedings; order books to record court decisions; and session papers kept by the Clerk of the Peace, the main court official. Informal mediation and meetings to discuss routine administrative matters might be recorded in unofficial papers kept by individual JPs.

RECORDS OF PROSECUTION

During the late sixteenth and early seventeenth centuries, overcrowding in or around towns and cities was a major concern, mainly due to the increased risk of fire or disease. Yet at the same time, population growth and urban expansion meant that there was pressure to provide sufficient accommodation for people who were drifting into urban areas. To prevent 'slums' appearing on the edges of towns, various statutes were passed that restricted new house building. The most important was 31 Elizabeth c.7 (1588–9), which stipulated that no new dwelling could be constructed without first assigning four acres of land to the site, thereby preventing overcrowding. One of the most important areas this affected was London and the surrounding counties. Punishment was potentially severe. An offender was liable to an initial £10 penalty, followed by 40 shillings per month for maintaining an illegal dwelling. Furthermore, if more than one family lived in the cottage there was an additional penalty of 10 shillings per month. Offences against this statute were usually prosecuted at the quarter sessions, and records can be found in surviving quarter-session rolls. These can be difficult to use as, like most formal courts, they were written in Latin until 1733; but a large number have been calendared and indexed, although knowing the name and date of a case would make searching for evidence much easier.

RECORDS OF LOCAL ADMINISTRATION

Other matters relating to the local community fell within the remit of the quarter sessions. Repairs to roads and highways were usually the responsibility of the relevant parish, unless covered by a private turnpike trust, and so, if they were not maintained, the entire parish was liable to amercement. Surviving quarter sessions papers can often list stretches of road that needed repair, and used the names and addresses of residents as landmarks to identify the worst sections. However, the chances of finding such information about your house will be slim.

Records of other types of property can be found in the quarter sessions papers. For example, JPs were effectively responsible for granting licences to alehouses. They issued recognizances that were valid for one year, which bound over alehouse owners to keep the peace; if law and order had been maintained, a new recognizance was issued for the following year. You will often find the name of the alehouse keeper listed, plus the names of two others who would act as sureties for the original recognizance. Usually alehouse keepers acted as a group and stood surety for each other, and where the records survive, you can find a wealth of information about local hostelries in a community.

HOUSE OCCUPANCY

9

9.1 Introduction

You will find that one of the most important and interesting ways to trace the history of your house is through the life stories of the people that either owned the property, or who used to reside there. Furthermore, you will start to put flesh on the bones of your chronology by empathizing with the people who considered your house as their home as well; this process tends to personalize your findings and move your research beyond a simple history of the bricks and mortar. The people you uncover in the documents helped to shape the way your house looks today, and their experiences are a valid and important avenue to explore when trying to understand how your area evolved into the community that you now live in.

This chapter will outline ways in which you can utilize sources for genealogy to extract information about previous owners or occupants. The best place to start is with census returns because, unlike people who have a habit of moving around, houses stay fixed in one place and are easier to find in the records. You can create a research framework for your property by examining the valuation survey of 1910–15 and the tithe maps and apportionments of c.1836–58, both described in Chapter 3, and then use the existing census returns from 1841 to 1901 to fill in some of the gaps.

Records generated within the parish will often tell you about the community in which your house was situated, as well as recording the major events in an occupier's life – baptism, marriage and burial. In particular, marriages often acted as a catalyst for constructing extensions to existing property and undertaking rebuilding schemes or major redecorations. Other unusual architectural features can be explained by looking in trade directories – houses also doubled up as places of work, and may have retained some of the original layout.

Earlier sources for genealogy are also suggested, such as inquisitions post mortem for major estate owners, and assignments of dower. Although not all houses will be old enough for you to able to use these sources, they can provide a remarkably vivid insight into previous dwellings that perhaps existed on the site of your current home. You may even uncover the story of why an older house was demolished to make way for a more modern property.

Census returns

CENSUS RETURNS 1801–31

Since Roman times, assessments of population numbers have been made to assist governments with their work. The first nationwide census in the United Kingdom was undertaken in 1801, and thereafter repeated every ten years. Between 1801 and 1831 only very basic information was recorded; in essence, the number of people who resided in a parish or street, with perhaps the heads of household listed and statistics that refer to age or occupation. The number of inhabited and uninhabited houses was also compiled.

As such, these official returns will be of minimal use to the house historian, as they provide basic statistics for an area. However, partial assessment returns and the working papers of the enumerators do survive for some regions, and these can provide information that can be utilized in conjunction with additional sources. To cite two examples, there are census records in the Shropshire Record Office for 1821 that record heads of household on a street by street level for parts of Shrewsbury; and a notebook compiled by a census enumerator for Saxmundham, Suffolk, provides an insight into the 1831 assessment, linking names with a general survey of property occupancy dating from the 1790s.

CENSUS RETURNS 1841–1901

It was with the 1841 census that the returns became an invaluable source for house history on a nationwide basis. For the first time, they record the names of all occupants for specific properties, as opposed to a general total by parish. Although street names are usually provided, house numbers are often omitted, and consequently the returns in isolation can be difficult to use. Nevertheless, you will obtain the names of all occupants, and where street numbers are not provided, the place where one property ends and another begins is marked on the return, usually with two dashes under the last name in the house. Households within a single property are also indicated, and are separated by a single slash. The full name, age, gender and occupation of all inhabitants are provided, although the ages of all over the age of 15 were rounded down to the nearest five years.

However, the subsequent census records from 1851 to 1901 provide far greater detail about the occupiers (*see* FIGURE 20) and should therefore allow you to positively identify your property with a greater degree of confidence. Each person will be identified by his or her full name, exact age,

The undermentioned Houses are situate within the Boundaries of the [Page 7]

Civil Parish [or Township] of Northop	City or Municipal Borough of	Municipal Ward of	Parliamentary Borough of	Town or Village or Hamlet of	Urban Sanitary District of	Rural Sanitary District of Holywell	Ecclesiastical Parish or District of 7

No. of Schedule	ROAD, STREET, &c. and No. or NAME of HOUSE	HOUSES (Inhabited / Uninhabited (U.) or Building (B.))	NAME and Surname of each Person	RELATION to Head of Family	CON- DITION as to Marriage	AGE last Birthday (Males / Females)	Rank, Profession, or OCCUPATION	WHERE BORN	If (1) Deaf-and-Dumb (2) Blind (3) Imbecile or Idiot (4) Lunatic
			Florence Foster	daur	Unmar	4	Scholar	Cheshire Ashton Mersey	
			William Lewis do	Son		2		Flintshire Northop	
34		1	Margaret Williams	Head	Unmar		Laundress	do Holywell	
			Mary Broughall	Sister	Widow		Publican Licensed Victualler	Hampshire Newcastle	
35	Park View	1	Job Kearsley	Head	Mar	38	Grocer, Master	Cheshire Bebington	
			Martha do	Wife	Mar	28		do Parkgate	
36	Glan y Rafon	1	William Griffiths	Head	Mar	61	Blacksmith, Master	Flintshire Northop	
			Elizabeth do	Wife	Mar	55		do do	
37	Glan y Rafon	1	Annie Ebaldiston	Head	Widow		Dress Maker employing...	Lancashire Liverpool	
38	The Yacht	1	Edward Foulkes	Head	Mar	38	Butcher, Master	Flintshire Northop	
			Elizabeth do	Wife	do	40		do Eidon District	
			do do	daur		8	Scholar	do Northop	
			Annie do	daur		6	do	do do	
			Edward Read do	Son		3		do do	
			Richard Henry do	Son		1		do do	
			Catherine Jones	Servant	Unmar	18	General Servant, Domestic	do do	
			Emily Jane Jones	do	do	14	Nurse, Domestic	do do	
39			John Thomas	Lodger	Unmar	31	Curate of Northop	Cardiganshire Llandysul	
			John Henry Evans	Visitor	Mar	34	Curate of Wrexham	Denbighshire Wrexham	
40		1	William G. Hancock	Head	Unmar	70	Agricultural Labourer	Flintshire Mold	
41		1	Jane Jones	Head	Widow	78		do Northop	
42			Robert Jones	Head	Mar	40	Coal Miner	do Flint	
			Sarah Jane do	Wife	Mar	34		Denbighshire Castle Dinas	
			Mary Rogers do	daur		9	Scholar	Flintshire Wood Hall	
			John Morgan do	Son		5	do	Flintshire Northop	

Total of Houses... 7 | Total of Males and Females... 11 14

NOTE.—Draw the pen through such of the words of the headings as are inappropriate.

Eng- Sheet F.

Figure 20 The 1881 census return for 'The Yacht', in Northop, Flintshire, formerly 'The Yacht Inn'. Its change in status is demonstrated by the occupation of Edward Foulkes, who is described as a master butcher. He resides there with his wife, four children and two house servants. Also listed is a lodger, the curate of Northop, and his visitor, the curate of Wrexham.

marital status, relationship to the head of the household, gender, occupation, parish and county of birth and various medical disabilities. The later the records are, the easier they are to use; so if you are researching a property, it makes sense to start with the 1901 census and work backwards.

As a source for house history, the census returns are a rich series of records that will tell you about the people who dwelt in your house, with details of their families, their occupations or whether more than one household was resident in your property. This social and economic data will allow you to assess what the community was like, and therefore permit an evaluation of the status of your house. One of the main benefits of census returns is that they exist in a continuous series, and so you can work backwards decade by decade to build up a picture of change or continuity. This data can then act as a foundation for other areas of research, such as parish records, trade directories and electoral lists that are described later in this chapter.

However, it is important to beware of the pitfalls of using census returns to provide a picture of who lived in your house. For a start, they record occupation on only one given day of the year; it might be the case that your house was unoccupied and therefore will not appear in the records. Furthermore, house names and numbers, and even the name of the street it was built in, were subject to change over time, so it is important to check these details in advance to ensure you are researching the correct property. Even some of the later census returns do not always include street names or house numbers, making positive identification very difficult, and it is entirely possible that your house had not yet been constructed. One final point – census returns provide the names of house occupiers only, which is fine when the occupier was also the owner. However, non-resident owners will be important figures in your house history, as it was they who transferred property and influenced who occupied it; you will have to use other sources to obtain this information.

LOCATING LATER CENSUS RECORDS IN ARCHIVES
A complete set of the census returns from 1841 to 1901 for England and Wales has been made available at the Family Records Centre in Myddleton Street, London. The records from 1841 to 1891 are on open access as microfilm copies of the original returns, while 1901 returns are on microfiche. A duplicate set of 1901 records can also be viewed at the National Archives. A summary of the record series is provided in TABLE 9.1.

Table 9.1 Census records

DATE OF CENSUS	RECORD SERIES
Available on microfilm at the Family Records Centre:	
1841	HO 107/1–1465
1851	HO 107/1466–2531
1861	RG 9/1–4543
1871	RG 10/1–5785
1881	RG 11/1–5632
1891	RG 12/1–5643
Available on microfiche at the National Archives:	
1901	RG 13/1–5338

For organizational purposes, the census adopted the registration districts and sub-districts established in 1837, which in turn were based on the Poor Law unions created in 1834. The FRC stocks place-name indexes for rural areas and street indexes for towns with a population in excess of 40,000 people. These provide the registration district and sub-district, and therefore allow you to locate the relevant document reference, having first consulted the appropriate volume in the search room. In turn, the reference corresponds to a microfilm that will contain the census returns.

As well as the official finding aids, there are separate name and place indexes available. The most comprehensive is for the 1881 census, now available on CD; and regional indexes for other years, most notably 1851, have also been compiled. While these are a good place to begin looking for people, they will be of less use to a house historian, as they are mainly designed for personal name searches. If travel to London is inconvenient, you will find that most CROs have microfiche or film copies for the relevant county. In addition, many local record societies have prepared separate indexes for census years other than 1851 and 1881. The Latter Day Saints maintain Family History Centres where you can hire in films for any county on request.

CENSUS RETURNS ONLINE

In 2002 the 1901 census was released online, one of the first datasets to be available in such a format. Since then, other sets of census records have been digitized and can now be viewed via the Internet. The National Archives website acts as a platform for access to census records from 1851 to 1901, and this is an amazing resource for family historians as each set of census returns has a name index. However, at present the online access has only limited use for the house historian as there is limited scope for searching by address – if indeed your house had a name or number actually recorded – and consequently you might find it easier to adopt some of the traditional searches outlined above and trawl by hamlet, village or town.

RESEARCH TECHNIQUES

When looking at census returns that do not have a house number, there are a couple of techniques you can employ to get round this problem. First, start with the 1910 Valuation Office survey – for information about accessing these records, see CHAPTER 3. You should be able to locate your house in the street, and then find out who lived there from the Field Book; but don't just stop at your property, obtain occupancy data for the entire street, and look out for any particular landmarks such as pubs, large named houses or other substantial buildings.

You can use these landmark buildings, along with the pattern of occupation, to make a reasonable attempt to locate your property in the 1901 census returns. For example, your house in 1910 may be only three doors down from a pub, and two in the other direction from a large identifiable house; you can use these fixed local coordinates to work out which unlisted property in the census is yours, particularly if the neighbours remained the same as in 1910. Of course, this is only a rough rule of thumb, and you should always attempt to verify the names you discover from other sources. However, once you have discovered a pattern, you can try to examine earlier census returns in the same way – bearing in mind that census enumerators often reversed the routes they took, or occasionally visited houses out of turn. Similarly, at the start of the period for which census returns survive, you have the tithe apportionment surveys that can serve a similar purpose; these are covered in CHAPTER 3.

So it should be possible to work forward from 1841 or 1851 in the manner outlined above, and there are a number of local history projects, usually stored at the relevant CRO, that have attempted to plot data from census returns on copies of tithe maps. The lesson to be learnt here is that one document used in isolation may be of little use; but when examined in combination with at least one other, the data it contains suddenly becomes relevant.

SCOTLAND AND IRELAND

The 1841–1901 census returns for Scotland, stored by the Registrar General for Scotland, are available at New Register House, Edinburgh. A fee is currently charged for access to the microfilms. Alternatively the entire 1881 census is available on CD-ROM, as it is for England and Wales. Digitized images of the 1891 and 1901 censuses are available at New Register House, and indexes to the 1881, 1891 and 1901 censuses (plus images for 1891 and 1901) can be obtained via the Internet at **www.scotlandspeople.gov.uk**. Material for Ireland is held by the National Archives, Dublin. However, most of the nineteenth-century returns have been destroyed, although the returns for 1901 and 1911 are reasonably complete and are available for public inspection. Copies are also available at PRONI. Copies of Irish and Scottish films can also be hired at Latter Day Saints Family History Centres.

Electoral lists and registers   9.3

Electoral rights have not always been as inclusive as they are today. The right to vote has gradually been extended throughout the twentieth century to include all men and women over the age of 18, but before 1918 not all men and very few women were eligible. From the earliest times until the nineteenth century, the right to vote was based on the amount and type of land or property that a man held, and lists of voters were compiled. From the eighteenth century these were usually based on Land Tax returns, as the right to vote was linked to holding freehold property. Therefore, early lists, often known as poll books, provide a guide to freeholders in your area, and on occasion will provide a precise address. The Guildhall Library, Society of Genealogists Library and the Institute of Historical Research all have large collections of poll books.

From 1832, electoral registers were compiled that listed the names of all those entitled to vote, with a brief description of the property that provided eligibility. The right to vote was extended from 1867, and consequently the lists became more comprehensive and provided greater details of property. Modern electoral registers from 1928, when women over 21 were enfranchised, provided street names and house numbers, and can give a useful indication of who lived at your house.

The National Archives does not hold any electoral lists in a distinct series, and the best place to begin your research will be the CRO, local studies centre or nearest branch library, where printed electoral registers are usually stored. However, a partial series of electoral registers for the early 1870s can be located in the National Archives Library and Resource Centre.

As with census records, it is advisable to start with the most recent set of records and work back in time. You will find that the boundaries of constituencies altered on a regular basis, so you need to keep an eye out if your house or street suddenly disappears; there are resources on hand to help you keep track of parliamentary boundary changes. As you work back in time, you will find that the quality of data starts to decrease; the most recent records are usually arranged alphabetically by street, but you will soon find that the lists change so that the names of eligible voters are sorted alphabetically instead. Gradually, less information about individual properties is recorded, and by the time you've worked back to the outbreak of the Second World War it can be very difficult to pinpoint the right family, as house numbers tend to disappear around this date, if not later. It is easier to track people further back in urban areas, but even then you might have to enlist the help of other sources, such as rate books (*see* CHAPTER 10.5).

9.4   Street and trade directories

Domestic dwellings were often used as places from which occupants also traded, and from the late eighteenth century street and trade directories were compiled to provide indexes to the whereabouts and occupation of tradespeople, and the private addresses of wealthier residents were often listed as well. The earliest lists will give only partial coverage for a town or parish, but those in the nineteenth and twentieth centuries can provide street indexes and maps that are more inclusive. Trade directories tended to cover a county or group of counties and list residents by parish, arranged under the types of occupation of the tradespeople. Street directories proliferate in urban areas, and usually give more detail. Rival directories may well give different information, so it is worth checking a variety if possible. Furthermore, they can contain incorrect data, as it was often down to the traders to inform the compilers that they had moved or ceased trading. Alternatively, the agents working for the compilers sometimes used information from earlier directories to prepare new versions. It is always sensible to corroborate your evidence from other sources. As you will see from the first case study in CHAPTER 15, the proprietors of a public house continued to be listed in one directory for five years after they were buried in the local churchyard!

The National Archives Library and Resource Centre has a selection of trade directories for the London area, but you should head for the relevant CRO or, in some cases, branch library for the best collection of local directories. The Guildhall Library in London has an excellent collection of London and provincial directories, as does the London Metropolitan Archives whose holdings include Buff Books, listings for the London suburbs from the late nineteenth to the early twentieth centuries. In general you will find that there are many different directories, but the main publications to look for will be Kelly's and the Post Office Directory, as these developed nationwide editions. You can even search for historic directories online at **www.historicaldirectories.org**.

Parish registers   9.5

If you are attempting to trace the history of a family in a local community, parish registers are an excellent place to begin. These are the records of baptisms, marriages and burials for a parish, and can date back to as early as 1538 when the post-Reformation regime stipulated that they should be maintained. Although early parish registers are of little immediate use for locating details of property, by the nineteenth century places of residence were recorded alongside the individual's name, especially in parishes in or around cities. Very few parish registers are stored at the National Archives and the vast majority can usually be found in the relevant CRO. Various publications exist to help you locate their whereabouts, while the Church of the Latter Day Saints has placed the collections of the International Genealogical Index online at **www.familysearch.org**.

In addition to parish registers, the parish chest may contain a variety of other useful documents. For example, assessments of parish rates were compiled that may record house names and property values, and these are considered in the next chapter. You might also find agreements among parishioners concerning rotas of duties for parish offices, such as parish constable or overseer of the poor; these are often arranged by house row.

Inquisitions post mortem   9.6

For earlier property or estates, you may find information contained in inquisitions post mortem (IPMs), particularly if you are tracing a substantial property or if your house was built on land that once formed part of a large estate. The records start in the thirteenth century and continue into the mid-seventeenth, and were compiled by the Crown at the death of a tenant-in-chief to determine whether an heir at law was sane, or of age (21 years) to inherit. If he was, he would pay a relief to enter into his lands; if not, then the lands would default to the Crown until lucidity or majority was reached, and

Table 9.2 *Inquisitions post mortem and relevant indexes*

1236–1418	
C 132 (Henry III), C 133 (Edward I), C 134 (Edward II), C 135 (Edward III), C 136 (Richard II), C 137 (Henry IV), C 138 (Henry V), E 149	Printed *Calendars of IPMs* (in English)
1418–85	
C 138 (Henry V), C 139 (Henry VI), C 140 (Edward IV), C 141 (Richard III) E 149	Original Latin documents – Chancery files indexed in c 138 series list, plus four volumes of calendars. Four manuscript indexes for Exchequer series.
1485–1509	
C 142 E 150	Printed *Calendar of IPMs* (in English)
1509–1640	
C 142 E 150 WARD 7	Original Latin documents – published *Index of IPMs*

the heir would become a ward of the Crown; the estates would be administered on the heir's behalf, but the Crown would take the profits. Royal officials known as escheators conducted the inquisitions, and they filed the returns in Chancery, the Exchequer or, from the reign of Henry VIII, the Court of Wards.

At the very least, IPMs can confirm that the estate on which your house was built was passed to a descendant, thereby making a search for relevant archives that bit easier. However, the original documents are in Latin and can be difficult to interpret. A summary of the National Archives series is provided in TABLE 9.2.

To order an original IPM from an entry in the calendar for the periods 1236–1418 and 1485–1509, you will need to convert it into a National Archives reference. Copies of this IPM were deposited in both Chancery and Exchequer, with a separate copy being enrolled in the Exchequer. The regnal year is Richard II, so the Chancery series will be c 136. The entry also provides the piece number, in this case 84, so you would need to order c 136/84. When the document arrives you will see that several IPMs were stitched into one file, and the number in brackets, in this case 10, provides the relevant IPM within the file. The Exchequer series will be E 149, and the same conversion principle

Example The IPM of Edmund Mussenden, taken 18 Richard II, includes a cottage and tenement at Guildford, Surrey. There are three calendar entries: C.Ric.II file 84(10), E.Inq.PM File 64(5) and E.Enrolment etc. of Inq. no. 307.

applies – so the document reference will be E 149/64 and the IPM will be the fifth in the file. The enrolment conversion is similar – the key sheet at the front of the calendar shows that the records are stored in E 152, and the relevant file is number 307, giving an ordering reference of E 152/307. Later records for the Palatinates of Chester, Durham and Lancaster and the Duchy of Lancaster can be found in CHES 3, DURH 3, PL 4 and DL 7 respectively, and for the period 1509–1640 are included in the published *Index of IPMs*.

Assignments of dower 9.7

Since medieval times, a dower was assigned to the bride as part of the marriage agreement. Normally this took the form of money or goods, but the practice of including houses was common amongst wealthier classes. Furthermore, dower houses were often especially constructed for the bride, and would become her residence if her spouse pre-deceased her. Many high-status yet relatively small houses on the edge of large estates can be traced to this practice, and building accounts or personal papers in estate records can provide relevant information. Quite often such properties can contain salvage from higher-status houses that may provide misleading architectural clues. The National Archives is not the best place to start looking for such material, and you should begin at the relevant CRO.

In some cases, assignments of dower that involved the legal transfer of property were enrolled to provide legal evidence of title. For example, the dower arrangement for Agnes Brown included a house near Billingsgate in London, and an indenture confirming this arrangement by the executors of her late husband's will was enrolled on the Hustings Roll in 1463, listing the layout of the property in great detail.

However, if a dower was disputed, you may find traces in one of the courts described in CHAPTER 8, in particular the Court of Requests. Furthermore, you may find inquisitions held into right of dower in lands or property that was part of a general IPM (known as an inquisition *de assignatione dotis*).

Diaries and personal correspondence 9.8

If you know the name of a house owner or occupier, you may be lucky enough to discover private correspondence or even a diary from the time that he or she lived in your property. These revealing insights are not only valuable for the light they throw on the way people used to live, but also for the evidence they contain about the house in which they lived. Not all diaries will be of use; but others have been known to include room by room descriptions of a house, even providing details about the room decorations.

As these are personal documents, the most logical place to begin a search is at the CRO or specialist collections, including personal or family archives. Diaries and correspondence occasionally turn up at the National Archives in the various exhibit series, and in the PRO series there are non-public collections and family papers, accumulated through gift, purchase or deposit, that contain correspondence. Some of these are calendared, but others will provide no clues as to their contents. You will find them of use only if you know that your house once formed part of a large estate whose owners deposited material at the National Archives.

10

Introduction

Taxation records may not sound the most fascinating area in which to look for information relating to your house, but throughout the centuries the Crown and its governments have found it expedient to raise levies that were assessed on land and property. We may grumble about paying taxes, but we should be thankful that previous occupiers of our houses have done so, as whenever assessments and payments have been made in the past, records were generated. It is therefore possible to obtain crucial information about houses and property from the assessments that were made upon them.

The most comprehensive and useful taxation source for house historians was perhaps the Valuation Office survey of 1910–15, described in CHAPTER 3, as it provided assessment data and maps that combined to give a nation-wide snapshot of property at the start of the twentieth century. The sources described in this chapter are not as easy to use, widespread or comprehensive. However, in combination with other sources, plus a working knowledge of your local area, you will find that the forms of taxation listed below might yield some surprising results and take you a few decades further back in the documentary tale of your house's history. Some tax records might also help to explain any puzzling architectural anomalies in your house, as assessments were often based on the number of fixed features, such as hearths and windows. Evasion was widespread, and one of the simplest ways to reduce your tax bill was to remove these features by bricking them up. The data contained in these records should allow you to make a comparison between contemporary assessment data and the equivalent modern number of these features.

You will usually find that tax records list the names of the house owners and occupiers and are arranged by parish, rather than by house number in the modern sense. However, some will be arranged by street and maintain a continuous order or sequence of names from year to year, and by employing related sources, such as trade directories or electoral lists, you should be able to identify your property with a degree of confidence.

The National Archives is a good place to start looking for some of the tax records listed in this chapter, but you will also need to undertake research at your CRO as well. Not only will you find tax records in 'official' sources, but also among the private papers of estate managers and assessors who were responsible for paying them. Several guides on the location, use and interpretation of tax records have been written to assist you, and are listed under 'Useful publications'.

10.2 Hearth Tax

HISTORY OF THE RECORDS

The earliest comprehensive and national assessed tax on property was the Hearth Tax, introduced in 1662 to raise money for the recently restored monarchy of Charles II. Although the tax was continued until 1688, only the assessments for 1662–6 and 1669–74 provide useful data for the house historian. The rate of tax for the period 1662–74 was a half-yearly payment of one shilling for each hearth in all occupied property worth more than 20 shillings per year in terms of rent; the occupier also had to be a local ratepayer of church and poor rates.

TYPES OF HEARTH TAX RETURNS

When the Hearth Tax was first introduced, various types of document were generated that related to the assessment and collection of the tax. The most relevant for the house historian were the liability assessments, which were compiled by local assessors. The assessor was usually the parish constable, who visited each property to obtain the number of hearths from the occupier. If he suspected that he had been provided with false information, he had powers of entry so that he could check for himself. The records can be difficult to use, as they list the name of the householder rather than provide a description of the property that was being assessed, and although not unknown, it is rare to find the name or location of properties specified. Therefore you will need to know either the number of hearths your property would have had, or the name of the householder who was being assessed. The problems associated with owner/occupier confusion were partially addressed in later assessments. Individuals who owned several properties were assessed where they were currently resident, and were issued with a certificate of residence as proof of payment. Earlier certificates of residence, which can be found in series E 115, list the place of abode where the person was assessed, and are arranged by the name of the individual.

Figure 21 Hearth Tax return for Titchfield, Hampshire, c.1665. 'St Margarets' was formerly the property of the Earl of Southampton and in all probability had been constructed as a dower house, then later converted into a hunting lodge. (E 179/176/565)

To identify the potential number of hearths that would have been liable, you will need to do some basic arithmetic. First, identify the section or sections of your house that you think were contemporary at the time of the tax. Second, count the number of chimney stacks. Third, count the number of rooms that abut each chimney stack. The maximum number of hearths can be obtained by allowing for a hearth in all rooms on each floor for every chimney stack. For example, a two-storey house with a chimney stack at each end and a room on each floor should have four hearths.

In addition to assessment data, you may find certificates of exemption to be of some use, as these can provide more information about the householder or the house itself. They might be issued on grounds of poverty, or because a house was uninhabited or undergoing repairs. For example, bricks uncovered in a house in Saxmundham, Suffolk, bore the date 1672, a Hearth Tax year, and it is tempting to imagine the occupier rebuilding sections of the property, leaving the hearths until last to avoid paying extra taxation. However, it is unlikely that he escaped for long, because periodical reassessments were conducted to pick up just this sort of evasion. Where reassessment or exemption records survive, they will be listed with the liability assessments at the National Archives.

LOCATING THE RECORDS

Hearth Tax returns can be found in National Archives series E 179 (*see* FIGURE 21). There are typed indexes, arranged by county, available on open access in the reading rooms that provide details of the tax, the area covered (usually a hundred or other county division), the type of Hearth Tax record, and whether names of individuals are recorded. However, the best means of access is via the National Archives website, www.nationalarchives.gov.uk, where you can search a database of tax returns in E 179 by place, type of tax, date of tax and type of tax record.

A general summary of Hearth Tax returns inside and outside the National Archives is provided in Gibson's guide to the Hearth Tax (*see* 'Useful publications'), while many counties have published Hearth Tax returns that are available at the CRO.

10.3 Land Tax

HISTORICAL BACKGROUND

An important method of taxation was the fixed quota, which had existed since 1334 and was frequently used by Henry VIII to raise subsidies. In 1696 this principle was adopted for the Land Tax. Instead of making assessments on individual properties based on an architectural feature such as the hearth, where widespread evasion was possible, a fixed sum of money was agreed that was to be levied from an entire county. The division of this tax burden fell to local assessors, who in turn created fixed quotas per parish to be paid by the proprietors of land. The tax was assessed on land units – although in principle these were restricted to landed property only – which were arranged in Land Tax parishes, the boundaries of which sometimes differed from ecclesiastical parishes. From 1780 an individual who paid Land Tax on freehold property worth £2 a year or more was entitled to vote, and so Land Tax returns were enrolled at the quarter sessions to provide lists of eligible voters. When a parliamentary election was due, large landowners often sold plots of land that were just above this value in order to increase their voter numbers and thus secure the election of their favoured candidates, so it is always worth searching for related records prior to an election.

From 1798 Land Tax assessment forms were printed and contained the following information: rentals (yearly value of the property); name of proprietor or copyholder; name of occupier; name or description of property (usually from 1825). From 1832 there was less need to collect Land Tax assessments for electoral purposes, and so the forms were less frequently filed at the quarter sessions. Indeed, after 1798 it was possible to purchase redemption from the Land Tax, and once the compulsion to register names for electoral purposes was removed, the names of many who had purchased Land Tax redemption were thereafter omitted from the Land Tax lists. Returns will therefore be of less use after 1832. Indeed, compulsory redemption was introduced in 1949, and the tax was finally abolished in 1963.

Most of the surviving records will be found in CROs, either in the quarter sessions records or among the private papers of the assessors and collectors of the tax, and the majority of surviving records tend to date from the late eighteenth century. Many CROs maintain separate lists of Land Tax returns, and a Gibson guide (*see* 'Useful publications', under Taxation) outlines where you can locate surviving records for each county.

LAND TAX RECORDS AT THE NATIONAL ARCHIVES

The National Archives holds a few accounting documents relating to Land Tax, but only one set of comprehensive returns for the entire country. In 1798 changes were introduced to the system under the Land Tax Perpetuation Act (38 George III c.60), and a series of returns was compiled for all landholders so that the tax could be levied as a fixed annual charge. For each property these provide the name of the occupier, the name of the proprietor (if different), the amount assessed and the rate of redemption (if applicable). The National Archives series IR 23 contains these assessments, which are indexed by county via a series of four volumes on open access. From these you can obtain the folio number for the relevant tax parish, which can then be matched to a National Archives reference in the series list.

From 1798 it became possible to purchase an exemption from paying the Land Tax. You may find data recorded in IR 23, such as the contract number and date of redemption. The records of such transactions are recorded in IR 22 (Parish Books of Redemptions) and IR 24 (Registers of Redemption Certificates), and are arranged by Land Tax parish. As well as providing details of individuals who were thus exempt, and will therefore disappear from future records in CROs, maps and plans of the properties in question can also be located.

In addition, material may be found in series E 182. The documents are arranged chronologically and by county, but the boxes are largely unsorted and there are no contemporary indexes. Therefore it can be a lengthy and frustrating process to wade through the material, with no guarantee of results at the end. However, many bundles seem to contain lists of people in arrears, changes in liability and those with double liability (such as Roman Catholics, aliens and denizens).

USING LAND TAX DATA

The Gibson guide to Land Tax is the best place to start, if you wish to locate Land Tax returns. Surviving records can contain some useful data if viewed in conjunction with other contemporary sources. Where a sequence of Land Tax returns exist for a long period, it is possible to discern fixed patterns in the list of names that tend to reflect their respective positions in the street, which is particularly useful when no house names or numbers are provided. Parish rate books are particularly useful for this type of analysis. Although there will be a degree of uncertainty over the reliability of using sequential data of this nature, you can start to identify when occupiers came and went from your property by using known data about neighbouring properties as points of reference; this shows the benefit of researching the surrounding area. If possible, work backwards from the modern era, where house names and numbers survive in greater detail, or from the known to the unknown. For urban areas, trade directories are a good corroboratory source for this method of analysis, while manorial surveys and, from 1840, tithe and census returns can be of use in rural communities or villages. You may also find changes in the assessment level for your property, which can indicate a substantial rebuild or extension, thereby accruing a higher level of Land Tax.

10.4 Other assessed taxes

In addition to the Hearth Tax and Land Tax, a variety of other features associated with houses and their contents were subject to assessment, and after 1784 they were all grouped together to be jointly described as 'assessed taxes'. In particular, the Window Tax and Inhabited House Duty featured assessments based on property; but the problem with these records is that survival tends to be scarce.

WINDOW TAX

The main component of the Window Tax was an assessment based on the number of windows in a property. The tax was introduced in 1696 and eventually repealed in 1851, and proved remarkably unpopular and difficult to collect. Properties were assessed in a series of bands, and a charge was levied on houses with over ten windows from 1696 to 1766, seven windows from 1766 to 1825 and eight windows from 1825 to 1851. There were many rules and regulations that permitted exemptions from the tax, which will affect whether your property was liable. However, you may still be able to use the data to identify periods when your property underwent rebuilding work or extensions, based on any changes in the Window Tax assessments from comparable returns over a series of years. Most assessments will provide the name of the taxpayer, plus the number of windows assessed and the amount of tax due. In most cases the taxpayer was also the occupier, and so you will not obtain much information on property owners unless they were the official resident. Furthermore, most of the individuals who were liable for the tax were already assessed for parish rates, which are described below. Another problem associated with Window Tax was evasion, as many people temporarily or permanently blocked up windows to avoid paying the duty. It was also possible to obtain an exemption by making the assessor believe that the property was a place of business.

Very few Window Tax returns now survive, as there was no compulsion to enrol the material at the quarter sessions. Where they still exist, they are listed in Gibson's guide to Land Tax and assessed taxes. The National Archives contains returns and particulars of assessed taxes in series E 182, but the records are largely unsorted. However, they do contain an enormous amount of material, although the qualifications in section 10.3: Land Tax records at the National Archives still apply, but if you have time to spare, you may be able to uncover a series of Window Tax returns for your particular area. Otherwise, you might find stray returns in CROs or amongst private and estate papers of landowners.

One of the places with the best Window Tax coverage is Scotland, as records were maintained by central government. These can be found at NAS in series E 326, and the returns also list properties with window numbers below the nominal tax liability.

HOUSE TAX AND INHABITED HOUSE DUTY

Although this was in theory a separate tax, returns for House Tax were usually made alongside those for Window Tax. It too was introduced from 1696, and assessed the number of actual occupiers of inhabited houses that were liable to church and poor rates. The vast majority of surviving records will be found at the relevant CRO, usually with the Window Tax returns, and are listed in the Gibson guide. The tax was repealed in 1834, despite the continuance of Window Tax, but Inhabited House Duty, one of the general 'assessed taxes', continued until 1924.

As with Window Tax, you will find material in E 182, although you will require time and patience if you want to extract any useful data from this unsorted series. The National Archives also holds IR 68 (precedent books and composition cases). These were compiled in cases where taxpayers were relieved from paying an annual assessment, and instead paid an agreed annual amount for three years. The series contains limited data for selected properties, but there are no indexes available to the two books.

To illustrate that all sorts of property were subject to Inhabited House Duty, the Brighton Aquarium was assessed for the tax in 1880 when a party of visiting Zulus slept in the aquarium during the course of an exhibition (PRO reference IR 40/1157).

THE 1695 MARRIAGE ASSESSMENT IN THE CITY OF LONDON

A tax peculiar to the City of London was in operation between 1694–5 and 1704, and is often referred to as the 1695 Marriage Assessment. It was liable on all births, marriages and burials, plus annual dues on bachelors over 25 and childless widowers. The records are stored in the Corporation of London Record Office and are arranged by parish, although the records for 17 parishes no longer survive. Furthermore, there are name indexes available for the assessment. The records can be used to identify the streets where people lived, although house names and numbers are rarely recorded.

10.5 Rates

'Rates' is an umbrella term that has been used to cover various forms of local taxation, all of which were designed to contribute to the community in which individuals lived. The levies took many shapes and forms, but can provide some basic information about property, as later documents for urban areas have been known to include assessment lists that denote house numbers. The following are the most common sources that the house historian may find of some use. However, as the records were created or maintained at a parochial level, or were administered by local authorities, rate books and assessments are not stored at the National Archives. Nevertheless, a brief outline of the material you may come across at your CRO is provided.

POOR, CHURCH AND HIGHWAY RATES

Poor, church and highway rates were assessed on parishioners by the parochial church wardens to raise revenue for poor relief, to provide money to fund church repairs and ecclesiastical activity in each parish, or to maintain the highways within the parish. Where returns and assessments survive, they are to be found among the papers kept in the parish chest and subsequently deposited at the CRO. Alternatively, the private papers of individuals who acted as church wardens may also yield assessment records, as will quarter sessions records that relate to the failure of a parish to maintain a highway. They usually date from the eighteenth and early nineteenth centuries, although earlier returns from the sixteenth and seventeenth centuries can be found.

Parish rate books rarely list individuals by their place of abode, but will provide a list of eligible parishioners that can be cross-referenced with other sources. You will usually find a list of parishioners followed by the amounts they paid, and in some cases you may find an address attached. However, this can be a useful supplementary source for other records, such as Land Tax or Window Tax; and where material on parish rates survives for the seventeenth century, it can also add to your knowledge of Hearth Tax. Data for towns and urban areas is often more detailed, and you will be more likely to find references to individual properties.

LOCAL AUTHORITY RATE BOOKS

After the Poor Law Amendment Act of 1834, Poor Law unions replaced the parochial system for poor relief administration. In consequence, new ways of financing improvements to the local community were introduced, including rates that were levied and collected by the relevant Poor Law union. With changes to the administration of local affairs, the responsibility for raising and collecting rates gradually passed to the appropriate borough, rural, district, municipal or urban councils that were set up from the late nineteenth century onwards. The local authorities maintained rate books to record the details of the amounts levied, and these are now stored at the relevant CROs. Rate books normally recorded the name of the occupier, and sometimes included the name of the owner; an assessment of the value of the property in question; the amount to be collected; and, most important, the name or description of the property. They were often annotated to record changes of occupancy. As with Land Tax returns, it is sometimes easier to work from the modern era backwards, especially if there is a good sequence of books and you know the names of the householders. Even if you do not, you can use supplementary information such as trade directories, or a comparative analysis of neighbouring returns, to work backwards. Increases in assessment data can often indicate a rise in the value of the property, usually as a result of building work or other extensions to the property.

SEWER RATE BOOKS

Sewer rate books are similar in format to local authority rate books, but exist for urban areas from the late eighteenth and particularly the nineteenth centuries where the construction and maintenance of sewers was necessary to maintain standards of public health. Local contributions were paid for sewers to be repaired and built, the terms of which were often specified in the original building lease; and, where sewers were maintained by the local authority, sewer commissioners were appointed to assess and collect the revenue. Their records are known as sewer rate books, and will be found in the relevant CRO or municipal, urban or metropolitan record office. In addition to the name of the contributor, they can often contain street names and house numbers. Some of the best records survive for London, when the Metropolitan Board of Works was established in 1855 to construct an ambitious network of sewers across the capital. To pay for the works, the Board was granted a £3 million loan, to be recouped from rates that were voted for in 1858 to pay for the works, to be levied over the following 40 years. The assessment books for these records survive at the London Metropolitan Archives.

Walcot Square, Southwark, London

There is much potential material to research if you live in a property in or around London, not only because you can use standard techniques and documents, but also because there are sources specific to the capital, such as the records of the Metropolitan Board of Works, which was set up to oversee the development of London in the mid-nineteenth century. Furthermore, as this case study shows, you can use your property as a barometer for the changing times and social status of the neighbourhood in which it stands. What follows is the story of the rise, fall and resurrection of a south London estate.

Walcot Square lies in the parish of Lambeth in southeast London. The land is owned by the Walcot Charity, which was established by the will of Edmund Walcot in 1667 to raise money from his lands and estates to provide funds for the poor of Lambeth and Southwark. The charity was able to extend his lands through canny purchases of neighbouring property, back in the days when London was much smaller and land as close to the centre as Lambeth and Southwark consisted of open fields. Yet throughout the eighteenth century, and especially during the early decades of the nineteenth, London's need for cheap and affordable housing and accommodation that was within easy reach of the City increased dramatically, thanks to the capital's expanding population. The rapid expansion of London across the Thames led the trustees of the charity to decide that the best way of fulfilling their charge to cater for the poor was to develop the estate into building plots, and erect suitable dwellings that could be leased for rent. A series of maps and plans in the Lambeth Archives shows exactly how the estate changed over time, from little more than gardens in the late eighteenth century and a few streets and building plots marked out in the early 1800s, to the gradual development of the estate in the 1820s and

1830s, causing it to spread over the area in which Walcot Square now stands. Later Ordnance Survey maps continue to record the process of growth, demonstrating that the expansion continued around the Walcott lands as other owners followed suit; it is even possible to pinpoint tram lines in the streets, as transport linked the area with the centre of the city.

If you are researching older properties in London, one of the best publications to start with is 'The Survey of London'; and the entry for Walcot Square reveals that the architect and builder John Woodward, of Paradise Street, laid out parts of the estate in 1837–9, while Charles Newnham built other sections. Indeed, Newnham was so taken with the properties in Walcot Square that he decided to move into one of them; the earliest schedule of leases dated 31 August 1840 shows that he took No.1, along with Nos. 1–4 St Mary's Square (which was situated nearby), for a term of 67 years from 24 June 1840 for an annual rent of £15.3.0. From this point, census records reveal the names of all the occupiers of the house from 1841 to 1901, and permit an analysis of the changing social conditions in the area. In 1841 no house numbers were recorded in the schedules, but the occupant of the first house in Walcot Square – following immediately after St Mary's Street – is Charles Newnham, whose occupation was a builder. He lived with his wife Miriam and daughter Elizabeth, though sharing the house are Sarah, Mary and Katherine Nock, listed as dressmakers. The impression given by the occupations of the inhabitants of the Square is that they were all middle class; Newnham's neighbour was a commercial traveller, while two doors down lived an accountant, followed by a bookseller. A number of occupants of the Square are of 'independent means' and many had servants.

In 1851, Charles (51) and Miriam (45) were

still living there, looking after their grandson Charles Roswell (1). The couple were still in residence ten years later as well, though Charles is now listed as a 'house proprietor'. However, by 1871 it seems as though the house had passed to their daughter Elizabeth Roswell and son-in-law Austin, possibly after the death of Charles and Miriam. The Roswells had four children living at home with them, but times were probably hard. Austin Roswell was listed as a tailor 'out of business'; this must have been even more galling for him, since his neighbour was a draper (James Cowan) who could afford a housekeeper, butler and general servant. The general standard of occupant in the Square remained middle class, and if anything had risen since the 1840s; for example, a parliamentary clerk and family occupied No.3 Walcot Square.

There is a sense that the Square has dropped in social status by the time the 1881 census was taken. The Roswells were still at No.1, though two daughters are described as 'assistant at home', suggesting that one or both parents were perhaps frail or invalid. This supposition gains credibility with the information that Austin had retired by this date, aged only 54. In an era before the welfare state, people who were unable to work became a real burden on their family, and one of the few options was the dreaded workhouse. The drop in status of the Square is confirmed when the households elsewhere are examined; other properties are occupied by a journeyman joiner, a smith, a teacher, a waiter, a chair and sofa maker and a police constable.

Yet Austin and Elizabeth hung on, appearing in the same property in 1891, which meant that they had been living in the same house for over 30 years. Nevertheless the Square's downward drift towards boarding houses and multiple-occupant tenancy had continued, with general labourers and warehousemen listed among the tenants. Two years later the house numbers were changed – a common pitfall if you are not careful, and one that can be avoided by cross-referencing census records with other sources such as rate books, street directories and estate rentals, indeed even the 1910 Valuation Office survey, as these sources often allow you to pinpoint when a renumbering exercise took place.

Sadly, the Roswells were no longer in place at the time of the 1901 census. Their house is occupied by Henry E. Stammers, a messenger, and his family, but the house is shared with a general labourer, a provision porter and a mosaic layer (Valentine Ricci) from Italy. It was clearly a very cosmopolitan world, far removed from the days of Charles Newnham, the builder of the Square. The switch to multi-occupancy tenancy was confirmed at the National Archives through an examination of the 1910 Valuation Office. In the Field Book, the property was described as a:

3 storey non-basement house, 1 [room] deep, but in sound repair, having a two-storey back addition. Drains alright. Accommodation: top 2–3 rooms; 1st storey 2 rooms and 1 anti-room; ground storey 2 rooms, kitchen and scullery and moderate sized yard. Frontage 16 ft. Owner: Trustees of Lambeth Walcot Charity Estate; Occupier: TW Swetman.

It is possible to follow the occupants of the house over the next 30 years or so, when the outbreak of the Second World War shattered the peace of the Square. It is clear from bomb census maps at the London Metropolitan Archives that Walcot Square suffered several direct hits during the Blitz; the colour coding used by the cartographer shows that the Roswell's house had been badly damaged following a terrifying raid on the night of the 17/18 September 1940. Casualty reports mask the full horror of the event:

18 Sep 1940, 0055 HRS
Supplementary Report
Walcot Square 1–9 and 2–12 demolished,
Bishop's Terrace 1A and 1–6 shattered.
Old type 2 storey with basements, brick
built, 145–169 odd nos Kennington Road
damaged. 1 dead 4 slight[ly wounded] ... No
panic. Road closed with red lamps. Approx
100 rendered homeless ... Crater 10ft wide,
full of water in Walcot Square at Junction
of Kennington Road ... A dead motor cyclist
on post 8 side, taken away in police van,
others by ambulance.

and:

18 Sep 1940, 1049 HOURS
Supplementary report
145 Kennington Road dangerous, 143
Kennington Road damaged, 141–121
Kennington Road slightly damaged,
14 Walcot Square slightly damaged.

**It is clear that the properties were rendered
uninhabitable, as four days later the tenants requested that their surviving furniture
be removed to alternative locations, where
they were being put up. A formal report in
October reveals the true extent of the
damage.**

Short report on Air Raid Damage suffered
up to 10th Oct 1940. The estate has
suffered severely. In Kennington Road Nos
145/167 (odd) have been much damaged
and few tenants are in occupation. Nos.
104/112 (even) have many fallen ceilings
and little glass remains. Nos. 121/143 (odd)
with the latter houses at the moment are
not habitable. The damage does not appear
to extend substantially to the brickwork,
except at Nos. 143 and 145 where demolition may be necessary. The extent of
damage to roofs, plaster, doors and
windows is very large. Nos. 1/7 (odd) and
2/12 (even) Walcot Square and the
properties in Bishop's Terrace have been
wholly or partially demolished and a
preliminary survey suggests total demoli-

tion in the future rather than reconstruction. The premises are now uninhabitable.
The properties in Walcot Square, St Mary's
Street and St Mary's Gardens are less
damaged, with the exception of individual
houses such as those adjoining or near to
Bishop's Terrace. A number of tenants have
vacated. Arrangements for the execution of
first aid repairs by the Lambeth Borough
Council are in hand but the magnitude of
the damage and difficulties in connection
with labour and material is likely to prevent
any early completion of such first aid work.

**Although official reports show that a case
was made for the total demolition of No.14
in the light of this terrible damage, instead
the house was left to stand derelict. It was
eventually restored in the 1970s, and once
again became a family home.**

RECORDS OF NATIONAL EVENTS

11

11.1 Introduction

During the course of British history, there have been moments when national events have had a profound impact on local communities, and marked a turning point in the way our ancestors lived. Some of these events triggered large-scale house building or generated waves of property transactions, while others affected the way people thought about housing in general. The aim of this chapter is to present some examples of the records that these events have left behind. The house historian should always be aware that local history forms a crucial part of our understanding of national history. Indeed, the process of creating an empathy with previous owners or occupiers, and placing the house or property in its correct historical perspective, should form an important part of your research.

Events such as the dissolution of the monasteries and the English Civil War saw property and land change hands rapidly, and were often accompanied by enrolment of title deeds by the new owners, and law suits instigated by previous owners to get their property back; in the case of the former, new buildings were created out of the fabric of the old monastic institutions. The development of railway networks also produced great social and economic change, with new towns developing around stations, and industrial expansion running hand in hand with population growth. Destructive events such as the Second World War meant that the landscape of Britain was radically altered, forcing large areas to be rebuilt and reconstructed following devastating bomb damage in the Blitz. Even today we see Green Belt land disappearing under 'new towns'.

Yet alongside these 'nationwide' issues will be events that had a particular impact on your own community. During the period of industrial and population expansion from the late eighteenth century onwards, local trades and industries would have had an enormous influence on the surrounding community. You will also have to consider why people began to build houses at a particular time. For example, Britain experienced a large share of global commerce in the eighteenth century that enabled merchants and traders to build grander houses from their profits; town houses were constructed and country estates underwent renovation during the Georgian period. These wider topics are briefly considered in this chapter, although relevant material is more likely to be found at a local level.

The dissolution of the monasteries 11.2

HISTORICAL BACKGROUND

For centuries, monasteries and nunneries were an integral part of local communities, mainly because they had acquired large estates through land grants from private patronage. Hence, many people farmed land that was 'owned' by a monastery, paid their rents to the officials of the local abbot, inherited land through manorial courts presided over by the monks' representatives, and built property after obtaining the permission of the relevant institution. One of the most profound changes in English and Welsh social history occurred when Henry VIII broke away from the authority of the Church in Rome and established himself as the Supreme Head of the Church of England. The process went hand in hand with the suppression of monastic institutions, mainly as a means of generating new revenue for the government from the extensive lands that they possessed.

The dissolution process had begun as early as 1524–8, when Cardinal Wolsey obtained papal authority to suppress about 30 small religious houses to create new places of learning; their lands and possessions were used to found colleges at Oxford and Ipswich. However, it was only when Thomas Cromwell rose to power that a full-scale suppression occurred. In 1534 Crown commissioners surveyed all ecclesiastical income, including monastic houses, and the returns were entered in the *Valor Ecclesiasticus* (literally, 'value of the church'). As part of the Act of Supremacy, all monasteries were required to swear an oath of allegiance to the Crown, and visitations were made to check on their spiritual condition. The first phase saw the suppression of small religious houses with incomes valued at less than £200 per annum; they were dissolved by Act of Parliament in 1536. Thereafter, larger houses were also 'persuaded' to surrender to the Crown, and the last monastery closed in 1540.

The dissolution process saw the Crown, as head of the Church of England and therefore the alleged founder of the monasteries, take possession of all lands and estates that the monastic institutions previously enjoyed. It was then free to sell, re-grant or take the profits of these lands. Furthermore, the government stipulated that the buildings themselves were to be destroyed, with the minimum requirement that the roof of an institution should be razed, so that the monks could not return. The implications of these measures for the house historian are considered below.

DISPOSING OF THE MONASTIC ESTATES

II.2

The dissolution effectively created an unprecedented flood of land into private hands, as the Crown disposed of a large number of the new estates through sales and leases. The business generated by this land movement was so immense that a new section of government was created to manage the process, known as the Court of Augmentations; this became the Augmentations Office in 1554. The records generated by this institution have largely been stored among the papers of the Exchequer, as the entire process was designed to raise revenue for the government.

With the new department came waves of documentation detailing the size, content and value of each parcel of land, and how and where it was reassigned. In addition, the title documents of the former monastic possessions fell into the Crown's hands, a process that created an impressive archive of title deeds. Furthermore, the sales themselves have left many more records, not only in the papers of the Exchequer but also among the state papers of the era.

Locating monastic land

The first step is to determine whether dissolution documents are going to be of any use, and you should check whether your house was built on ex-monastic land. One of the best places to begin is with the various county histories that have been compiled, such as the *VCH*. This will outline the history of the monastery, but also describe the lands that formed its estate and what happened to them; alternatively, you can use manorial descents to establish if the manor within which your house is located was once owned by a monastic institution.

Evidences of title

If you suspect that there is a connection, then you can start to examine the many and varied monastic records that came to the Crown at the time of their suppression. Title deeds and cartularies were either presented to the new owners, or retained by the Crown. There is no single place of deposit at the National Archives for these documents, and they are scattered across many record series, although the majority have been deposited with the Court of Augmentations.

Conventual leases record agreements made between religious houses (convents) and lay tenants who leased land from the monastic estates. The leases were then transferred to the Crown. Similarly, Crown commissioners and surveyors gathered title deeds and records of former grants to provide proof of title of the new estates, thus enabling the Crown to establish its rights. Many other documents appear in the miscellaneous books and papers collected by the Court of Augmentations, and land revenue enrolment books were also used to record copies of previous transactions conducted by the religious houses. The jurisdiction of the Duchy of Lancaster encompassed many monastic estates, and their deeds, leases and papers can be found amongst the Duchy's records.

11.2

TABLE 11.1 is a summary of some of the most important National Archives series that contain the records described above. Most contain detailed descriptions of each item, and the National Archives has also prepared a research guide that lists where the records of major institutions are to be found. Other areas of the Exchequer might also yield useful results, and careful use of keyword searches of the catalogue should enable you to locate the majority of relevant entries.

Table 11.1 *Monastic evidence of title*

CHANCERY	
C 109, 115	Chancery Masters Exhibits

COURT OF AUGMENTATIONS	
E 303	Conventual leases
E 312	Leases and offices surrendered to the Crown
E 313	Original letters patent
E 314	Miscellanea
E 315	Miscellaneous books
E 326–30	Ancient deeds

OTHER EXCHEQUER SERIES	
E 118	King's Remembrancer: Conventual leases
E 135	Miscellaneous ecclesiastical documents

LAND REVENUE OFFICE	
LR 1	Enrolment books

DUCHY OF LANCASTER	
DL 25–7	Deeds
DL 36	Miscellaneous charters
DL 41	Miscellanea
DL 42	Enrolments, surveys and other books

Sales, grants and leases

Disposal of monastic land began when commissioners surveyed the possessions of each institution, and the documents they produced often included an assessment of its value, goods, estates, major tenants, rents and buildings. Most of the rentals and surveys are now in series SC 11 and 12, LR 1, 2 and 10, E 315, and DL 41 (for monasteries that formed part of the Duchy of Lancaster).

The National Archives finding aid *List and Index, vol. 25* will provide details of most surveys that have survived, though these can also be located by a keyword search of the catalogue. Others have turned up in Chancery Masters Exhibits series (c 103–15) among the private papers of individual surveyors.

One of the best places to begin looking for general information about ex-monastic lands are the printed *Letters and Papers Foreign and Domestic Henry VIII*, which cover the relevant period; later material can also be obtained from the *Calendars of State Papers* which exist for various chronological periods. All are indexed and on open access in the reading rooms, and there are separate manuscript keys that allow you to convert entries into the National Archives references.

Estates were initially taken into the hands of the Crown, and were administered by local officials. Their records can be found primarily among the ministers' and receivers' accounts in sc 6, lr 6 and dl 29 and are included in *List and Index, vol. 34*. A separate index lists surviving records for monastic estates. Although you are unlikely to find specific property listed, you may find references to expenditure on monastic buildings that were later converted into dwellings.

Records of lands that were granted to individuals can be found on the patent rolls. These are listed in the printed *Letters and Papers Foreign and Domestic Henry VIII*, on open access in the reading rooms. You will also find grants listed in land revenue enrolment books in lr 1. The details of the original grant appear in e 318, and a detailed index of grantees exists in the 9th and 10th DKRs. There is also a manuscript index to places, which might be of more use. Furthermore, the Court of Augmentations dealt with disputes that arose over the ex-monastic lands. Finally, leases of ex-monastic lands can be located in e 307–12. The series e 321, 314 and 315 will mainly contain sixteenth-century records, and thereafter you should search the records of the equity side of the Exchequer.

MONASTIC BUILDINGS

As well as providing rentals for lands, the surveys and inventories of monastic possessions compiled by the Crown commissioners can tell you a great deal about the monastic buildings themselves. They usually provide a room by room assessment of the goods and possessions of the houses that were to be offered for sale. Although most buildings were destroyed according to the directions of the government, many were either rebuilt to form large country houses, or converted into domestic dwellings. Some disputes arose about the dwellings themselves, and thus can appear in court cases. Ex-monastic buildings are frequently referred to in wills and legal transfers, and private papers of the purchasers can provide building accounts that shed light on the conversion process.

Figure 22 Detail from an inventory of the goods and possessions of Blackladies nunnery, Brewood, at the time of its dissolution in 1538. The survival of a later survey from 1650, with an identical room layout, suggests that, contrary to requirements, the original building was not demolished by its new owners but was converted into a domestic dwelling. (E 315/172)

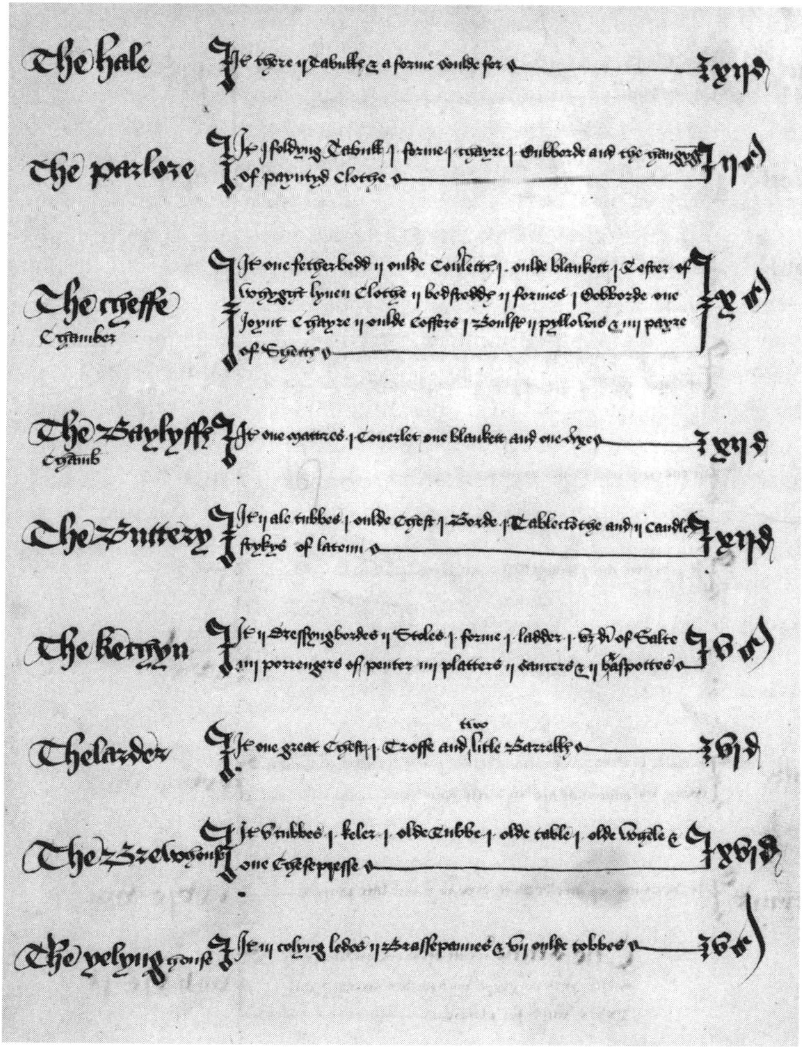

One of the best examples of a conversion comes from the papers of the Earl of Southampton, who purchased the estates and buildings of Titchfield Abbey. The Earl then built a large house on the site of the old monastery, converting many of the existing rooms into new accommodation. Letters which outline the conversion process exist in the state papers of Henry VIII, and can be located among the Wriothesley papers in SP 7.

In comparison, the fate of Blackladies nunnery (see FIGURE 22) in Brewood, Staffordshire, shows that the buildings themselves were sometimes sought as dwellings in their own right. (*See* the PROPERTY PROFILE on pages 73–5.) In this instance, the Gifford family bought the site of the nunnery and then used the house to provide accommodation for a younger branch of the family. Not only do estate papers exist, but there is also official correspondence in *Letters and Papers Foreign and Domestic Henry VIII* and a supplementary survey in C 115 to complement the official inventory in E 315.

However, the usual fate of the old monastic buildings was to be torn down and used as salvage for smaller dwellings. You may find stones in local houses, and architectural evidence should help you to determine monastic salvage.

11.3 The English Civil War

HISTORICAL BACKGROUND

The English Civil War was fought between supporters of King Charles I and those who backed the rule of Parliament. The first civil war raged from 1642 to 1645, and conflict broke out again between 1648 and 1649. The Parliamentary party was eventually victorious, and the execution of Charles I in 1649 enabled Parliament to establish the Commonwealth. An immediate problem facing the new regime was finance, and the lands of the Crown and the chief Royalist supporters were an obvious source of income.

As a result of the sequestration of Crown and Royalist lands, a land market was created between 1649 and 1660, with the profits initially used to pay for the wars and reward Parliamentary followers. However, the Commonwealth was dissolved and Cromwell was declared Lord Protector. No stable alternative to monarchy had been found, and on Cromwell's death Charles II was invited to return as King. In the aftermath of the Restoration, Crown lands and many Royalist estates were legally returned to their original owners (or their heirs). The resulting litigation, appeals and paperwork provided a convenient snapshot of property that was in dispute. Accordingly, there are various areas relating to the civil war period in which the house historian can look, although the best records survive for Crown lands and supporters of the Royalist cause.

DISPOSAL OF CROWN LANDS

After the final defeat of the Royalists in 1648–9, the victorious Parliamentarians were faced with the task of raising revenue to pay war debts, and army arrears in particular. An Act of Parliament dated 16 July 1649 permitted the sale of Crown lands with this specific aim in mind, and an administrative machine was set up to facilitate

Figure 23 A survey made by Parliamentary commissioners in 1650 on the manor house at Terrington St Clements, Norfolk. It describes the house in great detail, even providing dimensions for the outbuildings attached to the property. The occupier's name (Richard Pratt) is given, and the site was valued at a yearly rent of £5. (E 317/norf/16)

the process. First, Crown lands were legally vested in trustees, who collected the revenues accruing to the lands. Next, contractors were appointed to act as sale agents, who negotiated sales with the prospective purchasers. Treasurers collected and accounted for the sale money, while a registry enrolled the transactions and provided title deeds for the purchasers.

Parliamentary surveys

To start the process, documents known as Parliamentary surveys (*see* FIGURE 23) were compiled from 1649 to 1650. Local surveyors were appointed by the trustees to assess the revenue due from Crown manors and estates, and then to assign a sale value to the land. Two copies of each local survey were made, and the returns retained by the surveyor general are now in series E 317. The surveys covered all land that was nominally part of the Crown's estates, and therefore any property that was built on Crown land was included. The most informative types of survey covered manors and other properties sold under the 1649 Act, as these gave detailed descriptions of buildings on the land, plus details of leases. Other surveys were conducted by hundred to permit the sale of fee-farm rents, and during the course of the process evidence was collected relating to title.

Where Parliamentary surveys survive, they can prove an excellent source of information for the house historian, including room by room descriptions of houses, with valuations attached. The series is arranged by county and lists manors and hundreds covered. The documents are included in *List and Index, vol.* 25 (Rentals and Surveys), and can also be searched by place name via the catalogue. Duplicate copies are stored in LR 2, and material relating to the Duchy of Lancaster can be found in DL 32.

Other Crown properties are listed in great detail. For example, Richmond Palace was the subject of an individual survey, and it was demolished after the war to raise revenue from the sale of stones from the ruins. These were purchased for building purposes in the local community, and can still be seen in existing properties today.

Sale documents
In addition to the official surveys, the sales themselves generated swathes of documentation, including proofs of title; however, there is no overall composite index to the records, and so you may have to search through many series with little chance of finding particulars about your house. You should consider a search of these records only if you suspect your house was part of the sale process, or there is some evidence in the title deeds.

E 320 is a good place to begin looking for information, as it contains sale particulars drawn up by the registrar. You may also find various certificates that include details of purchaser and price, conveyance instructions and completion documents. There is a manuscript index to this series that is arranged by county. In addition, you can try the indexes to the close rolls to see if the title deeds were enrolled there. Other areas in which to start searching for certificates of sale include E 121 and 308/7 pt.II and SP 28/286 and 28/289.

In addition to the estates themselves, fee-farm rents were also sold to private individuals, and certificates of sale can be found in a variety of places. Particulars of sale will be of most use to the house historian, and are located in E 308 and among the particulars for leases in E 367; certificates of sale are in E 308/7 and 315/145, and enrolments can again be found on the close rolls in C 54. You may find references to individual properties in requests made to sale contractors (SP 28/286), counterpart deeds (E 307) and entry contract books (E 308/7 pt.I, 315/141 and 315/144), while a chronological summary of purchases can be found in SP 28/288. Another useful series will be the books of the trustees in SP 26, including entry books of agreement to purchase.

LANDS OF ROYALIST SUPPORTERS

From 1645 supporters of the Royalist cause faced severe repercussions under the Parliamentary regime. Technically they were viewed as traitors who had taken arms against the state, and therefore their lands were legally forfeited. However, the reality for most Royalist supporters was different, and they were allowed to pay a fine to retain their lands. This process, known as compounding, was administered by one of the new bodies created by the Parliamentary regime, entitled the Committee for Compounding with Delinquents. There are printed calendars available that enable you to locate the individuals who compounded, and properties are occasionally mentioned in detail. The records are in the National Archives series SP 23, and the most useful will be the lists of delinquents (the Royalists), as they often contain surveys of their estates. The committee compiled reports of individual compositions and sequestrations, and these can also contain particulars of the estates. Earlier records can be found in SP 20 (Sequestration Committee books and papers), for which a partial index survives in series ZBOX 1.

Royalists who refused to compound, or were not permitted to, found their estates sequestrated in a similar manner to Crown property. Property was transferred to the Treason Trustees, whose papers have largely disappeared. However, many lands were sold to private individuals, and you may find enrolments of deeds on the close rolls (C 54). New owners were required to notify the Committee for Compounding of each purchase, and you can once again track down the names of new owners, although some will be land agents acting on behalf of their clients, and others will be the names of those who sought to purchase property but were ultimately unsuccessful.

THE RESTORATION

With the Restoration of the monarchy in 1660, the task of recovering Crown lands began in earnest. The 'late pretended sales' of Crown estates between 1649 and 1660 were deemed to be illegal, and a new set of commissioners was appointed to assess the extent of the restitution payable to the purchasers of the land.

Commissions of enquiry survive among the records of the Exchequer, along with depositions taken from local witnesses who were questioned about the sales. These can be found in series E 134 and 178, and other references can be located among the state papers domestic (SP 29); these are calendared and on open access. Once the lands had been returned, the purchasers claimed restitution; information can be found in the Constat books that record details of Crown leases, in particular CRES 6/1–8 covering the period 1660–68. Local information can be traced through land revenue enrolment books in LR 1, which are grouped into counties and arranged chronologically.

Similarly, Royalist delinquents (or their heirs) whose lands had been sold after sequestration demanded a return of their possessions. As a result, many cases challenging the legality of the sales can be found in the equity courts after 1660. Compensation claims for war damage to property and houses were also filed in the courts, and the records generated by this procedure can provide great detail about houses and the damage they suffered, and this period can provide evidence of rebuilding programmes. Unfortunately, the indexes for this period are usually by the names of the plaintiff, so you will need to know the name of the former owner.

11.4 Trade and commerce

From the late seventeenth century and throughout the eighteenth century, Britain started to expand its commercial activities overseas. Trading companies flourished, and on the back of the wealth that was generated in the face of competition with their French and Dutch rivals, many merchants were able to purchase land in cities and maintain country estates. The result was a major period of building that changed the face of towns and cities across Britain during the Georgian period.

Ports were the communities that benefited the most from these developments. Trade links with the colonies in the West Indies, North America and the East Indies stimulated rapid growth in places such as Bristol, Liverpool, Southampton and London, not only in terms of the volume of business they conducted, but also in the many new properties that were built by merchants from their profits. The National Archives is not the best place to begin your research, as private records of the merchants are usually found in the CROs where they are deposited, or at specialist institutions such as the Oriental and India Office Library at the BL. For example, many of the papers of the former employees of the East India Company are deposited there. Before you begin searching, it is advisable to obtain clues about former merchant owners from existing title deeds, wills or later sales.

However, you might find records of properties built in the colonies themselves among the Colonial Office (CO) papers deposited at the National Archives, as well as at institutions such as the Oriental and India Office Library. If you wish to explore this line of research, there are publications to help you find the best place to look; but you ought to consider the historical background to this period before you begin, as many individuals became rich through their involvement with the slave trade. It is important to remember that, while such a practice may be abhorrent by today's standards, it was part of the fabric of life in the eighteenth century and funded the construction of many grand houses both in Britain and the colonies where the trade flourished.

It is sometimes easier to trace the records of the new urban areas that were developed in Britain during the eighteenth century. You will find many building leases assigned for individual properties and new 'estates' that date from this period. These were often specifically created for the rising merchant and gentry classes. High-status estates were often the work of local entrepreneurs who owned or purchased freehold land, but then sold the right to construct property to local builders. Once again you are more likely to find such material among private papers at municipal archives, specialist museums and institutions, as well as CROs, but printed local histories will probably provide good background information with document references for you to follow up. Furthermore, many building leases can be located in local deed registries, for example London or Yorkshire.

Railways and the Industrial Revolution   11.5

INDUSTRIAL EXPANSION

With the development of large-scale industrial sites and factories during the late eighteenth and nineteenth centuries, new dwellings were required to house increasing numbers of workers who flocked to the embryonic industrial towns from the countryside in search of employment. In contrast to the commercial expansion of ports and existing cities throughout the eighteenth century that was largely stimulated by the merchant and gentry classes, the requirement for industrial towns was for lower status housing close to the emerging factories, in particular in the Midlands and north of England. Building programmes would have been a combination of private enterprise with commercial support, and you will often find rows of workers' cottages springing up on the outskirts of towns near to the factories to form industrial suburbs.

It is therefore important to consider what the local industry would have been and where it was located, as this can often explain patterns of housing construction and lead you to the archives of the companies concerned, regardless of whether they were running mines, mills, dockyards, shipbuilding firms or ironworks. This material will be stored primarily at local archives and specialist labour history institutions, and you can use secondary sources, museum guides and local histories to track down industrial and urban development in your area. Although records of individual houses within these developments can be difficult to locate, you can use a combination of maps, trade directories and census returns (in particular from 1851 when the enumerators included more information in their returns) to create a sense of when new areas of housing were constructed, as urban growth was usually linked to periods of industrial expansion.

Larger industries often ran housing associations to provide accommodation for their workers, and the National Archives holds some material for nationalized industries, such as the papers of the National Coal Board. Correspondence and papers relating to housing for workers can be found in COAL 48 and 66. In addition, the Ministry of Housing maintained files in HLG 40 on rural housing and tied houses, which were built by industrial companies. Information on housing associations can be gleaned from the papers in HLG 101, and many records in local archives will also be relevant. Don't forget, though, that it is the texture of the past that you are looking to reproduce through your research, so visit as many local or specialist museums as possible, such as the National Coal Museum in Wakefield or the People's History Museum in Manchester (see 'Useful addresses').

RAILWAYS

In conjunction with the industrial revolution, one of the most significant changes in English social history was the widespread development of a railway network. Not only were communities joined together by a fast means of communication, but the network brought physical changes that left an indelible mark on the landscape. Townships underwent rapid expansion as new people settled or sought work, and property was often built around stations, which became the new focal point for communities. As part of this process, old houses were knocked down to make way for railroads, while railway companies often constructed new buildings to provide accommodation for their workers; these often took the form of housing associations.

Railway records were previously stored with the BTHR, and most have now been transferred to the National Archives along with records of the canal companies. The records are arranged by individual railway company, so you will need to identify which particular company operated along the line of track in your town or village. There are finding aids in the National Archives to assist you, such as the general card index compiled by the BTHR.

The best place to begin your research will be with the maps and plans created by the companies. The main series can be found in RAIL 1029–35, and you will also find maps and plans scattered among company papers in other RAIL series as well. You should also consider examining RAIL 1071, which contains maps and plans produced with private Acts of Parliament for railway construction, and accordingly there will be more records deposited at the House of Lords Record Office, London, where large numbers of private

Acts are now stored. Parliamentary papers in general (RAIL 1062–79) are worth consulting, as are collections of railway related material (RAIL 1014–19, 1038–60 and 1147–57). For example, RAIL 1189 holds files from the Surveyor and Estate Agent's branch of the Great Northern Railway, which contain correspondence dealing with the purchase of land required for new railways or the widening of existing railways, the disposal of surplus land, licensing of land and property to and by the company, enquiries from people and organizations outside the company concerning proposed purchases and sales of land and property, housing for staff and relocated residents, maintenance of property, and compensation paid to owners, lessees, tenants and residents affected by railway works. Similar material will be located with the records of the individual railway companies, in RAIL 1–799, and these are available for keyword searches on the catalogue. Material on accommodation for persons made homeless by statutory instruments for railway construction can be found in HLG 24, while other relevant material can be located at CROs.

Twentieth-century warfare   11.6

The first half of the twentieth century was marked by two world wars, and the records that were produced can provide information for the house historian. For example, many properties were requisitioned for military use during the Second World War, and the destruction caused to major cities during the Blitz stimulated post-war urban regeneration. These topics will be covered in more detail in the next chapter, but some of the series of documents that were used to detail the destruction caused by enemy bombing are described below.

REQUISITIONED PROPERTY IN THE SECOND WORLD WAR
There are no overall document series where requisitioned property is listed, but the following areas are worth investigating if you suspect that your house was once taken over for military purposes.

There are government property registers in WORK 50 that include 'blue books' (WORK 50/23–9). These are requisition, compensation and settlement registers that record transfers of property out of government hands and derequisitioned property. However, these documents cover only Berkshire, Buckinghamshire, Hampshire and Oxfordshire, with limited details for Hertfordshire and Surrey. Some policy material on the disposal of requisitioned property and land after the war can be found in HLG 102, with related files in HLG 101.

Compensation claims for loss of earnings, and war damage to requisitioned property, can be traced through compensation claims handled by the Land Tribunal in LT 6, to which there are indexes and registers to general claims in LT 7. In addition, it might be worth investigating various series of records that were maintained by the Ministry of Home Security. You will find many references to requisitioned property in HO 186 (Air Raid Precautions) under the headings Land and Accommodation, Finance, and Damage Reconstruction and Salvage, and there is similar material in HO 187 (Fire Brigades Division) under the heading Buildings and Land. In addition, correspondence and papers in HO 205 include several sections with files on requisitioned property, and there are further documents in HO 207 for each of the civil defence regions, particularly relating to compensation claims for damage. Other material relating to requisitions for emergency housing under special wartime functions of the Ministry of Health can be found in HLG 7.

BOMB DAMAGE IN THE SECOND WORLD WAR

To assess the extent of the damage caused by German raids during the Blitz, and to attempt to find ways of minimizing the damage caused by future raids, bomb census surveys were conducted; these can be a useful source of information about properties in cities affected by enemy action during the war. Maps, charts and plans were created that show the exact places where bombs were dropped, and can be found in HO 193. They are arranged by type of bomb (piloted and non-piloted aircraft), region and date. Documentation relating to the bomb census is in HO 198, although this will be of little use to the house historian. Other maps and plans that relate to bomb damage, along with associated casualty reports and demolition schedules of damaged property, can be found elsewhere, such as the London Metropolitan Archives and other municipal archives where urban areas were badly affected during the war.

The Ministry of Housing and Local Government created many files that relate to war damage and post-war reconstruction. Amongst the many series held by the National Archives, HLG 79 will be of most use as it is arranged by the name of each council authority; many files relate to proposals for reconstruction after war damage. HLG 7 is another important series, as the Ministry of Health held special wartime responsibility for coordinating the Ministries of Works, Health and Labour and the War Damage Commission to effect repairs in London to relieve homelessness. This series contains papers of the London Repairs Executive, which was replaced by the London Housing Committee in 1945 to integrate war damage repairs with other housing work.

Records of the Central Land Board are in HLG 98 (policy files), HLG 99 (case files) and HLG 112 (appeals files), which deal with cases that arose from the considerations of the War Damage Commission, whose papers are in IR 33–9. Papers relating to claims against damage caused by military personnel can be found in WO 306. Government papers on post-war rebuilding pro-grammes and the control of building materials can be found in WORK 45, 49 and 50. All of these series are technical in nature, and will not give specific details about individual properties. However, they do provide a context for some of the building programmes that began in the post-war years.

11.6

In addition to the bomb census records at the National Archives, an aer-ial survey was conducted after the war, whereby photographs were taken of various regions. These can be of some use to the house historian, and are stored at the Imperial War Museum.

IRISH HOUSING AFTER THE FIRST WORLD WAR
As a footnote to this section, there are records for houses and cottages con-structed in Ireland after the conclusion of the First World War. A trust fund for Irish sailors and soldiers was set up to provide land for men who had served in the armed forces in the First World War. The trustees first met in 1924, and their headquarters were based in London. The records are stored in series AP 1–8, and can provide detailed information about the properties that were constructed, and who lived in them.

AP 5 contains a register of properties from 1923 to 1927 for Northern Ireland, while correspondence about the initial construction of the houses and cottages and tenancy affairs are in AP 1 (London and Dublin) and AP 2 (London and Belfast). Registers of documents sealed by the trust are to be found in AP 8, where names and addresses of tenants who opted into the trust's sell and buy scheme are listed, along with information on sub-letting and mortgages. Treasury files on the sale to tenants scheme can be found in T 233/146, while the financial aspects of the policy of substituting flats for cottages between 1930 and 1947 are addressed in T 233/145. AP 7 contains other tenancy files, plus annotated OS maps, maps of building schemes and photographs of property; some of these can be matched with information in AP 1 and AP 2, although you will need to sign an undertaking in order to view these records. HO 351/199 also contains information on the requisition of land under the Irish Land (Provision of Sailors, Soldiers) Act 1919, and related material on land purchase is in CAB 27/85. Papers that describe the process of allocating housing to Northern Ireland from 1921 to 1924 are in HO 45/11708.

12

12.1 Introduction

Not every house can be traced very far back in time. However, there are plenty of excellent sources for late-nineteenth-century and twentieth-century houses that can tell you when your house was built, and perhaps what was there before it was constructed. The best place to begin will be with some of the sources already described, such as census returns (1841–1901), the Valuation Office survey (1910–15), the National Farm Survey (1940s), modern electoral lists, and trade and street directories. Furthermore, there is more chance that property transfers will be recorded in the Land Registry, and modern title deeds are going to be easier to track down. However, the twentieth century furnishes the house historian with many new sources that will reflect developments in housing policy to meet the needs of a growing population.

Some aspects of the Second World War have been considered in the previous chapter, but the long-term impact on urban regeneration and the immediate housing crisis that it produced can be traced through many important pieces of legislation that affected the remainder of the century. The Town and Country Planning Act of 1947 set out the guidelines for the post-war slum clearance, town planning and building techniques that shaped the landscape of the communities we live in today. Most of the records created by the central authorities are now at the National Archives in archives deposited by the Housing and Local Government Department, the Local Government Board, the Ministry of Health and the Ministry of Town and Country Planning; however, there will be many more files, maps and plans generated by local authorities and stored at CROs.

To write in detail on the changing nature of houses and housing policy would be to write a social and economic history of the twentieth century, so this chapter will focus on only the most relevant and easily accessible sources at the National Archives. In addition, files created by local authorities in response to specific housing matters are briefly considered, as are various sources that can provide additional information at a local level. Finally, advice about where to start research into building techniques and materials employed in twentieth-century housing is also provided.

Housing policy before the Second World War   12.2

BACKGROUND INFORMATION: TACKLING NINETEENTH-CENTURY POVERTY

During the nineteenth century, the rapid growth of towns and cities created problems of overcrowding, which in turn impacted upon public health. From the 1840s the spread of epidemics, such as cholera, prompted numerous Royal Commissions to investigate how to tackle the combined health and housing crises. Much of the work fell upon newly created Poor Law unions, which had responsibility for implementing Poor Law legislation. Some of the records and correspondence of the Poor Law Commission and subsequent Poor Law Board, which coordinated the work of the unions, are in MH 1 and 12, but these will give only background information rather than specific references to houses; however, indexes in MH 15 should allow you to locate relevant files in MH 12 that relate to early housing policy. Plans of land and buildings used by local authorities under the terms of the Poor Laws can be found in MH 14, HLG 6 and MH 48.

Of similar importance was the 1843 Royal Commission on the Health of Towns and Populous Places. Measures were drafted to prevent the spread of infectious disease, and a Board of Health was established. There are many records that deal with the problems caused by housing and overcrowding in correspondence located in MH 13 and HLG 1 and 46, but – as with the records of the Poor Law Board – the records will provide only background information rather than specific property details.

You will also find information on the housing conditions that were prevalent in the works of Charles Booth and Edwin Chadwick, who compiled reports based on specific houses in the urban slum areas. These can be accessed via the index to the Parliamentary Sessional Papers, available on CD-ROM from the National Archives Library. Copies of the papers themselves are stored on microfiche at Kew.

A publication that will provide further contemporary opinion on housing and sanitary conditions for the poor and working classes is *The Builder*, first published in 1842 and extensively developed under the editorship of George Godwin from 1844. It also focused on architecture and building debates of the age. Copies can be found at many main libraries, and there are annual indexes from 1842 to 1879 and half-annual indexes from 1880 bound with the relevant volume. Don't forget that you can also view Charles Booth's poverty maps, created from 1886 onwards, online as described in CHAPTER 3.

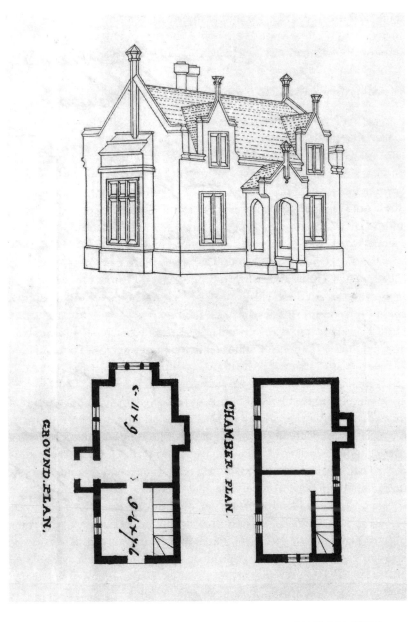

Figure 24 Plan for a worker's cottage in Delamere Forest, which cost £75 to construct in 1841. (CRES 2/132)

SLUM CLEARANCE, REDEVELOPMENT AND PLANNING SCHEMES

The establishment of the Local Government Board by Act of Parliament in 1871 created an institution with powers to tackle housing problems at a local level, and the Board inherited many of the responsibilities of the Poor Law Board. Early responsibility for housing fell to the Sanitary Department, but by 1910 a separate Housing and Town Planning Department had been formed. In an effort to address the problem of housing for the working classes, from 1875 local authorities were permitted to purchase areas that were considered to be slums under the terms of the Artisans' and Labourers' Dwellings Act and submit redevelopment schemes to the Board for approval. After the First World War, the Ministry of Health inherited most of the housing work of the Local Government Board, and also developed an interest in building control in general. An important piece of legislation was the 1930 Housing Act, which enabled the Ministry of Health (Housing Department) to establish clearance and improvement areas and then demolish unfit houses while building new ones.

In consequence, there are many useful records now with the National Archives that relate to urban regeneration in the late nineteenth and early twentieth centuries, housing for working classes and the creation of local authority housing estates. To make searching easier, you should begin by identifying which local authority your property falls within. Maps created by the Ministry of Health and previous departments that depict the boundaries of some of the Poor Law unions and district authorities can be found in HLG 6 for the period 1800–1900, with similar and related material in HLG 44. These will at least afford some assistance if you are unsure, and can include properties that were affected by boundary changes.

If you are trying to track down slum clearance and redevelopment plans in your area that commenced before the Second World War, the place to begin should be the registered files for the planning schemes themselves. HLG 4 contains the planning schemes developed by local authorities that were referred to the Local Government Board and its successors for approval under the Town and Country Planning Acts 1909–32. The records are arranged by the name of the local authority, and there is an introductory note in the series list to assist you. Alternatively, you can search for material in registers stored in HLG 95. Much of the material contained in the records will not be property specific, but you will obtain a general overview of the planning schemes and their extent. Extracted maps and plans that accompanied the schemes are in HLG 5, although you may find some material bound with the paperwork in HLG 4.

Local authorities were required to seek the permission of the relevant government department before they could start to proceed with their plans. Consequently, the department's legal branch gained responsibility for drawing up the housing instruments for the erection of houses and new streets. These records are stored in HLG 13, and contain maps, instruments and consents for land sales, leases and purchases, construction of new streets and sewers, and general housing issues. Registers to the series exist in HLG 14 and are arranged by date and type of local authority; the indexes will lead you to an instrument number, which is listed in HLG 13. Similar material will also be found in HLG 95.

Officially sealed orders made by the various institutions and departments that authorized permission for planning schemes to go ahead are to be found in HLG 26, with sealed plans in HLG 23; later post-war material is in HLG 111. The records can contain great detail, in some instances describing a property and listing the current or former occupiers, but the level of information will vary according to the type of order and the date. The main drawback is that there are no internal indexes to the orders themselves, so you may need to undertake a great deal of searching. Registers and indexes that allow you to identify relevant documents in all three series are contained in HLG 66, although the series lists can usefully be searched on the catalogue.

In addition to the planning schemes, orders, instruments and consents listed above, other material can shed tremendous light on the actual proceedings themselves. For example, HLG 49 contains a wealth of information relating to detailed surveys of the conditions and needs of areas under local authority control, with proposals, plans, acquisition of land and surveyors' reports into the ensuing redevelopment work. The records are generally arranged by the name of the street, area or planning scheme, and are further grouped under the relevant council or local authority. You will also find some material on housing associations. Furthermore, registers of progress for some of these schemes can be found in HLG 96, and are arranged by county between 1934 and 1941; however, they only provide basic statistical details of how many properties were demolished or built on given dates, and are not property-specific. HLG 47 will perhaps be of greater use, as it contains demolition and closing orders, papers relating to slum clearance, objections, compulsory purchase of property and correspondence, mainly relating to the period 1919–40, although earlier material can be identified. General correspondence on slum clearance, redevelopment and housing programmes can be found in HLG 118, although only a few places are listed by street or development scheme.

12.3 Post-war reconstruction and development

THE 1947 TOWN AND COUNTRY PLANNING ACT

The need for regeneration of urban areas was brought into sharp focus by the devastation caused by bombing raids during the Blitz, a topic that has been considered in the previous chapter. Although planning for urban and rural redevelopment had long been a function of the various bodies described above, an Act of Parliament in 1943 established a separate Ministry of Town and Country Planning. Its remit was to regulate local authority wartime construction, and subsequently to redevelop areas that had been worst affected by damage or blight caused by the war. The result of the ministry's work was the 1947 Town and Country Planning Act, which made fresh provision for planning development and use of land. It also gave additional powers to local authorities to develop land for planning. A Central Land Board was established, and councils were directed to create development plans for their area of authority. From 1951 functions formerly under the Ministry of Health were added to create the Ministry of Local Government and Planning.

All local authorities were required to survey their area and prepare a development plan, which was to be submitted to the Ministry of Town and County Planning. Maps and written statements for each county are stored in series HLG 119, along with amendments to the plans made under later surveys. In addition, HLG 79 contains the detailed submission of the proposals and plans by local authorities. The records are listed by the local authority, and cover a vast amount of material, such as housing programmes, war damage redevelopment, surveys, planning and reconstruction. Although the quality of information will vary from location to location, some records provide great detail, including maps and plans of the areas under consideration.

Other areas worth investigating include HLG 71, which contains general policy files. There is a subject index in the series list that displays the topics covered by the material, but the most important areas for property will include Planning, Land, Development Plans and Disposals. You will find many miscellaneous files, including planning appeals by local authority, aerial photographs, surveys, and even reports into 'moveable' dwellings such as caravan sites.

Many of the series listed in the previous section will also contain post-war information, in particular HLG 47, 49 and 118. In addition, HLG 101 contains general material on government building programmes, housing associations, flats, and building research. A list of subject headings is provided at the front of the series list, including one on housing, and similar material and information on the disposal of land and property requisitioned during the war are found in HLG 102. You might also wish to browse HLG 68 for general information on planning and development policy for the period, and background material on the Town and Country Planning Act is located in HLG 104.

NEW TOWNS

In addition to the work on redeveloping existing towns and rural areas, and providing a national coordinating body, the Ministry of Town and Country Planning, and after 1951 the Ministry of Local Government and Planning, were responsible for developing new towns. The first piece of legislation to consider developing new urban areas was the New Town Act 1946, which was based on the experiences of the 'garden' cities of Letchworth and Welwyn. New Town Development Corporations were established to project-manage the creation of new towns, covering the acquisition of land, development of all services required by the new towns, and provision of adequate housing.

Consequently, there are numerous records of use to the house historian who lives in one of the post-war new town developments. General correspondence and files relating to planning policy and development of new towns can be found in HLG 90, which lists several specific proposals. The records of the New Town Development Corporations are in HLG 91, and there is an index to the corporations in the series list. There are maps, plans and papers on the entire planning process required to create a community from scratch, including references to specific houses and streets. Development proposals for the new towns, plus registered files, are in HLG 115, which is arranged by town with a key at the front of the series list. Topics are listed under each town corporation. You may also find Treasury files in T 227 to be of interest, as the Social Services division contains files on housing, local government and new towns, and further background and policy information is in HLG 116.

LOCAL AUTHORITY RENT CONTROL

In 1946 Rent Tribunals were established under the 1946 Furnished Houses (Rent Control) Act. Their work involved hearing applications from landlords, tenants and local authorities wishing to seek a decision on the level of reasonable rent for furnished property. The Tribunals therefore held hearings to decide the rent that should be paid, and in the course of their work they often visited the property in question. Once they had reached a decision, they then notified the local authority in which the property was located. Local authorities were then required by law to maintain a register of decisions made about fixing a reasonable level of rent between landlords and tenants. The National Archives contains applications and Tribunal records for Devon, Cornwall and South Middlesex in HLG 97. This is an excellent source, as it is arranged by district and then by the address of the property in question, so it is easy to search for a specific property. You will find information on the name of the lessor, the name of the lessee, the dimensions of the property, details of rent, service provided by the lessor and general running costs of the property, such as rates, electricity and cleaning charges.

In addition, the 1965 Rent Act reintroduced rent control for unfurnished property, and rent officers decided an equitable level of rent that should be paid. Appeals by either landlords or tenants were made to Rent Assessment Committees, and selected cases are in series HLG 121. As with the Tribunal records, the assessment panel records are listed by the address of the property in question. HLG 122 contains similarly listed cases produced by the rent officers themselves. Background material on rent control, plus subjects such as house building, slum clearance and the impact of building regulations on house design and construction, can be found in HLG 118.

BUILDING RESEARCH AND BYE-LAWS

Most of the series at the National Archives that have been listed in this chapter will be of relevance to individual properties, or housing development plans that affect properties in a particular area. However, there are numerous other files created by government departments that will provide information on house construction, plus the rules and regulations that affect buildings in general. These may be of interest if you wish to know more about how and why your house was built.

Background information on the planning process and building research can be found in HLG 52, which contains many files that complement those in HLG 49. Subjects such as planning and development, including research into building techniques, are covered and can provide much background information about the specific records contained in the series listed above. Other series holding similar details include HLG 101 (housing policy and building research), which contains cross-references to many other series, and HLG 118 (the impact of building regulations on house construction). In addition, HLG 58 supplements this material as it contains files and papers on local authority bye laws that affect local planning and building. For those interested in Welsh local authority housing policy, case files, maps and plans, a search of BD 11 might prove fruitful.

As well as permanent housing, there are many records at the National Archives relating to the temporary housing that was introduced to ease the hardship caused by enemy bomb damage during the Second World War. The 1944 Housing (Temporary Accommodation) Act and the 1948 Local Government Act regulated the provision of post-war accommodation in the form of prefabricated houses. Records can be located in a variety of areas at the National Archives, particularly in many of the series already listed above. In addition, files maintained by the Building Research Station on prefabricated house-building techniques, plus technical reports, are in DSIR 4, while general development papers can be found in AVIA 65/230. The impact of local building bye-laws on prefabricated housing can be researched in HLG 58, and documentation on Treasury aid to the companies that constructed the houses is to be found in T 227. Series BD 11 contains relevant material for Wales.

12.4 Records maintained by local authorities

The records described above relate to official files maintained by the relevant government departments and institutions in response to legislation regarding housing. This is only one side of the story, as the local authorities themselves created and maintained similar files that can provide even more detail on these topics, plus more specific information on council housing in general.

The National Archives does not hold any records created by the various local authorities, and consequently CROs or city archives will be the logical place of deposit for the registered files that were created by these bodies. Most local authorities maintained departments with responsibility for housing, building contracts, architects, engineers, surveyors and urban development, and the records generated by these departments can be of great importance. Of particular use will be applications for planning permission to build or extend properties, as the relevant department would have to consider each application in turn before delivering a verdict; this process would create paperwork that lists names of owners and occupiers. Similar applications to council departments would have been made if a property were to be considered for listed buildings status, and records of surveys, assessments, judgments and justification of judgments will be of great use in determining the history of a property.

Similarly, local authorities had responsibility for all aspects of town planning, and in addition to the files listed above you will find reams of paperwork on decisions reached at a local level, plus deposited plans for the various schemes. The everyday administration of local towns and villages generated records that feature property in a number of surprising places. For example, sewers were fundamental in improving health conditions in the nineteenth century, and local authorities inherited the responsibility for maintaining them. They also inherited the maps and plans that accompanied the work, and these can be of great use to the urban house historian. Similarly, paving committees will list work in streets, often referring to particular houses or requests by house owners for work to be done.

Finally, the administration of council housing created under the various planning schemes and redevelopment plans listed above will contain a wealth of information on individual properties. Some archives will have a wider range of material than others, depending on the individual local authorities; and there may be restrictions on access depending on how recent the records are. However, if you suspect that your property was once maintained or owned by the local council, then you could find the names of previous tenants, evidence of rebuilding works and repairs, and even a construction or purchase date.

Records of utility companies

With the widespread introduction of water, electricity, gas and telephones from the late nineteenth century onwards, deposited records of pre-nationalization public utility companies can provide a useful guide to the location of properties from this period onwards. For example, when any of these services were installed in a street or community, maps and plans were usually created, and were amended as new connections were made. Similarly, papers relating to the installation of services within individual properties can provide the names of owners or occupiers. Some of the company records have been deposited at local archives, but others will still be with the companies themselves, so you may not automatically find records in the public domain.

13

13.1 Introduction

Most of this guide has been devoted to the documentary sources that are available to help you construct a chronology of your house's history, mainly by tracing the records generated by the owners and occupiers. However, it is easy to forget that these same individuals considered your house to have been their home too, and having established who these individuals were, your next step should be to find out more about how they would have lived, and in particular how they would have decorated or furnished your house to reflect their own personal taste. You can uncover a surprising amount of documentary evidence that should help you place the interior of your house in its original historical context, and many of the sources that have already been described can contain additional information about house interiors, furnishings and general layout. Although this guide is not the best place to undertake an analysis of period décor, this chapter describes some areas in which to look if you would like to begin investigating how your house once appeared.

Frequent mention has been made already of the personal papers of past owners and occupants, and once again they will be useful if you wish to uncover more about how life would have been for former residents. These recollections can be supplemented by clues left behind in the internal architecture of your house. In addition to beams, doors, windows and stairs, which can be useful in helping you to date the construction of the house, you may find surviving fixtures or fittings that can be researched and assigned a rough date. From the mid-nineteenth century onwards there are registers of designs and representations for patents and inventions, many of which relate to everyday household objects and decorations. Similarly, probate inventories and insurance records can shed light on how a house would have been furnished (*see* FIGURE 25), and sometimes provide

Figure 25 An extract from the inventory of personal effects found at the house of London lawyer Silvester Petyt. The inventory was made on 26 November 1723, and provides a vivid insight into the way a gentleman's early eighteenth century house would have been furnished. (PROB 5/2768)

	£	s	d
A peice of old Gold _____	00	08	06
Severall peices of old Coarse Silver medalls weighing 3:07:8 weights:	} 0	18	00
another parcell of old mixt Coarse Silver 3:8 w. worth about			
remaineing in Mr Lambs hands of moneys deposited with him by the Testator in his Life tim̄e _____	} 1264	17	04
Severall old Copper peices of no value _____	00	00	00
Copper Swedish money _____	00	08	09

1400. 14.

Testators pictures household Goods Books and wearing apparrell viz: _____

Eighty two old pictures of different Sizes _____	03	00	00
Mr petits and Mr Catersons pictures in Ovall Gilt Frames _____	01	01	00
one hundred and ninety four large & Smal prints Maps and Coats of Arms _____	} 02	10	00
Seven prints framed with Glass and one Dutch Glass two Ovall prints of Queen Anne & Prince George in Carved frames _____	} 00	15	00
An Indian Card table lined with Crimson plush, One Walnutt Tree inlaid Table A Smal Table & Tea board A writing Stand one Walnutt Tree ffilligree Table & eight Stands	} 00	15	00
One large Oval Wainscott Table one black Table with a Drawer broken one black and white Eight Square Table, one Smal ovall Table a Square Table and an old Deske _____	} 00	16	00
an Indian Beauroe _____	01	05	00
A Walnut Tree Scriptore & a Chest _____	01	10	00
a Smal inlaid Cabinet upon a Chest of Drawers _____	01	01	00
a Black Chest on a frame _____	00	10	00
a Smal Black Cabinet _____	00	05	00
Two playing Tables Box Dice & men _____	00	08	00
one Looking Glass in an inlaid Frame & one Weather Glass _____	01	05	00
Two Looking Glasses in Black frames and three Glass Stones _____	03	10	00
nine Cane Chairs and a Cane Couch Squab and Bolster and two Wosted Damaske Stools Seven Turkey workt & two Stuffed Chairs a Slip & Step Ladder _____	} 01	00	00
an Old Iron Grate one Warming pan some old Iron one Iron Fork and Koy belonging to the Chambers _____	} 00	14	00
One Worsted Damask Bed Compleat a Feather Bed and Bolster one pillow and two Ruggs _____	} 04	10	00
a Fiddle and Base a Glass Case & some odd things _____	00	02	06

detailed descriptions of the interior and layout of a property. You should not forget photographic evidence either.

Further reading on the subject of house interiors is provided under 'Useful publications', most of which will include tips about dating an interior from the surviving fixtures and fittings. If you are interested in restoring your house according to the manner in which it was once decorated, the addresses and websites of a few organizations are provided under 'Useful addresses'.

13.2 Rediscovering previous interiors

SEARCHING FOR CLUES

The best place to start is with the interior of your property. You can often use original fixtures and fittings to provide a date when the interior was constructed or decorated. Indeed, even original wallpaper can be used to date a property, and provide a feeling of how a property might once have looked. Various guides on dating techniques are listed under 'Useful publications'; interior dating should be done in conjunction with your architectural analysis when first attempting to construct a chronological framework.

In addition, you will find that many old household objects can turn up under the soil in your garden. Clay pipes, tiles, even remnants of contemporary household 'technology' were thrown away, and these can offer a tantalizing glimpse of the lifestyles of previous owners. Similarly, bags of dateable rubbish can be uncovered in attics or cellars. Some of the contents can be matched among the design registers and representations described below, and local museums can often provide advice about assigning a date to a particular object. Furthermore, the objects that you find may be linked to a previous use of the property, which might be reflected in the current or former name of the house.

DESIGN REGISTERS AND REPRESENTATIONS

If you have managed to locate old wallpaper, dateable objects, or perhaps a photograph showing how the house was decorated at a particular period, you can attempt to match some of this material with the original designs and sample representations that were registered by the proprietors who wished to protect their designs from competitors. The records are now with the National Archives as part of the holdings of the Board of Trade, and cover the period 1839–1964.

The records are arranged in various series, reflecting chronological periods and the type of design that was registered. There are two areas in which to start your research – the registers, which contain the names and addresses of the design owner, the number of items registered, and the registered number; and the representations of each design, arranged by registered number. From 1842 to 1883 the documents were given separate registration numbers according to the type of material, although you may sometimes find items misfiled in the wrong series. There is a useful research guide prepared by the National Archives that describes how to locate material, and summarizes the relevant series that contain the registers and representations.

Furthermore, items from this period may possess a diamond mark, which contains information that should allow you to identify the relevant registration details. Another National Archives research guide explains the conversion process, which can be a little tricky to perform.

The representations are a wonderful source if you wish to discover period wallpaper designs and contemporary household inventions, and should allow you to paint a vivid picture of how your house might once have been furnished and decorated. Some of the sketches include illustrations on how household devices would have been installed, and can explain strange alcoves or other inexplicable anomalies in the internal structure of a property.

PATENTS AND SPECIFICATIONS
In addition to the registers and representations, applications by inventors for patents for new inventions up to 1853, with specifications from 1711 that provide details of the invention, were enrolled in Chancery. Copies of the letter patent sent to the applicant were enrolled on the patent rolls in c 66, while the specifications of patents were enrolled in c 54 (Close Rolls), c 210 (Petty Bag Office, Specification and Surrender Rolls) or c 73 (Rolls Chapel, Specification and Surrender Rolls). There is a series of publications available on open access that act as an index to patents and their specifications, and will allow you to locate the relevant roll. Once you have found the date of a patent in the volume, you should then look this up in the respective patent roll calendar on open access, and then convert the entry into a National Archives document reference. Similarly, the volumes also list the relevant series in which you will find a specification.

Once you have matched an entry with the correct reference and ordered the document, you should find that the enrolment contains a description of the item that has been granted a patent, which in theory protected the invention from other designers, or a transcript of the relevant specification for the item.

Early applications for patents can be found in various series. From 1661 there are entry books for patents in sp 44, continued from 1782 in series ho 43. After 1853 copies of patents are available from the Patent Office Sale Branch (see 'Useful addresses'). Furthermore, printed transcripts of specifications enrolled before 1853 can be seen at the BL Science Reference Library, along with annual journals that provide information on the various historic trademarks that companies used, many of which appear on everyday household items.

COPYRIGHT FILES

You may also wish to examine the copyright entry forms maintained by the Stationers' Company at Stationers' Hall, London, under the various Copyright Acts from 1842, which have been deposited at the National Archives and assigned the series COPY 1. A wide variety of items are covered in the records, some of which were used in domestic property. The records cover the period 1837–1912, and you can obtain the copyright number from the registers and indexes in COPY 3, which should correspond with the files in COPY 1. However, the entry forms are arranged by type of material and by date, so the copyright number will be of limited use for search purposes. The Stationers' Company has retained the registers for the period 1554–1842.

COPY 1 will also be of use if you are searching for images, as part of the series is devoted to copyright of photographs. Many of these relate to individual houses or properties. However, there is no place index available in the series list, and so the records are not easily accessible.

13.3 Inventories

Inventories are lists of possessions or property belonging to a particular person or persons. They were compiled for many reasons, and some of the best places to begin looking are listed below.

PROBATE INVENTORIES

Probate inventories were compiled to quantify a deceased person's estate, excluding realty, so that the executors knew the extent and value of the possessions that they were to distribute. These are described in detail in CHAPTER 7, but in summary you will find that they generally listed all possessions and belongings that were contained in relevant properties or dwellings, and usually a value was assigned to the goods so that they could be sold. Consequently, you will find a room by room list of personal possessions, furniture, clothes and paintings. For example, when the London lawyer Silvester Petyt died in 1720, the contents of his house were described in great detail (*see* FIGURE 25 above); we are left with an impression of how an early-eighteenth-century gentleman would have furnished his lodgings, complete with furniture from India, Dutch glassware, Turkish carpets, four looking glasses, an eight-day clock, a musket, bayonet and sword, and nearly 200 prints and various pictures of family, royalty and judges (the National Archives reference PROB 5/2768).

INVENTORIES IN OTHER SERIES

You will find that many legal cases required inventories to be produced, particularly in the equity courts. A list of where to look for the National Archives series that contain exhibits is provided in CHAPTER 8.

In addition, there are a few distinct series that contain various inventories, such as E 154 (goods and chattels, 1207–1721), which mainly covers premises and shops but also incorporates merchants' dwellings and private residences. Many of these refer to individuals who had been indicted for treason or other felonies, and this will lead you to other areas in which to look for inventories, as criminal cases heard by the Crown often resulted in the seizure of an indicted criminal's possessions. However, these can be notoriously difficult to track down, and are not the best place for the house historian to begin. Generally, inquisitions will be fruitful, as will accounts of forfeited property, which usually take the form of an inventory. Series such as E 101, 143, 163 and 199 and FEC 1 contain such information, and inventories can also be found in E 140, 219, 314 and 315; IR 59; LR 1, 2 and 5; and SP 28 and 46.

13.4 Sale catalogues and prospectuses

To assist with the sale of a property, the estate or land agent who was handling the process often compiled a catalogue to provide information for the prospective purchaser. This is often listed among the business papers of the relevant firm of agents, who in the eighteenth and nineteenth centuries were usually solicitors. Occasionally you will find catalogues among the private papers of individuals who either bought the property or were involved in the sale process.

The format of the documents will vary from catalogue to catalogue, depending on what is being sold. The most useful records will be the sale of a deceased person's estate by an executor, as you will often find a room by room list of personal possessions that effectively forms an inventory, as well as serving as a guide to the layout of the house. Preliminary surveys to compile the official catalogue also survive among solicitors' or estate agents' papers, although these are quite rare. You will also need an idea of which firm of solicitors or estate agents handled the process. To identify contemporary local firms, you should examine relevant trade directories. If you are lucky, the firm may still be in operation, perhaps under a new name after previous mergers. There are a number of associations and societies that can be approached for further advice about tracking down company archives, and these are listed under 'Useful addresses'.

Most sale catalogues will therefore be deposited at the relevant CRO, often amongst the collections of local solicitors or estate agents, but the

National Archives holds a collection of catalogues dating from the late nineteenth century that were brought into the Supreme Court (Chancery Division) by solicitors. These related to forthcoming sales by auction by order of the court, and are located in series J 46. The documents are arranged by county and thereafter by the name of the place that is listed in the sale catalogue.

You can also obtain useful information about the layout or interior of a property from sale notices in local newspapers. This is even more appropriate for properties that are advertised for rent, as a description of the fixtures and fittings that accompany the property is sometimes given. However, notices of either type can be difficult to locate unless you have obtained a potential sale date from other sources such as title deeds or private papers. Some CROs have compiled basic indexes for the more important publications, but these tend to list names, places and events, and as such do not cover these notices. A comprehensive collection of local newspapers has been deposited at the BL Newspaper Library, Colindale. You can use their website www.bl.uk to see if they hold a newspaper title that covered the area in which your house stands.

13.5 Correspondence and diaries

The thoughts and recollections of past occupants or visitors can provide an evocative window to the past, and can contain some quite revealing insights into the way people lived in your local community. Diaries and personal correspondence are a rich source – where they survive. You will be very fortunate to find anything that directly relates to your house, but you may well be able to find references to life in your village or street in the personal recollections of others.

The National Archives has a limited range of diaries in its holdings. They are usually to be found amongst the exhibits brought to court as evidence and never collected by the litigants. Other areas to begin looking will be among the private papers of owners, where far more personal correspondence can be found. However, at the National Archives these tend to relate to major historical figures whose archives have been deposited or purchased due to their importance, and are mainly in the National Archives series. Nevertheless some surprising evidence can be uncovered; for example, in the Granville papers, correspondence survives from the Duke of Devonshire to his sister, Lady Granville, that describes his stay at a private house high on the cliffs at Cullercoats, a small village north of Tynemouth, Northumberland. The letter is written on headed paper that contains a printed depiction of the house in question (*see* PROPERTY PROFILE: Cliff house, Northumberland, on pages 105–7). Further research in the Duke of Devonshire's own archives revealed similar correspondence from his sister, describing the interior of the same house in great detail during a stay of her own; she writes of the spectacular view from her bedroom across the bay to the ruins of Tynemouth Priory in the distance. This shows that you may need to visit more than one archive to make the most of such personal material, incorporating national collections at the National Archives, local archives where many personal papers have been deposited, and even private archives that may not be that readily accessible to the public.

13.6 Fire insurance records

Fire insurance offices were established in London from the late seventeenth century, with wider coverage from the eighteenth century onwards. Most provincial companies restricted their practice to the local area, but the major London firms, such as the Sun, Royal Exchange and Phoenix, expanded their business to set up provincial offices. The companies insured all types of property against the risk of fire, and usually provided their own fire brigades as well. To identify an insured property, a fire mark was issued to the householder that was then fixed to the wall of the property; each company had a unique fire mark, which could also contain the policy number embossed in the corner.

The main type of record will be a policy register that details the policy number; name, status, occupation and address of the policyholder, plus the same data for tenants, if applicable; the location, type, nature of construction and value of the property to be insured; the premium paid to the company; the renewal date; and a brief outline of any endorsement. Entries in the registers were usually chronological, and each new entry was assigned a policy number. You may find that larger companies maintained concurrent registers, so the policies may not run in strict numerical order. The major companies also kept indexes to the registers, by name, place or policy number. Where contemporary indexes have failed to survive, limited indexing work has been undertaken for some companies.

The registers will give a rough indication of the layout of a property, and some individuals specified in great detail what was to be insured. However, these were usually much earlier policies, and the volume of business meant that the agents restricted the detail they recorded in the registers. Other records may be of use though. For example, endorsement books, claims records and surveyors' plans and reports exist for some companies, and these can provide great detail for any property covered.

Records for local companies will be deposited at the relevant CRO, either among the records of the company or in the personal papers of the individual agents that they employed. The Guildhall Library, London, has records of the Sun, Royal Exchange (both London and provincial business) and Hand-in-Hand (London only); the Phoenix records (London and provincial) are at Cambridge University Library, and the records of the Westminster Fire Office (London and limited provincial) are at the Westminster Archives Centre. The National Archives holds no fire insurance records. More information can be found in David Hawkings' book on the subject, listed under 'Useful publications'.

PREPARING A RESEARCH PLAN

14

Some hints about beginning research have been provided in CHAPTER 2, but one of the most important 'first steps' is to sit down and sketch out a provisional research plan. Although every house will have a different research trail that reflects its own unique history, the majority of first-time house historians will find the following framework useful.

Furthermore, you should consider at the outset what you want to find out about your house. For some house historians, pinpointing a construction date will be sufficient reward for time spent in an archive; but for many others, the real excitement is provided by bringing the past back to life by finding out about the lives of the people who resided in your home, and how the local community evolved through the ages. Even if you live in a house built in the twentieth century, don't let this deter you from researching the previous history of the site.

First steps   14.1

(A) WORK OUT WHAT YOU WANT TO FIND.
  - Set your research parameters; these can change as you find out more, but you should try to limit yourself to one or two immediate goals.
  - Do you want to concentrate solely on the chronology?
  - Do you want to research previous owners?
  - Do you want to research previous houses on the site?
  - Do you want to look at the history of the local area and the influence it exerted on your house?

(B) MAKE YOUR GOALS REALISTIC.
  - How much research time do you have?
  - Are you prepared to travel to distant archives?
  - Research can be expensive – are you prepared to pay for photocopies (where available)?
  - Do you require any additional skills (e.g. language, paleography)?
  - Do you have access to necessary research tools (e.g. personal computer, the Internet, Latin dictionaries, guides to local history)?

14.2 Background research

(A) BEGIN WITH THE ARCHITECTURE OF YOUR HOUSE.
- Try to work out a rough date of construction for your house from the architectural clues that exist.
- You should also try to identify the dates of any major rebuilds or additions, as the cause of these might be important clues in your research.
- Compare your house to its neighbours – is it similar or different?
- Where is your house in relation to the village/town/city in which it is built? In general, if it is close to the centre it is probably older.

(B) PINPOINT THE LOCATION OF YOUR HOUSE IN THE LOCAL AREA. THIS WILL PROBABLY INVOLVE A TRIP TO THE LOCAL STUDIES CENTRE. IF POSSIBLE:
- Locate the manor in which your house was once situated.
- Locate the parish it was in; this might be different from today, and look out for differing ecclesiastical and civil parishes.
- Locate the administrative district – county division (hundred, rape, riding, etc.); local authority (urban district council, rural district council, borough); Poor Law union; tax district; registration district; parliamentary constituency.

(C) WHILE YOU ARE AT THE LOCAL STUDIES CENTRE, READ ABOUT YOUR LOCAL AREA AND ITS HISTORY IN SECONDARY SOURCES.
- Local studies publications (e.g. *VCH*) may provide information and document references that you can follow up.
- Look for old photographs, newspaper clippings or any other items that can provide clues for your documentary research. It may be that some research has already been done on your property.

(D) TRY TO CONTACT YOUR MORTGAGE PROVIDER.
- Ask to see your title deeds, as they give the names of previous owners.
- You may be charged a fee to view these documents.
- They may not go back that far, so don't be too disappointed if the information they contain is limited.

(E) START YOUR ORAL RESEARCH.
- Talk to neighbours, local antiquarians, previous owners, estate agents and solicitors that handled the sale of the property – they might be able to provide you with evidence or stories for you to research.
- In particular, solicitors may have earlier title deeds, although they are most likely to have been lost many years ago, or be with previous owners who paid off their mortgage.

- Remember to exercise diplomacy and courtesy when approaching any of these people.

(F) START TO LOCATE RELEVANT ARCHIVES.
- Based on where parish, manorial, estate and relevant local records are located, you should start to plan where to continue your research.
- Consult the publications listed at the end of this book under 'Useful publications', or browse the National Archives website under the National Register of Archives, or the ARCHON directory of archives and repositories.
- Contact potential archives and ask about opening times, entry requirements and document availability.

Archival research: creating a document framework   14.3

You can construct a document framework that in theory will provide names of owners and occupiers. The documents listed below mainly cover the period from 1840 to 1940. Although they are not appropriate for all houses and sometimes may not have survived, they cover the majority of properties in England and Wales and are recommended as the starting place for all house historians.

(A) THE NATIONAL ARCHIVES: VALUATION SURVEY
- Provides maps and names of owners/principal occupiers *c*.1910, plus a basic description of the property.

(B) THE NATIONAL ARCHIVES/CRO: TITHE APPORTIONMENT
- Provides names of owners/principal occupiers *c*.1840s.

(C) FRC/THE NATIONAL ARCHIVES/CRO: CENSUS RETURNS
- Provides names of all occupiers 1841–1901.

(D) THE NATIONAL ARCHIVES/CRO: ENCLOSURE AWARDS
- Provides useful background information on local landowners and tenants, with maps; from 1780s, mainly nineteenth century.

(E) THE NATIONAL ARCHIVES: NATIONAL FARM SURVEY
- Provides maps and names of owners of farm properties *c*.1940s.

14.4 Archival research: following up leads

Armed with the data from your document framework, plus information gleaned from your pre-research in step 2, you can start to plan your unique research trail. This will lead you to various archives, but it is usually best to start with the relevant CRO. The main documents you will probably use are listed below in descending order of potential value, although this will vary depending on the history of your house and what you find from your document framework.

(A) RELEVANT CRO
- Start with maps and plans of the local area (including OS).
- Starting from the present day, use electoral lists to track down all the modern occupiers of your house as far back as possible.
- Street and trade directories can help you to work even further back in time, if used in conjunction with the electoral lists and census returns.
- Rate books and other tax assessments that span the nineteenth and early twentieth centuries can also provide a link between electoral lists, street directories and census returns.
- Look for manorial records (court rolls if copyhold).
- Chase down other estate records (if copyhold, freehold or part of a larger estate).
- Always see if there are any deposited title deeds or leases.
- Check for sale catalogues (among estate agents' papers).
- Wills and probate material (deposited, plus existing local consistory court registers).
- Personal papers of known owners/occupiers.
- Land Tax (and other assessed taxes).
- Parochial material (for occupancy and local rates).
- Local newspapers (for listed sales).
- Local fire insurance registers.
- Records of local industries.
- Records of utility companies.
- Miscellaneous local records. (Be bold, be imaginative – you never know what you might uncover!)

Don't forget that you may need to visit other local record offices, such as borough or metropolitan archives, and the chances are you will have to return to these archives more than once as you make new discoveries elsewhere. The local studies centre at your library may also have a collection of relevant documents.

(b) THE NATIONAL ARCHIVES
- Maps and plans.
- PCC wills and administration pre-1858 (also at FRC).
- PCC inventories.
- Records of land transfer, conveyance and enrolled deeds.
- Legal disputes.
- Hearth Tax (and other assessed taxes).
- Records of national events.
- Records of modern houses.
- Private papers of known owners/occupiers.

(c) OTHER ARCHIVES (IN NO PARTICULAR ORDER OF RELEVANCE)
- FRC, Myddleton Street, London, for censuses, wills and registration of births, marriages and deaths.
- LMA for property in Greater London.
- Corporation of London Record Office for property in the City of London.
- BL for maps, plans and records of private individuals.
- Guildhall Library for fire insurance registers for London companies (which will include records of provincial insurance).
- Borthwick Institute, York, for PCY wills, administrations and inventories pre-1858.
- First Avenue House, Holborn, London, for post-1858 probate material.
- NLW, Aberystwyth, for Welsh property not covered at the National Archives.
- NAS, Edinburgh, for Scottish property.
- PRONI, Belfast, for property in Northern Ireland (some earlier material in Dublin at the National Archives of Ireland).

You will find that your research takes you to any number of these archives, and you will use various combinations of the documents listed above. The next chapter uses a real case study to demonstrate how the history of your house can lead to some surprising discoveries.

15

This chapter provides a detailed case study of a single property, Plymouth House in Northop, Flintshire, whose history has also provided examples of research elsewhere in this book. This chapter takes you through the detective process step by step, from basic initial searches to more complicated lines of enquiry.

You will also find four other, summarized, case studies – 'Property profiles' – in this book; they and Plymouth House are collectively intended to inspire you in your research, and perhaps persuade you to undertake more detailed work than you might otherwise have considered.

15.1 First steps

The aim of the research was to find out as much as possible about the history of Plymouth House. The primary goal was to attempt to provide a construction date, but also to discover some of the social history associated with the property. There were various local stories about the history of the property, and one of the most important was the legend that it was once a coaching inn called 'The Yacht' that served the Holyhead to Chester mail-coach route in the eighteenth century.

There were also stories about a property in the village called Ty Mawr (translated as 'Great House'), which once had a plaque on the wall inscribed with the words 'Woe to Him That Buildeth in Unrighteousness, 1674'. No such house exists in Northop today, but given that Plymouth House is the largest property in the village, there is the intriguing possibility that it was once known by the name of Ty Mawr.

15.2 Background research

The first step was to place the house in the locality. The village of Northop is situated in the county of Flint, and the CRO is located at Hawarden; there is no main separate local study centre. The village also formed part of the parish of Northop; parish registers can be found at Hawarden or on

Figure 26 Plymouth House, Northop, formerly a coaching inn called 'The Yacht'.

microfilm at the National Library of Wales.

From the secondary sources at Hawarden it became apparent that the village of Northop once formed part of a manor with the same name, which itself was a component part of the estates of the Earl of Plymouth from 1706 until the early nineteenth century. A search of the NRA at the National Archives showed that records of the Plymouth estates were deposited at the NLW, Aberystwyth, with some rentals at the Glamorgan Record Office, Cardiff.

An article on Northop by the local antiquarian Thomas Edwards, published in the *Cambrian Quarterly Magazine*, suggests that The Yacht and Ty Mawr were separate buildings – Ty Mawr was situated in the centre of the village, and 'according to the style of building, entrance, garden, etc., would appear to be a dwelling of some significance'. However, The Yacht is listed separately as one of the six inns in Northop. So from this evidence it would appear that The Yacht was not Ty Mawr.

Archival research: creating a document framework   15.3

(A) AT THE NATIONAL ARCHIVES, LONDON
Valuation survey
- From the finding aids, the relevant map (Flintshire IX.16) was identified as reference IR 131/10/85 and ordered. The property is clearly depicted, set back from the road, with a marked path leading from the door to the road.

This is unique in the village centre.

- On inspection, the hereditament number assigned to the property was 1685, which meant that the correct valuation book had the reference IR 58/94483.
- The Field Book recorded that the name of the owner was Edward Foulkes, who was also the freeholder and occupier. The name of the property was Plymouth House, 'an old property but substantially built', the outbuildings of which also contained 'an old coach house' (for storing coaches).

Tithe apportionment
- Northop parish was identified in Kain and Oliver's publication, and the references were IR 30/50/32 (map) and IR 29/50/32 (apportionment).
- The plot number on the map was B38, and the apportionment for this plot showed that the owner was Benjamin Bellis and the occupant was Joseph Joynson; the property is described as a public house and yard called The Yacht. Bellis also rented 12 acres of land to Joynson.
- As with the valuation map, the house is clearly set back from the road, connected by a marked path.

(B) AT THE FAMILY RECORDS CENTRE, LONDON
1841–1901 census returns
- The indexes were searched to find which district Northop was in, and document references for each census were obtained.
- 1841 (ref. HO 107/1407/18): 'Yacht Inn' not listed by name, but Joseph Joynson and family listed as an innkeeper in the village.
- 1851 (ref. HO 107/2501): 'Yacht Inn' listed in possession of Joseph Joynson, wife Catherine, two daughters Ann and Mary, and servant (Elizabeth Bellis).
- 1861 (ref. RG 9/4272): 'Yacht Inn' listed, in possession of John and Ann Whaley, two children and servant.
- 1871 (ref. RG 10/5643): 'Yacht Inn' no longer listed; 'Yacht House' in possession of Diana Davies.
- 1881 (ref. RG 11/5505): 'The Yacht' in possession of Edward Foulkes, master butcher, plus wife and four children, and two servants.
- 1891 (ref. RG 12/4607): 'Yacht House' in possession of Edward Foulkes and family.
- 1901 (ref. RG 13/5211): 'Plymouth House' in possession of Edward Foukes and family.

(C) IN SUMMARY
- Plymouth House was formerly The Yacht, as its position on the tithe map and valuation map is the same.
- In 1840 it was owned by Thomas Bellis and was rented to Joseph Joynson.

- At some point between 1861 and 1871 it ceased trading as an inn and became a private residence.
- It was in the hands of Edward Foulkes and family by 1881, probably via Diana Davies.
- By 1901 its name had changed to Plymouth House.

Archival research: following up leads   15.4

Further research was continued at Hawarden based on the data found in the framework research.

(A) LOCAL RECORDS CONFIRMED SOME OF THE DETAILS.
- Trade directories periodically listed the innkeepers of The Yacht – Slater's directory in 1844, 1850 and 1856 list The Yacht in the possession of Joseph Joynson; in 1868 and 1874 Ann Whaley is listed as proprietor; Ann and Mary Joynson (daughters of Joseph) are running another inn nearby in Pentre, also called The Yacht.
- From 1876, The Yacht is not mentioned. However, parish registers show that John Whaley was buried in 1866 and Anne Whaley was buried in 1867, suggesting that the information in the trade directories is inaccurate; this also fits in with the census data for 1871.
- Church rates from 1826 list contributions from Mrs Bellis (owner) and Joseph Joynson (occupier), although the property concerned is not named.
- Quarter sessions records show that in 1823 four locals were bound over to keep the peace against Joseph Joynson, publican, following an affray in a local inn; it is likely that this is The Yacht.

(B) OTHER USEFUL EVIDENCE WAS UNCOVERED.
- An estate map created for the Earl of Plymouth in 1717 depicts a house on the site of the modern Plymouth House, partly drawn in profile. It appears to be the largest house in the village, and has land attached to it. As with the tithe and valuation maps, it is set back from the road and appears to have a strange entrance or path marked on it. Frustratingly, a survey book linking tenants with property has been lost, and all that survives is a list of names on the map with no means of reference. However, it would appear that this house, on the site of The Yacht and Plymouth House, once formed part of the Plymouth estates.
- A survey of the parish by Edward Llewyd c.1695 lists all the important property in the village. There is no mention of Ty Mawr, although a property named Kort Mawr is listed. 'Kort' translates as 'court', which refers to a court or manor house (where the manorial court could also be heard if the lord of the manor lived elsewhere), so is this an early reference to Ty

Mawr? To follow up some of the leads about the Earl of Plymouth, the trail led to the NLW, which holds large sections of the Plymouth archives.

(c) SALE CATALOGUE 1812.

- A crucial link between 'The Yacht Inn', the Earl of Plymouth and the Bellis family was uncovered among the Wigmore estate papers in a sale catalogue dated 1812. It listed all properties and land parcels to be sold from the Earl of Plymouth's estates, and notes that all properties to be sold were freehold estates of inheritance. This meant that they should (in theory) be listed among the estate papers of the Earls of Plymouth. However, court rolls would be of no use as they cover only copyhold property.
- Lot IX – 'The Yacht Inn, a substantial and commodious house, with excellent stabling, and every requisite for a respectable Inn, upon the much frequented road from Chester to Holyhead.' The inn included nine acres of land. Lots XIII–XVII were in the tenancy of John Bellis 'of the Yacht'.

(d) WITH THIS CLUE, THE BELLIS FAMILY HISTORY WAS FURTHER INVESTIGATED.

- Will of Edward Bellis, 1832 – son of Elizabeth Bellis, brother of John Hughes Bellis – leaves his share of property in Northop under the licence/occupation of Joseph Joynson to his wife for life, and then equally to his son John and daughter Elizabeth; if all were to die, then to his brother Benjamin.
- Will of John Hughes Bellis, 1830 (the innkeeper listed in 1812) – son of Elizabeth Bellis – described as gentleman, leaves his share of property in Northop to John Bellis, son of brother Edward.
- Will of Elizabeth Bellis, 1827 (listed in the Northop church rates) – widow of Benjamin Bellis – leaves all her property and possessions to her sons, Edward and Benjamin.
- The Northop parish registers provide dates for some of these events, plus the following entry – 'memorandum: the above correction and addition in the entry of John Bellis, christening 1825 was made by me this 14th day of May, Henry Jones, vicar, signed in the presence of us, Robert Jones parish clerk and Joseph Joynson, Yacht, Northop' – further evidence of ties between the Bellis family and Joseph Joynson, their tenant.

(e) A RETURN TO THE PLYMOUTH ARCHIVES PRODUCED TITLE DEEDS FOR THEIR ESTATES, AND THREW UP SOME NEW NAMES TO TRACK DOWN.

- The descent of the manor of Northop was listed in great detail in the schedule of deeds for the Plymouth estate.
- 1706 marriage between Elizabeth Whitley, heiress of Roger Whitley, to Earl

of Plymouth – marriage settlement includes the manor of Northop, previously held by the Whitley family. Various properties are listed as part of the manor, including 'The Courthouse'; The Yacht is not listed. Is this Kort Mawr alias Ty Mawr?

- Other deeds belonging to the Whitley family provide more detail about the Courthouse – 1703 Richard Lucas is the occupier; 1701 'formerly in the possession of Richard Sneade'; the earliest reference is in 1670, when Roger Whitley purchased Northop from the Earl of Bridgewater. The Courthouse and 12 acres of land is in the possession of Richard Sneade.
- Earlier descent of Northop: 1537 Thomas Billington esquire settles land in and title of Northop on his son Randall, who in 1578 sells it all to Thomas Egerton, later Lord Chancellor to James I; it then passes through the Egerton family (the Earls of Bridgewater) until 1670.

(F) IN SUMMARY

- The house was sold in 1812 to the Bellis family, who were tenants of the Earl of Plymouth before this date. Thereafter, and from at least 1823, it was let to Joseph Joynson.
- The inn was linked to the Chester–Holyhead coach route.
- No earlier references to The Yacht appear before this date.
- No mention is made of Ty Mawr, although the Courthouse is listed to c.1670.
- The descent of the manor of Northop is clear from 1537.

A search of the NRA showed that papers of Roger Whitley were held at various archives, including the Bodleian Library, Oxford; John Rylands University, Manchester; and the Post Office Archives, London. More research on Whitley showed that a history of his career had been compiled, and a copy deposited at Hawarden. From this, it appears he was a fervent Royalist who was rewarded at the Restoration with the position of Postmaster General, and used the wealth this generated to buy lands, including the manor of Northop.

However, this did not progress the story of the Yacht Inn before 1812. To change tactics, the history of the Chester–Holyhead mail-coach route was investigated, starting with the Chester Record Office, as the start venue of the route, and followed by the National Archives, which held a report into the route c.1810.

Archival research: further investigations 15.5

(A) COACHING ADVERTISEMENTS IN LOCAL NEWSPAPERS.

- The *Chester Chronicle* contained many notices about coach routes.

Figure 27 The doorway of Plymouth House.

Although searching was a time-consuming task, it was a worthwhile exercise.

- 16 May 1776 – Thomas Carter announced that he intended to address the complaints about the lengthy and uncomfortable journey along the mail-coach route from Holyhead to Chester by funding a series of high-class inns along the route so that travellers could stop in comfort.
- 25 July 1776 – Thomas Carter proclaimed the first of his coaches, designed for the nobility and gentry travelling through North Wales, was ready to leave The Yacht, Chester, and make its way to the Walsh's Head, Holyhead, stopping at various inns along the way. The first stop out of Chester was the Yacht Inn, Northop, run by Thomas Bellis.

(B) REPORT INTO THE CHESTER–HOLYHEAD ROAD AT THE NATIONAL ARCHIVES.
- A report into the Chester to Holyhead road in MT 27/69 showed that the mail-coach route through Northop took longer than the coastal route, and so the village was bypassed *c*.1810. The entire route was later dropped in favour of a new road that ran from Shrewsbury after 1812.

In summary
- These are crucial leads. First, it appears that Thomas Carter was creating a private coach route; and that from 1776 it included the Yacht Inn in Northop. If that is so, there is a possibility that the Earl of Plymouth was renting the property to either Carter or Bellis, and therefore it should appear in estate rentals.

- Second, the removal of the mail-coach route *c.*1810 meant a loss of business for Northop, and hence the coaching inn would have lost trade. This may explain why the Earl of Plymouth decided to sell the property in 1812. Following up the lead on Thomas Carter, rentals for some of the Earl of Plymouth's lands were discovered at Glamorgan Record Office, Cardiff.

(C) PLYMOUTH ESTATE RENTALS AT GLAMORGAN.
- No properties were assigned names in the rentals, but for the year ending March 1777, Thomas Carter is listed as renting two pieces of property from the Earl, valued at £16.10.0 and £4.10.0. They are described as 'late Edwards', meaning that they were previously rented to a tenant named Edwards.
- By tracking the rentals back, it is possible to determine who previously rented these properties.
    1773–6 rented by Widow Davenport, late Edwards.
    1772 Thomas Davenport.
    1771 Samuel Crew now Thomas Davenport.
    1770 Samuel Crew.
    1768–9 Thomas Edwards.
- Another entry in 1771 provides crucial information. It lists 'repairs for the Courthouse and barn in Northop, Thomas Edwards late tenant thereof failed and now in gaol', and provides expenditure for renovating the property.

In summary
- Not only has the earliest recorded date of The Yacht been brought back to 1776, but it can also be linked to the Courthouse listed in the Plymouth deeds.
- The repairs listed for 1771 show that the tenant, Thomas Edwards, had let the house fall into a state of disrepair; yet the repairs provided the first stage of renovation from a private high-status dwelling to a coaching inn under Thomas Carter.
- The link between The Yacht, the Courthouse and Kort Mawr is now very strong. The trail therefore leads back to Roger Whitley, as it was his purchase of Northop in 1670 that provided the first documentary proof of the Courthouse. Roger Whitley was Postmaster General under Charles II, and some of his personal papers were deposited in the Post Office Archives in London. This is also an excellent source for records of the Chester–Holyhead post route.

(D) WHITLEY'S POST OFFICE LETTER-BOOKS.
- These record correspondence with his deputy postmasters about postal affairs. Records show that from 1667 the postmaster for Northop was

Richard Sneade, who was also listed in the Plymouth deeds as the tenant in the Courthouse in 1670.

- POST 94/13: 14 June 1673, letter from Whitley to Sneade, Northop – 'I pray present my service to my cousin Evans and family, tell him I will speedily send the length of the timber I would have cut for your house, as for slates, I would have the best and most useful, resolving to make it handsome. Remember Midsummer is at hand, make your rent ready also which is due to the office.'
- POST 94/15: 23 January 1674/5, letter from Whitley to Sneade, Northop – 'Let me advise you (once more) to send me an exact account of what money you have paid my brother and also give me a full assurance, that I shall be speedily and punctually paid for the remainder. If you fail herein I am resolved to get another postmaster for Northop, and also a new tenant for my house.'
- POST 94/15: 13 April 1675, letter from Whitley to Sneade, Northop – 'My brother informs me, he can get no money from you, I wonder, you use me so ill, let me prevail with you, to pay him what is due, immediately upon receipt of this letter (and before the next post returns on Saturday next) or I will give direction to put you out of employment, and place a more careful and just man in it.'
- Further correspondence shows that Mrs Sneade acts as postmaster for Northop from 1676.

In summary
- We now have a potential explanation for the cryptic plaque on Ty Mawr, if it is the same as Kort Mawr. 'Woe to Him That Buildeth in Unrighteousness' could refer to Richard Sneade, the non-payment of funds, and his presumed death by 1676; the date of a major reconstruction of the Courthouse/Ty Mawr is c.1673–4.
- This ties in with the purchase date for the manor of Northop in 1670, and perhaps represents an attempt by a non-resident lord of the manor to renovate the manor (court) house. Tying up the loose ends, we find from the parish records in Hawarden that Richard Sneade was buried in Northop parish churchyard on 25 September 1675 – perhaps another chilling reference to the inscription on the plaque?

In 1670 Roger Whitley purchased Northop from the Egerton family. Having checked the NRA at the National Archives, it would appear that records of the Egerton family before 1670 were largely with the Ellesmere papers, which are stored in the Huntington Library, San Marino, California, USA. After an email research request, it was confirmed that rentals for Northop did exist but no names linked to the Courthouse were found.

(E) FINAL CHRONOLOGY OF PLYMOUTH HOUSE
- Plymouth House from *c*.1900 onwards.
- Private residence, known as Yacht House, from *c*.1870 to *c*.1900.
- The 'Yacht Inn' from 1776 to 1870; part of private high-class coaching chain run by Thomas Carter and sub-let to the Bellis family, yet owned by the Earl of Plymouth until its sale to the Bellis family in 1812.
- The 'Courthouse' from 1670 to 1775; residence of the Northop postmaster Richard Sneade from *c*.1667 to 1675, and thereafter his widow. Underwent an extensive rebuild *c*.1673–4 on the orders of the lord of the manor, Roger Whitley; thereafter passed to private hands until the fall from grace of Thomas Edwards in 1769–70, and renovated *c*.1771.
- The house was probably known as Ty Mawr, a derivation of Kort Mawr (1695).
- Records before 1670 may exist, but are in the USA.

Conclusion   15.6

This case study demonstrates that you will have to employ some lateral thinking in your research, as well as educated guesses and a great deal of searching. You may also be left with an inconclusive answer – in this example, it is highly likely that Plymouth House *was* Ty Mawr, but it is not possible to prove this through the documents as a certain *fact*. You should also note that the research led backwards and forwards between archives, following clues as and when they became relevant. You may find that some evidence initially seems inconsequential, but then becomes vital in the wake of later discoveries. You should never assume that you have 'finished' with an archive, as you may have to return to re-check sources you thought you had discarded. You may achieve an end result as satisfactory as this one!

The National Archives series containing title deeds

1. Private deeds

COLLECTION	FINDING AIDS

CHANCERY

C 146	Ancient Deeds Series C c.1100–1695 11,087 deeds	Pieces 1–8060 in *Descriptive Catalogue of Ancient Deeds*;* pieces 8061–11087 in transcript with index.
C 147	Ancient Deeds Series CC c.1100–16 1,310 deeds	Series list, pieces 1–373; card index to persons and places, pieces 1–315.
C 148	Ancient Deeds Series CS 1256–1603 171 boxes	Typescript list, pieces 1–169, manuscript list pieces 170–171; card index (with c 147).
C 149	Modern Deeds Series C c.1600–c.1800 65 boxes	Unlisted and unsorted.

EXCHEQUER OF RECEIPT

E 40	Ancient Deeds Series A c.1100–1603 15,912 deeds	Pieces 1–13672 in *Descriptive Catalogue of Ancient Deeds*; pieces 13673–15068 and 15069–15910 in *List and Index* *vols 151* and *152* respectively.
E 41	Ancient Deeds Series AA c.1100–1642 533 deeds	Pieces 461 and 464 printed in *The Pipe Roll Society*, X (1888).
E 42	Ancient Deeds Series AS c.1100–1590 549 deeds	Pieces 1–549 in *List and Index Society*, vol. 158.
E 44	Modern Deeds Series A 20 Hen VII–4 Geo III 535 deeds	Series list.

* *A Descriptive Catalogue of Ancient Deeds in the Public Record Office*, 6 volumes (HMSO, 1890–1906).

COLLECTION	FINDING AIDS

E 132	Transcript of Deeds Edward 1–James 1 66 files and rolls	Series list.
E 210	Ancient Deeds Series D 1120–1609 11,325 deeds	Pieces 1–1330 in *Descriptive Catalogue of Ancient Deeds*.
E 211	Ancient Deeds Series DD c.1101–1645 724 boxes	Pieces 1–724 in *List and Index Society, vol. 200.*
E 212	Ancient Deeds Series DS 1228–1582 139 deeds	Series list.
E 214	Modern Deeds Series D 1603–1851 1,679 deeds	Series list, indexed for persons and places.

EXCHEQUER AUGMENTATION OFFICE

E 326	Ancient Deeds Series B c.1200–1592 13,677 deeds	Pieces 1–4232 in *Descriptive Catalogue of Ancient Deeds*; pieces 4233–4827, 4838–9000 and 9001–12950, plus index to 4233–12950, in *List and Index Society*, vols *95, 101,* *113* and *124* respectively.
E 327	Ancient Deeds Series BX Hen I–1543 783 deeds	All deeds published in Thomas Madox, *Formulare* *Anglicanum* (London, 1702).
E 328	Ancient Deeds Series BB 1225–1667 441 boxes, files	Index to pieces 1–433 in *List and Index Society, vol. 137.*
E 329	Ancient Deeds Series BS 1148–1560 484 deeds	Series list.
E 330	Modern Deeds Series B 1548–1803 50 deeds	Series list.

EXCHEQUER PIPE OFFICE

E 354	Ancient Deeds Series P 1524–1608 50 deeds	Series list.
E 355	Ancient Deeds Series PP c.1500–c.1600 7 boxes	Unsorted, restricted access.

2. Private deeds for semi-autonomous jurisdictions

COLLECTION		FINDING AIDS

DUCHY OF LANCASTER

DL 25	Deeds Series L c.1100–34 Chas II 3,652 documents	Various pieces are published in several sources – see series list for details.
DL 26	Deeds Series LL 6 Edw I–10 Geo III 106 deeds	Pieces 1–7 in introduction to series list.
DL 27	Deeds Series LS to 12 Jas I 332 documents	Various pieces are published in several sources – see series list for details.
DL 36	*Cartae Miscellanae* c.1125–17th century 3 volumes	TNA *Lists and Indexes, Supplementary Series, vol. 3.*

PALATINATE OF DURHAM

DURH 21	Chancery Deeds Series G 1557–1799 9 bundles	Unsorted, with restricted access.

PALATINATE OF LANCASTER

PL 29	Deeds, etc. Series H 1501–1844 63 papers	Series list.

PALATINATE OF CHESTER

WALE 29	Ancient Deeds Series F c.1270–1602 516 deeds	Series list.
WALE 30	Ancient Deeds Series FF 1508–1634 53 deeds	Typescript list available on open access, indexed by person and place.
WALE 31	Modern Deeds Series F 1297–1830 11 boxes of deeds	Transferred to National Library of Wales (NLW).

3. Deeds for Crown properties

COLLECTION		FINDING AIDS

Crown Estate Commissioners

CRES 38	Title deeds: property acquired, sold or leased by the Crown Edward 1–1967 2,219 pieces	Series list.

Office of Auditors of Land Revenue

LR 14	Ancient Deeds Series E 1223–1730 1,178 deeds	Pieces 1–1178 in *List and Index Society, vol. 181.*
LR 15	Ancient Deeds Series EE 1349–1731 322 deeds	Typescript calendar, indexed by people and places on open access.
LR 16	Modern Deeds Series E Jas I–*c.*1800 14 deeds	Unsorted, with restricted access.

Office of Land Revenue

LRRO 5	Deposited Documents Henry VIII–1917 69 volumes, rolls and bundles	Series list.
LRRO 37	Miscellaneous Records 1629–1921 137 rolls, volumes, etc.	Series list.

Office of Works

WORK 7	Deeds Series I *c.*1700–1915 84 boxes	Series list.
WORK 8	Deeds Series II 1710–1904 82 boxes	Ancient monuments, historic buildings; series list.
WORK 13	Deeds Series III 1844–1951 1,395 rolls	Public offices and buildings; series list.
WORK 24	Deeds Series IV 1614–1929 8 boxes	Property in Westminster; series list.

Glossary

AFFIDAVIT a voluntary statement made on oath.

ALIENATE to transfer property away from the normal line of inheritance.

AMERCEMENT a financial penalty.

ANCIENT LIGHTS the light that falls on the windows of a house from the heavens, and which the owner claims to enjoy unobscured by obstructions erected by his neighbours.

ASSIZE a biennial court presided over by itinerant royal justices who toured a circuit of neighbouring counties.

BAR (AN ENTAIL) to destroy the normal line of descent.

BEQUEATH to leave possessions to another by will.

CALENDAR a summary of the contents of a document, usually in printed form.

CAPITAL MESSUAGE the main property in a manor, commonly referred to as the manor house.

COMMON LAW the laws developed from the common customs of England.

COMMON SOCAGE agricultural service owed to a lord.

COMPOUNDING a payment made by Royalists to retain their forfeited lands after the English Civil War.

CONTINGENT REMAINDER – a remainder (in an entail) that might happen but was not certain.

CONVEYANCING the legal transfer of title to property from one party to another.

COPYHOLD LAND 'unfree' land, held according to the custom of the manor and transferred through the manorial court.

CUSTOMARY TENANT a manorial tenant who held land according to the custom of the manor; also referred to as copyholder.

DEMESNE land reserved by the lord of the manor for his own use.

DEMISE to lease land for a given period.

DEPOSITION a sworn statement made in response to a specific interrogatory.

DEVISE to leave by will, usually with reference to realty.

DOWER property or income settled on a woman at marriage by her husband's family that she enjoyed on her husband's death.

ENCLOSURE a wide-ranging term that describes changes in land use or status (*see also* encroaching and engrossing).

ENCROACHING amalgamation of smaller plots of land.

ENFRANCHISEMENT with regard to land, the term applied to the conversion of copyhold into freehold.

ENGROSSING amalgamation of two farms.

ENTAIL *see* fee tail.

EQUITY a body of law based on judgments according to the merits of the case rather than the confines of common law.

ESCHEAT the return of land to the original grantor, either through the death of the last heir or default.

ESSOIN a payment made to excuse a tenant's attendance at the manorial court.

ESTATE with regard to land, the type of interest in the land is called the 'estate' (fee simple, fee tail, life interest, or term of years).

FEE FARM an alternative name for a lease.

FEE SIMPLE an interest in property limited to a man and his heirs.

FEE TAIL an interest in property limited to a man and the heirs of his body.

FINE with regard to land, a legal document that ended a fictitious lawsuit.

FREEHOLD LAND land held from the lord of the manor on fixed terms.

GAVELKIND inheritance where property is divided equally between sons, a practice prevalent in Kent.

HEREDITAMENT NUMBER a number assigned to a plot of land, used as part of the 1910 valuation survey.

IMPARTIBLE INHERITANCE property that could not be divided on death, and therefore passed intact.

INTERROGATORY a list of specific questions relevant to a legal case.

LEASE an interest in land fixed for a set period known as a term of years.

LEGACY personal property left to another in a will.

LIFE INTEREST an interest in property limited to the life of the tenant.

MAJORITY the age at which an heir was entitled to inherit, traditionally 21 years until 1969.

MEMORIAL an abstract of a deed.

MESSUAGE a term used in manorial documents for a house.

MORTGAGE conveyance of real estate as security for a loan.

PALEOGRAPHY the term used to describe handwriting and abbreviations used in documents.

PARTIBLE INHERITANCE a form of inheritance where land could be divided between several parties according to the customs of the manor.

PERSONALTY personal property that can be devised by will; this can include leases and uses.

POSSESSION the legal holder of land was deemed to be in possession.

PRIMOGENITURE inheritance through the first-born male.

PROBATE notification that a will had been proved in the relevant court.

PUR AUTRE VIE a lease or grant that could be held for only as long as the lessor or grantor lived; literally 'for the life of another'.

QUARTER SESSIONS a quarterly local court presided over by JPs that dealt with administrative matters and minor offences.

QUIT RENT the conversion of agricultural services to monetary payments.

REALTY land, also defined as real estate.

REGNAL YEAR a method of dating using the first day of the monarch's reign as the first day of the year. Hence the regnal year '1 Henry VIII' ran from 22 April 1509 to 21 April 1510.

REMAINDER a future interest in land beginning at the end of another interest.

RENTCHARGE rent that was charged on a plot of land, as opposed to rent service that was owed to a feudal lord as a condition of holding the land.

REPERTORY ROLL a roll fulfilling the task of a list, index, catalogue or calendar.

REVERSION land that would revert to the original grantor at the end of the term was held 'in reversion'.

ROTULUS the Latin name for a roll, used to describe the individual sheets of parchment in a document.

SETTLEMENT a land grant that involved the creation of a succession of interests in the land.

STRICT SETTLEMENT a settlement that restricted inheritance to certain persons.

TENANT-IN-CHIEF one who holds land direct from the Crown.

TENEMENT a term used in manorial documents for a house.

TENURE the terms by which land was held.

TERM OF YEARS *see* lease.

TITHE payments in kind of a tenth of the annual produce of land by way of crops and animals.

TITHE APPORTIONMENT a formal agreement that set a monetary value to commuted tithes for a parish, and then divided it amongst liable individuals.

TITLE DEEDS the collected legal documentation for past transfers of a particular piece of land or property that conveys legal possession.

TRUST the interest of a person who is invested with property for the benefit of another.

TRUSTEE the person to whom an estate was conveyed in trust for another.

TURNPIKE TRUST a body responsible for the finance and administration of the roads (turnpikes) in its jurisdiction.

USE the older name for trust.

WARDSHIP the control of the land of an under-age heir by his lord.

List of abbreviations

BL	British Library
BTHR	British Transport Historical Records
CARN	County Archive Research Network
CRO	County Record Office
DKR	Deputy Keeper's Report
FRC	Family Records Centre
HMC	Royal Commission for Historical Manuscripts
IPM	Inquisition post mortem
ITP	Income Tax Parish
JP	Justice of the Peace
LMA	London Metropolitan Archives
MAF	Ministry of Agriculture and Fisheries
MDR	Manorial Documents Register
NAS	National Archives of Scotland
NLW	National Library of Wales
NRA	National Register of Archives
OS	Ordnance Survey
PCC	Prerogative Court of Canterbury
PCY	Prerogative Court of York
PRO	Public Record Office
PRONI	Public Record Office of Northern Ireland
TNA	The National Archives
VCH	*Victoria County History* series

Useful addresses

ASSOCIATION OF GENEALOGISTS AND RESEARCHERS IN ARCHIVES,
29 Badgers Close, Horsham, West Sussex RH12 5RU.

BODLEIAN LIBRARY, Broad Street, Oxford OX1 3BG. *Tel*: 01865 277158.

BORTHWICK INSTITUTE FOR ARCHIVES, Borthwick Institute, University
of York, Heslington, York. *Tel*: 01904 321166.

BRITISH ASSOCIATION FOR LOCAL HISTORY, PO Box 1576, Salisbury,
Wiltshire SP2 8SY. *Tel*: 01722 332158.

BRITISH GEOLOGICAL SURVEY, Kingsley Dunham Centre, Keyworth,
Nottingham NG12 5GG. *Tel*: 0115 936 3100.

BRITISH LIBRARY, 96 Euston Road, London NW1 2DB.
Tel: 020 7412 7676. Also houses the SCIENCE REFERENCE LIBRARY,
ORIENTAL AND INDIA OFFICE LIBRARY and MAP LIBRARY.

BRITISH LIBRARY NEWSPAPER LIBRARY, Colindale Avenue, London
NW9 5HE. *Tel*: 020 7412 7356.

BRITISH RECORDS ASSOCIATION, c/o Finsbury Library,
245 St John Street, London EC1V 4NB. *Tel*: 020 7833 0428.

CAMBRIDGE UNIVERSITY LIBRARY, West Road, Cambridge CB3 9DR.
Tel: 01223 333000.

CITY OF LONDON, LONDON METROPOLITAN ARCHIVES,
40 Northampton Road, London EC1R 0HB. *Tel*: 020 7641 5180.

CITY OF WESTMINSTER ARCHIVE CENTRE, 10 St Ann's Street, London
SW1P 2DE. *Tel*: 020 7641 5180.

COLLEGE OF ARMS, Queen Victoria Street, London EC4V 4BT.
Tel: 020 7248 2762.

DEPARTMENT OF ENVIRONMENT, FOOD AND RURAL AFFAIRS
(DEFRA), Records Review Section, Lion House, Willowburn Trading
Estate, Alnwick, Northumberland NE66 2PF. *Tel*: 01665 602881.

ENGLISH HERITAGE *see* National Monuments Record (England).

GENERAL REGISTER OFFICE FOR ENGLAND AND WALES, Family Records
Centre, 1 Myddleton Street, London EC1R 1UW. *Tel*: 020 8392 5300.

GENERAL REGISTER OFFICE (NORTHERN IRELAND), Oxford House,
49–55 Chichester Street, Belfast BT1 4HL. *Tel*: 028 9025 2000.

GENERAL REGISTER OFFICE FOR SCOTLAND, New Register House,
Edinburgh EH1 3YT. *Tel*: 0131 314 4433.

GEOLOGISTS' ASSOCIATION, Burlington House, Piccadilly, London
WC1V 0JU. *Tel*: 020 7434 9298.

GUILDHALL LIBRARY, Aldermanbury, London EC2P 2EJ. *Tel*: 020 7332 1863.

HOUSE OF LORDS RECORD OFFICE, House of Lords, London SW1A 0PW.
Tel: 020 7219 3074.

IMPERIAL WAR MUSEUM, Department of Documents, Lambeth Road, London SE1 6HZ. *Tel*: 020 7416 5221.

INDIA OFFICE LIBRARY *see* British Library.

INSTITUTE OF HISTORICAL RESEARCH, University of London, Senate House, London WC1E 7HU. *Tel*: 020 7862 8740.

LAND REGISTRY, HM, Lincoln's Inn Fields, London WC2A 3PH. *Tel*: 020 7917 8888.

LAW SOCIETY, Chancery Lane, London WC2A 1PL. *Tel*: 020 7242 1222.

LAW SOCIETY ARCHIVES, Ipsley Court, Berrington Close, Redditch, Worcestershire B98 0TD. *Tel*: 020 7242 1222.

LONDON METROPOLITAN ARCHIVES *see* City of London.

MANORIAL DOCUMENTS REGISTER *see* National Archives, The.

MINISTRY OF DEFENCE, Defence Geographic Centre, Elmwood Avenue, Feltham, Surrey TW13 7AH. *Tel*: MOD Map Library 020 8818 3196.

MUSEUM OF ENGLISH RURAL LIFE, The University of Reading, Redlands Road, Reading RG1 5EX. *Tel*: 0118 378 8660.

NATIONAL ARCHIVES, THE (England and Wales), Kew, Richmond, Surrey TW9 4DU. *Tel*: 020 8876 3444.

NATIONAL ARCHIVES OF SCOTLAND, HM General Register House, Edinburgh EH1 3YY.

NATIONAL ARCHIVES OF SCOTLAND (West Register House), Charlotte Square, Edinburgh EH2 4DF. *Tel*: 0131 535 1314.

NATIONAL LIBRARY OF SCOTLAND, George IV Bridge, Edinburgh EH1 1EW. *Tel*: 0131 226 4351.

NATIONAL LIBRARY OF WALES, Aberystwyth, Ceredigion SY23 3BU. *Tel*: 01970 623816.

NATIONAL MONUMENTS RECORD (ENGLAND), English Heritage, Great Western Village, Kemble Drive, Swindon SN2 2GZ. *Tel*: 01793 414600.

NATIONAL MONUMENTS RECORD OF SCOTLAND, RCAHMS, John Sinclair House, 16 Bernard Terrace, Edinburgh EH8 9NX. *Tel*: 0131 662 1456.

NATIONAL MONUMENTS RECORD OF WALES, Plas Crug, Aberystwyth, Ceredigion SY23 1NJ. *Tel*: 01970 621200.

NATIONAL RAILWAY MUSEUM LIBRARY, Leeman Road, York YO26 4XJ. Tel: 01904 621261.

PATENT OFFICE SALE BRANCH, St Mary Cray, Orpington, Kent BR5 3RD.

PRINCIPAL REGISTRY OF THE FAMILY DIVISION, First Avenue House, 42–49 High Holborn, London WC1V 6NP. *Tel*: 020 7947 7000.

PUBLIC RECORD OFFICE OF NORTHERN IRELAND, 66 Balmoral Avenue, Belfast BT9 6NY. *Tel*: 028 9025 5905.

REGISTRY OF DEEDS, King's Inn, Henrietta Street, Dublin, Republic of Ireland. *Tel*: 003531 760 7500.

RIBA British Architectural Library Drawings and Archives Collection, Victoria and Albert Museum, Cromwell Road, London sw7 2rl. *Tel*: 020 7307 3708.

Royal Institute of British Architects Library, 66 Portland Place, London win 4ad. *Tel*: 020 7580 5533.

Society of Genealogists, 14 Charterhouse Buildings, Goswell Road, London ec1m 7ba. *Tel*: 020 7251 8799.

Stationers' Hall, Ave Maria Court, London ec4m 7dd. *Tel*: 020 7248 2934.

Victoria and Albert Museum, Cromwell Road, South Kensington, London sw7 2rl. *Tel*: 020 7942 2000.

Useful websites

ARCHIVES AND OTHER INSTITUTIONS
ARCHON www.nationalarchives.gov.uk/archon/
BODLEIAN LIBRARY, OXFORD www.bodley.ox.ac.uk
BRITISH LIBRARY www.bl.uk
BRITISH RECORDS ASSOCIATION www.britishrecordsassociation.org.uk
COLLEGE OF ARMS www.college-of-arms.gov.uk
ENGLISH HERITAGE www.english-heritage.org.uk
FAMILY RECORDS CENTRE www.familyrecords.gov.uk/frc/
GETTING STARTED www.arts-scheme.co.uk
LAND REGISTRY www.landreg.gov.uk
LAW SOCIETY www.lawsociety.org.uk
NATIONAL ARCHIVES, THE (England and Wales) www.nationalarchives.gov.uk
NATIONAL ARCHIVES OF SCOTLAND www.nas.gov.uk
NATIONAL REGISTER OF ARCHIVES www.nationalarchives.gov.uk/nra/
PUBLIC RECORD OFFICE OF NORTHERN IRELAND (PRONI) http://proni.gov.uk

GENEALOGY
FAMILIA www.familia.org.uk
FAMILY HISTORY PORTAL www.familyrecords.gov.uk
GENEALOGY IN UK AND IRELAND www.genuki.com
ORIGINS www.origins.net
SOCIETY OF GENEALOGISTS www.sog.org.uk

HOUSE HISTORY
HOUSE HISTORY www.house-detectives.co.uk

LOCAL HISTORY
BRITISH ASSOCIATION FOR LOCAL HISTORY www.balh.co.uk
GAZETTEER OF BRITISH PLACE NAMES www.gazetteer.co.uk
VICTORIA COUNTY HISTORY www.englandpast.net

MAPS
ONLINE ACCESS TO AERIAL AND STREET MAPS
   www.getmapping.com www.multimap.com www.streetmap.co.uk

PERIOD PROPERTIES
BRITANNIA (HISTORIES OF COUNTRY HOUSES) www.britannia.com
PERIOD PROPERTIES www.periodproperty.co.uk
SOCIETY FOR THE PROTECTION OF ANCIENT BUILDINGS www.spab.org.uk

Useful publications (by alphabetical category)

DOCUMENT INTERPRETATION

W. S. B. BUCK, *Examples of Handwriting 1550–1650* (Society of Genealogists, 1996)

C. R. CHENEY, revised by M. Jones, *Handbook of Dates for Students of British History* (Cambridge University Press, 2000)

E. GOODER, *Latin for Local History*, 2nd edn (Longman, 1978)

B. H. KENNEDY, revised by Sir J. Mountford, *Shorter Latin Primer* (Longman, 1974)

R. E. LATHAM, *Revised Medieval Latin Word List* (Oxford University Press, 1989)

C. T. LEWIS and C. SHORT, *A Latin Dictionary* (Clarendon Press, 1886)

D. STUART, *Latin for Local and County Historians: A Beginner's Guide* (Phillimore, 1995)

C. TRICE-MARTIN, *The Record Interpreter* (Phillimore, 1982)

GENEALOGY / FAMILY HISTORY

GENERAL

S. COLWELL, *Dictionary of Genealogical Sources in the PRO* (Weidenfeld & Nicolson, 1992)

J. S. W. GIBSON and M. WALCOT, *Where to Find the International Genealogical Index* (FFHS, 1985)

S. RAYMOND, *County Genealogical Bibliographies*, published by county

CENSUS

C. CHAPMAN, *Pre-1841 Census and Population Listings* (Lochin Publishing, 1994)

J. S. W. GIBSON and E. HAMPSON, *Census Returns 1841–1891 on Microform: A Directory to Local Holdings* (FFHS, 1997)

E. HIGGS, *A Clearer Sense of the Census* (HMSO, 1996)

S. LUMAS, *Making Use of the Census,* 6th edn (PRO, 2002)

ELECTORAL MATERIAL

J. S. W. GIBSON and C. ROGERS, *Electoral Registers since 1832 and Burgers Rolls* (FFHS, 1990)

J. S. W. GIBSON and C. ROGERS, *Poll Books c.1696–1872* (FFHS, 1994)

J. SIMS, *A Handlist of British Parliamentary Poll Books* (University of Leicester History Department, 1984)

PARISH REGISTERS

National Index of Parish Registers (Society of Genealogists, 1968 continuing)

C. HUMPHREY-SMITH, *The Phillimore Atlas and Index of Parish Registers* (Phillimore, 1984)

W. TATE, *The Parish Chest* (Cambridge University Press, 1969)

TRADE DIRECTORIES

P. J. ATKINS, *The Directories of London 1677–1977* (Mansell Publishing, 1990)

G. SHAW and A. TIPPER, *British Directories: A Bibliography and Guide* (Leicester University Press, 1989)

HOUSE HISTORY (GENERAL GUIDES)

D. AUSTIN, M. DOWDY, J. MILLER, *Be Your Own House Detective* (BBC Books, 1997)

M. W. BAILEY, *The English Farmhouse and Cottage* (Sutton, 1987)

B. BRECKON and J. PARKER, *Tracing the History of Houses* (Countryside Books, 1998)

R. W. BRUNSKILL, *Illustrated Handbook of Vernacular Architecture* (Faber, 1970)

P. BUSHELL, *Tracing the History of Your House* (Pavilion Books, 1989)

H. M. COLVIN, *A Biographical Dictionary of British Architects 1600–1840*, 3rd edn (Yale University Press, 1995)

D. CRUICKSHANK and P. WYLD, *Georgian Town Houses and Their Details* (Butterworth, 1990)

N. CURRER-BRIGGS, *Debrett's Guide to Your House* (Headline, 1993)

A. FELSTEAD, J. FRANKLIN and L. PINFIELD, *Directory of British Architects 1834–1900* (Mansell, 1993)

J. H. HARVEY, *Sources for the History of Houses* (British Records Association, 1968)

D. IREDALE and J. BARRETT, *Discovering Your Old House* (Shire Publications, 1991)

C. L. KINGSFORD, 'A London Merchant's House and Its Owners', *Archaelogica*, 74 (1923–4), pp. 137–58

N. PEVSNER *et al.*, *The Buildings of England* (Penguin, 1951–)

M. WOOD, *The English Medieval House* (Ferndale, 1981)

HOW WE USED TO LIVE

E. ARBER (ed.), *A Transcript of the Registers of the Company of Stationers of London 1554–1640* (London, 1875–94)

J. S. BATTS, *British Manuscript Diaries of the 19th Century: An Annotated Listing* (Totawa, NJ, 1976)

M. W. BERESFORD, 'Building History from Fire Insurance Records', *Urban History Yearbook* (Leicester University Press, 1976)

H. A. L. COCKERELL and E. GREEN, *The British Insurance Business, 1547–1970*, 2nd edn (Sheffield Academic Press, 1994)

B. EYRE (ed.), *A Transcript of the Registers of the Worshipful Company of Stationers 1640–1708* (London, 1913–14)

D. T. HAWKINGS, *Fire Insurance records for Family and Local Historians, 1696 to 1920* (Boutle, 2003)

J. MILLER, *Period Details Sourcebook* (Mitchell Beazley, 1999)

LAND LAW AND CONVEYANCING

B. ENGLISH and J. SAVILLE, *Strict Settlement: A Guide for Historians* (University of Hull, 1983)

J. KISSOCK, 'Medieval Feet of Fines: A Study of Their Uses', *The Local Historian*, XXIV (2) (1994)

R. E. LATHAM, 'Feet of Fines', *The Amateur Historian*, I (1) (1952)

J. G. RIDDALL, *Introduction to Land Law*, 5th edn (Butterworth, 1993)

A. W. B. SIMPSON, *A History of the Land Law* (Clarendon Press, 1986)

LEGAL DISPUTES

J. H. BAKER, *An Introduction to English Legal History* (Butterworth, 1990)

W. H. BRYSON, *The Equity Side of the Exchequer* (Cambridge University Press, 1975)

SIR JULIUS CAESAR, ed. L. M. Hill, *The Ancient State, Authority and Proceedings of the Court of Requests* (Cambridge University Press, 1975)

R. E. F. GARRETT, *Chancery and Other Legal Proceedings* (Pinhorns, 1968)

J. S. W. GIBSON, *Quarter Session Records for Family Historians: A Select List* (FFHS, 1995)

J. A. GUY, *The Court of Star Chamber and Its Records to the Reign of Elizabeth I* (PRO, 1984)

H. HORWITZ, *Chancery Equity Records and Proceedings 1600–1800*, a guide to documents in the PRO, revised edn (PRO, 1998)

H. HORWITZ, *Exchequer Equity Records and Proceedings 1649–1841*, a guide to documents in the PRO (PRO, 2001)

A. MARTIN, *Index to Various Repertories, Books of Orders, and Decrees, and Other Records Preserved in the Court of Exchequer* (Society of the Inner Temple, 1819)

H. SHARP, *How to Use the Bernau Index* (Society of Genealogists, 1996)

LOCAL HISTORY

Alphabetical List of Parishes and Places in England and Wales, 2 vols (HMSO, 1897)

English Place Name Society series (published by county)

Victoria History of the Counties of England series (published by county)

J. S. W. GIBSON, *Local Newspapers 1750–1920* (FFHS, 1987)

M. D. HERBER, *Ancestral Trails* (Sutton, 1997)

D. HEY, *Oxford Companion to Local and Family History* (Oxford University Press, 1996)

S. LEWIS, *Topographical Dictionary of England* (London, 1840)

S. LEWIS, *Topographical Dictionary of Ireland* (London, 1846)

S. LEWIS, *Topographical Dictionary of Scotland* (London, 1846)

S. LEWIS, *Topographical Dictionary of Wales* (London, 1840)

A. MACFARLANE, *A Guide to English Historical Records* (Cambridge University Press, 1983)

L. MUNBY, Rev. K. M THOMPSON, *Short Guides to Records, 2 series* (Historical Association, 1994, 1997)

P. RIDEN, *Local History: A Handbook for Beginners*, 2nd edn (Batsford, 1998)

C. D. ROGERS and J. H. SMITH, *Local Family History in England, 1538–1914* (Manchester University Press, 1991)

W. B. STEPHENS, *Sources for English Local History* (Phillimore, 1994)

F. A. YOUNGS Jr, *Guide to the Administrative Units of England*, 2 vols (Royal Historical Society, 1980, 1991)

MANORIAL AND ESTATE RECORDS

M. ELLIS, *Using Manorial Records* (PRO, 1997)

P. D. A. HARVEY, *Manorial Records* (British Records Association, 1984)

R. HOYLE, *The Estates of the English Crown, 1558–1640* (Cambridge University Press, 1992)

D. STUART, *Manorial Records* (Phillimore, 1992)

A. TRAVERS, 'Manorial Documents', *Genealogists' Magazine*, XXI (1983)

MAPS, PLANS AND LAND SURVEYS

GENERAL

Maps and Plans in the British Isles 1410–1860 (PRO, 1967)

Royal Historical Society Guides and Handbooks No. 18, 'Historians' Guide to British Maps' (London, 1994)

W. FOOT, *Maps for Family History* (PRO, 1994)

J. B. HARLEY, *Maps for the Local Historian: A Guide to British Sources* (National Council for Social Service, 1972)

P. D. A. HARVEY, *Maps in Tudor England* (British Library, 1993)

B. P. HINDLE, *Maps for Local History* (Batsford, 1988)

O. MASON (ed.), *Bartholomew Gazetteer of Places in Britain* (Bartholomew, 1986)

ENCLOSURE

M. W. BERESFORD, 'Habitiation versus Improvement: The Debate on enclosure by agreement' in F. J. Fisher (ed.), *Essays in the Economic and Social History of Tudor and Stuart England in Honour of R. H. Tawney* (Cambridge University Press, 1961)

W. E. TATE, *A Domesday of Enclosure Acts and Awards* (University of Reading, 1978)

W. E. TATE, *The English Village Community and the Enclosure Movements* (Gollancz, 1967)

W. E. TATE, 'Some Unexplored Records of the English Enclosure Movement', *English Historical Review*, LVII (1942)

NATIONAL FARM SURVEY

P. S. BARNWELL, 'The National Farm Survey 1941–43', *Journal of the Historic Farm Buildings Group*, VII (1994)

J. A. EDWARDS, *Historical Farm Records* (University of Reading, 1973)

P. EDWARDS, *Farming: Sources for Local Historians* (Batsford, 1992)

TITHE APPORTIONMENTS

E. J. EVANS, *The Contentious Tithe* (Routledge & Kegan Paul, 1976)

R. J. P. KAIN and R. R. OLIVER, *The Tithe Maps and Apportionments of England and Wales* (Cambridge University Press, 1994)

R. J. P. KAIN and H. C. PRINCE, *The Tithe Surveys of England and Wales* (Cambridge University Press, 1985)

VALUATION SURVEY

B. SHORT and M. REED, 'An Edwardian Land Survey: The Finance (1909–1910) Act 1910 Records', *Journal of the Society of Archivists*, VIII (1) and VIII (2) (1986)

B. SHORT and M. REED, *Landownership and Society in Edwardian England and Wales: The Finance (1909–10) Act 1910 Records* (University of Sussex, 1987)

MODERN HOUSING

J. D. CANTWELL, *The Second World War: A Guide to Documents in the PRO*, 3rd edn (PRO, 1998)

A. COLE, *An Introduction to Poor Law Documents before 1834* (FFHS, 1993)

For background information on the Poor Law reforms and housing conditions in the mid-nineteenth century, consult *Index to Parliamentary Papers* (also available on CD-ROM).

THE NATIONAL ARCHIVES AND THE FAMILY RECORDS CENTRE
A. BEVAN (ed.), *Tracing Your Ancestors at the PRO*, 6th edn (PRO, 2002);
7th edn, forthcoming (The National Archives, 2006)
S. COLWELL, *The Family Records Centre: A User's Guide* (PRO, 2002)
S. COLWELL, *The National Archives: A Practical Guide for Family Historians*
(The National Archives, 2006)

NATIONAL EVENTS
G. E. AYLMER and J. S. MORRILL, *The Civil War and Interregnum: Sources
for Local Historians* (Bedford Square Press, 1979)
E. CARTER, *An Historical Geography of the Railways of the British Isles*
(Cassell, 1959)
W. C. RICHARDSON, *History of the Court of Augmentations, 1536–1640*
(Louisiana State University Press, 1961)
J. YOUINGS, *The Dissolution of the Monasteries* (Allen & Unwin, 1971)

PROPERTY INHERITANCE
A. J. CAMP, *Wills and Their Whereabouts*, 4th edn (British Records
Association, 1974)
J. COX, *Hatred Pursued Beyond the Grave* (HMSO, 1993)
B. ENGLISH, 'Inheritance and Succession in Landed Families 1660–1925',
Genealogists' Magazine, XXIV, pp. 433–8
E. MCLAUGHLIN, *Wills before 1858* (FFHS, 1994)
E. MCLAUGHLIN, *Wills from 1858* (FFHS, 1995)
M. SCOTT, *Prerogative Court of Canterbury: Wills and Other Probate
Records* (PRO, 1997)

RECORD OFFICE GUIDES
Royal Commission on Historical Manuscripts, *Record Repositories in Great
Britain*, 11th edn (PRO, 1999)
J. FOSTER and J. SHEPPARD, *British Archives: A Guide to Archive Resources
in the United Kingdom* (Macmillan, 1995)
J. S. W. GIBSON and P. PESKETT, *Record Offices and How to Find Them*
(FFHS, 1998)
S. GUY, *English Local Studies Handbook: A Guide to Resources for Each
County Including Libraries, Record Societies, Journals and Museums*
(University of Exeter Press, 1992)

TAXATION
'A Supplement to the London Inhabitants List of 1695 Compiled by Staff
at Guildhall Library', *Guildhall Studies in London History*, vol. 2, no. 2
(Part 1: surnames beginning A–M) and no. 3 (Part 2: surnames
beginning N–Z, plus index of trades) (April and October 1976)

J. Gibson, *Hearth Tax Returns and Other Later Stuart Tax Lists and the Association Oath Rolls* (FFHS, 1996)

J. Gibson, M. Medlycott and D. Mills, *Land and Window Tax Assessments 1690–1950* (FFHS, 1997)

D. V. Glass, *London Inhabitants within the Walls 1695*, vol. 2 (London Record Society Publications, 1966); Corporation of London Record Office has a typescript index of *London Inhabitants without the Walls*

M. Jurkowski, C. L. Smith and D. Crook, *Lay Taxes in England and Wales* (PRO, 1998)

TITLE DEEDS

A Descriptive Catalogue of Ancient Deeds in the Public Record Office, 6 vols (HMSO, 1890–1906)

N. W. Alcock, *Old Title Deeds* (Phillimore, 1986)

A. A. Dibben, *Title Deeds* (Historical Association, 1971)

F. Sheppard and V. Belcher, 'The Deed Registries of Yorkshire and Middlesex', *Journal of the Society of Archivists,* VI (1978–81), pp. 274–86

K. T. Ward, 'Pre-registration Title Deeds: The Legal Issues of Ownership, Custody and Abandonment', *Journal of the Society of Archivists,* XVI (1995), pp. 27–39

Index

Page numbers in *italics* denote
a figure or table

PICTURE ACKNOWLEDGEMENTS

PAGE 73 Staffordshire Record Office (c/p/65/5/1/6/87/2)
PAGE 135 image courtesy of Strutt & Parker, estate agents
PAGE 183 Mike Pearcy/Words and Pictures

PLATE 1 Michael Jenner/Collections
PLATES 2, 9 The National Archives
PLATES 3, 4, 5, 6, 7, 14, 15 Derry Brabbs
PLATE 8 Quintin Wright/Collections
PLATE 10 Mike Kipling/Collections
PLATE 11 Robert Pilgrim/Collections
PLATE 12 Brian Shuel/Collections
PLATE 13 Oliver Benn/Collections
PLATE 16 David M. Hughes/Collections

All other images The National Archives